THE OG AND TH VERSIONS OF DANIEL

SOCIETY OF BIBLICAL LITERATURE
SEPTUAGINT AND COGNATE STUDIES SERIES

Series Editor
Bernard A. Taylor

Editorial Advisory Committee

N. Fernández Marcos, Madrid
I. Soisalon - Soininen, Helsinki
E. Tov, Jerusalem

Number 43

THE OG AND TH VERSIONS OF DANIEL

by
Tim McLay

THE OG AND TH VERSIONS OF DANIEL

by

Tim McLay

Scholars Press
Atlanta, Georgia

THE OG AND TH VERSIONS OF DANIEL

by
Tim McLay

© 1996
Society of Biblical Literature

Excerpt from p. 231–32 of *Semantics*
(John Lyons, ©1977 Cambridge University Press),
reprinted with the permission of Cambridge University Press.

Library of Congress Cataloging-in-Publication Data
McLay, Tim.
    The OG and Th versions of Daniel / by Tim McLay.
       p. cm. — (Septuagint and cognate studies series ; no. 43)
    Revision of the author's thesis (Ph.D) University of Durham, 1994.
    Includes bibliographical references. (p.   ) and indexes.
    ISBN 0-7885-0269-7 (cloth : alk. paper)
    1. Bible. O.T. Daniel. Greek—Versions—Septuagint. 2. Bible.
O.T. Daniel. Greek—Versions—Theodotion. 3. Bible. O.T.
Daniel—Criticism, Textual. I. Title. II. Series.
BS1555.2.M35 1996
224'.5048—dc20   96-14160
                                                                                 CIP

ISBN 978-1-58983-486-6 (paperback : alk. paper)

Printed in the United States of America
on acid-free paper

Table of Contents

Abbreviations xi

Preface xv

Chapter I Introduction 1

    I.1. Purpose of this Volume 1
    I.2. Translation Technique and Textual Criticism 2
    I.3. The Book of Daniel and the OG and Th Versions ... 12
    I.4. The Methodology for the Analysis of TT 16
    I.5. Introduction to the Analysis 22
    I.6. Texts and Witnesses Consulted 25
    I.7. Computers and the Analysis of TT 26
    I.8. A Note on the Citation of the Texts of Daniel 27
    I.9. Plan of Study 28

Chapter II Daniel 1:1-10 29

    II.1. TextualNotes 38
    II.2. Analysis of 1:1-10 40
        II.2.i. Morphology 40
        II.2.ii. Syntax 41
        II.2.iii. Lexicology 43
        II.2.iv. Summary 54
    II.3. The Relationship Between OG and Th 55

II.4. Text-Critical Problems 60

Chapter III Daniel 2:1-10 63

    III.1. Textual Notes 72
    III.2. Analysis of 2:1-10 78
        III.2.i. Morphology 78
        III.2.ii. Syntax 79
        III.2.iii. Lexicology 86
        III.2.iv. Summary 107
    III.3. The Relationship Between OG and Th 108
    III.4. Text-Critical Problems 110

Chapter IV Daniel 3:11-20 115

    IV.1. Textual Notes 125
    IV.2. Analysis of 3:11-20 126
        IV.2.i. Morphology 126
        IV.2.ii. Syntax 127
        IV.2.iii. Lexicology 132
        IV.2.iv. Summary 144
    IV.3. A Note on the Additions to Chapter Three 146
    IV.4. The Relationship Between OG and Th 148
    IV.5. Text-Critical Problems 149

Chapter V Daniel 8:1-10 153

    V.1. Textual Notes 160
    V.2. The Relationship Between OG and Th 160
    V.3. Summary 172

Table of Contents   ix

Chapter VI Daniel 12:1-13 175

    VI.1. Textual Notes 186
    VI.2. Analysis of 12:1-13 186
        VI.2.i. Morphology 186
        VI.2.ii. Syntax 188
        VI.2.iii. Lexicology 196
        VI.2.iv. Summary 205
    VI.3. The Relationship Between OG and Th 207
    VI.4. Text-Critical Problems 208

Chapter VII Summary 211

Chapter VIII Th and Kaige 219

    VIII.1. List of Kaige Characteristics 222
    VIII.2. Evaluation of Readings in Daniel 227
    VIII.3. Does Th belong to kaige? 239

Conclusion 241

Appendix 245

Bibliography 249

Author Index 277

Index of Biblical References 279

Abbreviations

A. Journals and Series

AB	Anchor Bible
AASF	Annales Academiæ Scientiarum Fennicæ
ANRW	Aufstieg und Niedergang der römischen Welt
AOAT	Alter Orient und Altes Testament
AUSS	Andrews University Seminary Studies
BASOR	Bulletin of the American Schools for Oriental Research
Bib	Biblica
BIOSCS	Bulletin of the International Organization for Septuagint and Cognate Studies
BZ	Biblische Zeitschrift
CBQ	Catholic Biblical Quarterly
CBQMS	Catholic Biblical Quarterly, Monograph Series
ConBOT	Coniectanea Biblica, Old Testament Series
DJD	Discoveries in the Judean Desert
ETL	Ephemerides Theologicae Lovanienses
FN	Filologia Neotestamentaria
HSM	Harvard Semitic Monographs
HTR	Harvard Theological Review
HUCA	Hebrew Union College Annual
IBA	Proceedings of the Irish Biblical Association
IEJ	Israel Exploration Journal

JAOS	Journal of the American Oriental Society
JBL	Journal of Biblical Literature
JBLMS	Journal of Biblical Literature, Monograph Series
JJS	Journal of Jewish Studies
JNSL	Journal of Northwest Semitic Languages
JQR	Jewish Quarterly Review
JSOT	Journal for the Study of the Old Testament
JSP	Journal for the Study of the Pseudepigrapha
JSPS	Journal for the Study of the Pseudepigrapha Supplement Series
JSS	Journal of Semitic Studies
JSSM	Journal of Semitic Studies, Monographs
JTS	Journal of Theological Studies
KAT	Kommentar zum Alten Testament
MIO	Mitteilungen des Instituts für Orientforschung
MSU	Mitteilungen des Septuaginta-Unternehmens der Akademie der Wissenschaften in Göttingen
NAWG,I.phil.-hist. Kl.	Nachrichten der Akademie der Wissenschaften in Göttingen, I. philologisch-historische Klasse
OBO	Orbis Biblicus et Orientalis
OTL	Old Testament Library
OTS	Oudtestamentische Studiën
PTA	Papyrologische Texte und Abhandlungen
RB	Revue Biblique
SBS	Stuttgarter Bibel-Studien
SCS	Septuagint and Cognate Studies

Abbreviations *xiii*

Septuaginta	Septuaginta, Vetus Testamentum Graecum Auctoritate Academiae Scientiarum Gottingensis editum
TSK	Theologische Studien und Kritiken
TR	Theologische Rundschau
VT	Vetus Testamentum
VTSup	Supplements to Vetus Testamentum
WMANT	Wissenschaftliche Monographien zum Alten und Neuen Testament
ZAW	Zeitschrift für die alttestamentliche Wissenschaft

B. Cited Works and Sources
(See Bibliography for full citations)

BA	Biblical Aramaic
BAG	Bauer, Arndt and Gingrich, *A Greek-English Lexicon of the New Testament*
BDF	Blass, Debrunner and Funk, *A Greek Grammar of the New Testament*
BDB	Brown, Driver and Briggs, *Hebrew Lexicon*
BH	Biblical Hebrew
CATSS	Computer Assisted Tools for Septuagint Studies
GBA	Rosenthal, *Grammar of Biblical Aramaic*
HA	Hebrew/Aramaic
HR	Hatch-Repath, *A Concordance to the Septuagint and the other Greek Versions of the Old Testament*

KB	Koehler-Baumgartner, *Lexicon in Veteris Testamenti Libros*
LEH	Lust, Eynikel, and Hauspie, *A Greek-English Lexicon of the Septuagint*
LSJ	Liddell-Scott, Jones, *A Greek English Lexicon*
LXX	Septuagint, not necessarily in its oldest recoverable form (according to Rhalfs)
Mayser	Mayser, *Grammatik der griechischen Papyri*
MT	Masoretic Text
OG	Old Greek text of Daniel
P	Peshitta
Th	Theodotion text of Daniel

C. Text Critical Sigla

+	plus
>	minus
1,3,2	different order of words
√	root

Preface

This volume is a revised version of my Ph.D. thesis, which was completed at the University of Durham in 1994. The content and presentation of the bulk of the material is essentially the same, but the introduction is a condensation of several chapters. The changes do not affect the thrust of the argument developed here, but some readers who would like more background on the theory of translation technique and the importance of papyrus 967 as a witness to the Old Greek of Daniel may want to consult my thesis.

The idea for the thesis germinated during my M.Div. studies while I was reading on the theory of Translation Technique and working in the texts of Daniel. It occurred to me that Daniel would be the perfect book to explore the differences between "literal" and "free" translations and the question of what makes a recension, because it is the only book where we have witnesses to two complete Greek versions. However, as often happens during the course of one's research, new questions arose and my answers to others were modified. The most significant conclusion, which is bound to raise a few eyebrows, is that the available evidence indicates that the Theodotion text in Daniel is an independent translation and not a revision of the Old Greek. I arrived at this conclusion over a lengthy period and through a number of steps, and I believe that the content of this book is presented in such a way that you, the reader, can follow my footprints. I would only urge from the outset that you set aside any presuppositions about the Theodotion text of Daniel and allow the evidence to speak for itself.

There are some people to whom I wish to take the time to thank publicly, because the opportunity and ability to move across the ocean with my wife and four children to pursue a dream that has culminated in the wordprocessing of this volume did not come without their unfailing support, generosity, and love. My teachers and fellow students, past and present, have stimulated my thinking in countless ways. However, I have to single out some for their specific contributions. First, it was a privilege to have Dr. Robert Hayward to supervise my research. He listened to the ramblings of an enthusiastic student with unfailing patience and constant encouragement. I thank him for his counsel and I hope that I can pass on his wisdom to others. Rev. Glenn Wooden, my friend and colleague in Danielic research, also made an invaluable contribution. Besides our constant exchange of ideas courtesy of e-mail, he read the first draft of most of my thesis and offered many helpful suggestions. I also must acknowledge the helpful comments and suggestions of my examiners. Dr. Anthony Gelston, my internal reader, was a model of academic excellence throughout the course of my stay in Durham. Dr. Alison Salvesen, my external reader, had incisive questions and helpful suggestions, and it has been my privilege to work with her in Septuagint studies.

The overall support and congeniality in the Theology Department on Palace Green made my time of research in Durham one of the most pleasurable experiences of my life. I shall miss the exhilaration of walking up to the square and the majesty of Durham Cathedral and Castle. The friends I made in Kepier Court and at Durham City Baptist Church will always remain close to my heart. The fellowship at Grange Road Baptist Church in Jarrow also offered both personal and financial support, and for this I am thankful. I received an ORS award from the Committee of Vice-Chancellors and Principals of the Universities of the United Kingdom, and for this I am most grateful. The Theology Department in Durham also provided me with a small fellowship. Thanks also to Bernard Taylor and Scholars Press for accepting this volume for the *Septuagint and Cognate Studies* series.

Preface

I would never have made it this far without the constant support of my parents and extended family, but my wife and children have made the greatest sacrifices so that a perpetual student could achieve his goal. In particular, my best friend and lifelong partner, Martha, has made countless sacrifices, and it is to her that this book is dedicated.

Finally, I hope that this study will in some way honour Him whose Word is studied here.

Chapter I

Introduction

I.1. *Purpose of this Volume*

The primary purpose of this monograph is to analyze the Translation Technique (TT) employed in the Old Greek (OG) and Theodotion (Th) versions of the Book of Daniel in order to compare their relationship and demonstrate how that knowledge can be applied to textual criticism of the Hebrew/Aramaic (HA) version of Daniel.[1] Although the aim is stated in one sentence, it encompasses two important subjects. The first is the Greek texts chosen for the study: the OG and Th versions of Daniel. The second is the study of TT and how the study of TT can

---

[1] The relevant secondary literature on the Old Greek and Theodotion versions of Daniel is extensive. At this point we note the number of theses that have recently been devoted to the study of the Greek texts of Daniel. See A. McCrystall, "Studies in the Old Greek Translation of Daniel" (D.Phil. Dissertation, Oxford University, 1980); S. Pace Jeansonne, *The Old Greek Translation of Daniel 7-12* (CBQMS 19; Washington: Catholic Biblical Association, 1988); D. O. Wenthe, "The Old Greek Translation of Daniel 1-6" (Ph.D. Dissertation, University of Notre Dame, 1991); P. S. David, "The Composition and Structure of the Book of Daniel: A Synchronic and Diachronic Reading" (Ph.D. Dissertation, Katholicke Universiteit, Leuven, 1991); T. J. Meadowcroft, "A Literary Critical Comparison of the Masoretic Text and Septuagint of Daniel 2-7" (Ph.D. Dissertation, University of Edinburgh, 1993); T. McLay, "Translation Technique and Textual Studies in the Old Greek and Theodotion Versions of Daniel" (Ph.D. Dissertation, University of Durham, 1994). The classic study of the OG version was by A. Bludau, *Die Alexandrinische übersetzung des Buches Daniel und ihr Verhältnis zum Massorethischen Text* (Freiburg: Herder'sche Verlagshandlung, 1897).

inform the scholar's use of a version for the textual criticism of the Hebrew Bible.

In the course of this thesis, then, we will begin with the textual criticism of OG and the analysis of the TT of the Greek texts of Daniel and follow this process through to its ultimate end: textual criticism of MT. There are those who might express reservations about the wisdom of "lone rangers" attempting to combine too many areas of research and manufacturing tendentious "do-it-yourself" methodologies,[2] and, the shortcomings of this research may well prove their doubts well-founded. On the other hand, though it is more difficult nowadays to employ a multi-disciplinary approach in one's research, the necessity of doing so remains.[3] If one of the main reasons for reconstructing the critical text of the versions is to serve textual criticism of MT and, furthermore, if the primary reason why we analyze TT is also to serve textual criticism of MT, then a study that combines these exercises is in order.

I will comment more fully on the aims of this research below.

I.2. *Translation Technique and Textual Criticism*

Foremost in the research of TT in the OG is the need for a model that is appropriate for the analysis of two very different ancient languages. In recent years there has been an increasing emphasis on the features of literalism in a translation, but it is our contention that the focus on literalism is inadequate to describe the TT of any book,

---

[2] For example, see the excellent discussion of the difficulties of employing modern linguistic methods to the analysis of TT by J. De Waard, "La Septante: une Traduction," *Études sur le Judaïsme Hellénistique* (ed. R. Kuntzmann and J. Schlosser; Paris: Les Éditions du CERF, 1984), 133-45, especially p. 143.

[3] See also the article by Moshe Goshen-Gottstein, in which he raises concerns about the increasing specialization and fragmentation within biblical scholarship, in "The Textual Criticism of the Old Testament: Rise, Decline, Rebirth," *JBL* 102 (1983): 365-99.

Introduction 3

particularly a free translation like the OG of Daniel.[4] The emphasis on literalism has been influenced by two scholars who have set forth most clearly the means for defining literalism: James Barr and Emanuel Tov. In separate works first Barr and then Tov proposed criteria for literalism, which were very similar in content.[5] The research on the characteristics of literalism has concentrated on generating statistics that measure the degree to which various books formally reproduce the source text in the receptor language. Although these statistics are helpful as a general guide to TT, they are insufficient to describe how the translator understood the text before him in any particular case.

Our thesis is that the analysis of TT should be informed by the insights of modern linguistic research. The science of linguistics has made great gains in the past century and the last 30 years of Biblical scholarship reveal the growing influence of linguistics in biblical studies.[6] Though some scholars have used linguistic principles in their research of TT in the LXX (notably Ilmari Soisalon-Soininen and his

---

[4] For studies which focus on the criteria for literalism see, G. Marquis, "Consistency of Lexical Equivalents as a Criterion for the Evaluation of Translation Technique," ed. C. Cox, *VI Congress of the IOSCS* (SCS 23; Atlanta: Scholars Press, 1988) 405-424; "Word Order as a Criterion for the Evaluation of Translation Technique in the LXX and the Evaluation of Word-Order Variants as Exemplified in LXX-Ezekiel," *Textus* 13 (1986): 59-84; E. Tov, and B.G. Wright, "Computer Assisted Study of the Criteria for Assessing the Literalness of Translation Units in the LXX," *Textus* 12 (1985): 149-187; B.G. Wright, "The Quantitative Representation of Elements: Evaluating 'Literalism' in the LXX," ed. C. Cox, *VI Congress of the IOSCS* (SCS 23; Atlanta: Scholars Press, 1988) 311-335; *No Small Difference, Sirach's Relationship to Its Hebrew Parent Text* (SCS 26; Atlanta: Scholars Press, 1989). For a useful overview of what has been written on TT in the LXX, see S. Olofsson *The LXX Version: A Guide to the Translation Technique of the Septuagint* (ConBib.OT 30; Stockholm: Almqvist & Wiksell, 1990).

[5] J. Barr, "The Typology of Literalism in Ancient Biblical Translations," *MSU* 15 (1979): 294; E. Tov, *The Text-Critical Use of the Septuagint in Biblical Research* (JBS 3; Jerusalem: Simor, 1981) 54-60.

[6] James Barr justly deserves much of the credit for putting Biblical scholars on the right track in his book, *The Semantics of Biblical Language* (Oxford: University Press, 1961).

students Raija Sollamo and Anneli Aejmelaeus[7]), they have confined their investigations to specific areas of syntax and applied them to numerous books of the LXX rather than attempting to describe the TT of a particular book. However, there has been one publication that appeared during the course of this research that does offer a TT analysis of a biblical book by employing a linguistic approach.[8] H. Szpek offers a very thorough model for the analysis of TT; and our research employs a similar methodology, which was developed independently.[9]

The existence of two Greek versions of the book of Daniel, which are closely related to the same *Vorlage* (at least in chapters 1-3 and 7-12), furnishes us with ideal examples for the demonstration of our methodology for the analysis of TT. The two versions are particularly appropriate because they manifest important differences in how each rendered its parent text. It has become common to conceptualize these differences by referring to the OG version as a "free" translation, whereas Th's translation is described as "literal."[10] These characterizations, however, have tended to cast more shadow than light on the subject of TT. In fact, the majority of the books of the LXX were translated very literally; and the differences between "literal" and "free" translations have sometimes been overemphasized without due

---

[7] See I. Soisalon-Soininen, *Die Infinitive in der Septuaginta* (AASF B 132, 1; Helsinki: Suomalainen Tiedeakatemia, 1965); R. Sollamo, *Renderings of Hebrew Semiprepositions in the Septuagint* (AASF 19; Helsinki: Suomalainen Tiedeaka-temia, 1979); A. Aejmelaeus, *Parataxis in the Septuagint* (AASF 31; Helsinki: Suomalainen Tiedeakatemia, 1982).

[8] H. M. Szpek, *Translation Technique in the Peshitta to Job: A Model for Evaluating a Text with Documentation from the Peshitta to Job* (SBLDS 137; Atlanta: Scholars Press, 1992). See also J. De Waard, "Translation Techniques Used by the Greek Translators of Ruth," *Bib* 54 (1973): 499-515; "Translation Techniques Used by the Greek Translators of Amos," *Bib* 59 (1978): 339-50.

[9] The similarites and differences between the approach of Szpek and that which I employed are fully discussed in chapter four of my thesis.

[10] H. St. J. Thackeray, *A Grammar of the Old Testament in Greek* (Cambridge: University Press, 1909) 12-13; H.B. Swete, *An Introduction to the Old Testament in Greek* (rev. by R. R. Ottley; Cambridge: University Press, 1914) 43, 310.

attention to features that they have in common. James Barr draws attention to this very point when he states: "truly 'free' translation in the sense in which this might be understood by the modern literary public, scarcely existed in the world of the LXX, or indeed of much of ancient biblical translation in general."[11]

It has already been mentioned that the primary reason for the analysis of TT arises from the crucial role it plays in textual criticism.[12] TT and the science of textual criticism are inextricably interwoven, just as we cannot consider the reading of the OG or MT without recourse to the other. For these reasons our aim is to employ an approach to the analysis of TT that also serves the practical needs of the textual critic and we will demonstrate how the application of the methodology can serve textual criticism of both the OG and MT of Daniel. At this point, it is worthwhile to entertain a brief discussion of how TT and textual criticism relate and, more particularly, why specific textual problems in the texts of Daniel require that we give special attention to textual criticism.

Textual criticism involves two basic steps: first, the collection of variants and, second, the evaluation of the variants. However, the evaluation of the LXX as a source of variant readings for the proto-MT is complicated for three reasons. First, the LXX is a translation and one must attempt to reconstruct the hypothetical *Vorlage* of the Greek text by retroversion before one can assess the value of the OG as a witness. However, as Goshen-Gottstein warns, "there is no retroversion without a residue of doubt, and what seems self-evident to one scholar may look like a house of cards to his fellow."[13] In the second place, the process

---

[11] Barr, "Typology," 281.

[12] The need for clarity in our use of the LXX for textual criticism is well illustrated by L. Greenspoon in "The Use and Abuse of the Term 'LXX' and Related Terminology in Recent Scholarship," *BIOSCS* 20 (1987): 21-29.

[13] M. Goshen-Gottstein, "Theory and Practice of Textual Criticism," *Textus* 3 (1963): 132.

of retroversion is itself complicated in many instances because the original OG text must first be established before attempting to retrovert the semitic text from which it was translated. In essence, one must collect and evaluate the variant readings from the witnesses to the OG text of a book before one can evaluate the retroverted reading of the OG as a witness to the original semitic text.[14] There are, then, two stages of textual criticism in the use of an ancient version like the LXX for the textual criticism of the MT, and the exhaustive analysis of the TT in a given unit/book is essential for its text-critical use at both of these levels.[15]

It is all the more important to attempt to discern whether we have established a reliable critical text of OG because the Th version supplanted it at an early date, and the majority of manuscripts we possess witness to this later Th version. There are only two extant witnesses to the complete text of OG, and only one of them is in Greek. The Chisian (Chigi) manuscript, numbered 88 by Rahlfs and Ziegler,[16] is dated in the 9-11th centuries C.E. The other manuscript is the Syro-Hexapla (Syh) which was completed by Paul of Tella in 615-617 C.E. The Syh

---

[14] The *Text-Critical Use of the Septuagint* by E. Tov is by far the best introduction to this process. The Göttingen editions are indispensable for the task of textual criticism and it can only be hoped that the work on the remaining books will be accomplished as soon as possible.

[15] A. Pietersma writes that a thorough analysis of the TT:

> . . . might be called the quest for the Archimedean point, because only from this vantage point can the text-critic sit in judgment over the fidelity with which the manuscripts have preserved the original text, and hence determine the quality of individual texts.

A. Pietersma, "Septuagint Research: A Plea for a Return to Basic Issues," *VT* 35 (1985): 299.

[16] A. Rahlfs, ed., *Septuaginta, id est Vetus Testamentum Graece iuxta LXX Intepretes* (2 vols.; Stuttgart: Privilegierte württembergische Bibelanstalt, 1935); J. Ziegler, *Susanna, Daniel, Bel et Draco* (*Septuaginta* 16:2; Göttingen: Vandenhoeck & Ruprecht, 1954). Incorrectly numbered as 87 by H.B. Swete.

Introduction 7

is an extremely literal translation of Origen's Hexapla into Syriac.[17] One notable feature of 88 and Syh is the extent of their agreement. Ziegler refers to them as "sister manuscripts."[18] The only extant pre-hexaplaric manuscript of Daniel is papyrus 967, which was discovered in 1931 and required 46 years and the efforts of four editors before it was fully published.[19] Unfortunately, only the texts published by Kenyon were available to Ziegler when he prepared the critical edition of OG in the Göttingen series, so the volume lacks the readings of 967 in the editions published by Hamm, Geissen, and Roca-Puig. The necessity of reconstructing the OG for these sections is made obvious by the number of variants between 967 and Ziegler's text. There is also no doubt that 967 is the more faithful witness to the original OG text.[20] Therefore, our analysis of the texts will always be concerned with establishing what is the most likely reading of OG.[21]

---

[17] A. Vööbus, *The Hexapla and the Syro-Hexapla* (Wetteren: Cultura, 1971) 55-57.

[18] J. Ziegler, *Susanna, Daniel, Bel et Draco* (*Septuaginta* 16:2; Göttingen: Vandenhoeck & Ruprecht, 1954) 13.

[19] Sir F.G. Kenyon, *The Chester Beatty Biblical Papyri. Fasc. VIII Ezekiel, Daniel, Esther (Plates and Text)* (London: Emery Walker, 1937-38); A. Geissen, *Der Septuaginta-Text des Buches Daniel Kap. 5-12, zusammmen mit Susanna, Bel et Draco, sowie Esther Kap. 1,1a-2,15 nach dem kölner Teil des Papyrus 967* (PTA 5; Bonn: Habelt, 1968); W. Hamm, *Der Septuaginta-Text des Buches Daniel nach dem kölner Teil des Papyrus 967: Kap I-II* (PTA 10; Bonn: Habelt, 1969); W. Hamm, *Der Septuaginta-Text des Buches Daniel nach dem kölner Teil des Papyrus 967: Kap III-IV* (PTA 21; Bonn: Habelt, 1977); R. Roca-Puig, "Daniel: Dos Semifogli del Codex 967," *Aegyptus* 56 (1976): 3-18.

[20] See Ziegler, 19-21; Hamm, I-II, 19-55. Due to the limited number of witnesses to OG we also have to recognize the provisional nature of any critical reconstruction of the text. Given the obvious superiority of 967 it is odd that in his recent thesis Meadowcroft, 22, characterizes Ziegler's text as "biased" toward 967.

[21] All the variant readings from the aforementioned editions of 967 have been collated and evaluated against Ziegler's critical text in chapter 2 of my thesis. The variants have been published as "A Collation of Variants from 967 to Ziegler's Critical Edition of *Susanna, Daniel, Bel et Draco*," *Textus* 18 (1995): 119-32; a modified form has been used to supplement the variant files for Daniel in the CATSS project.

Obviously, it would have been more practical for our purposes to have analyzed an established critical text, and, if a revised edition of Ziegler's text were not already in preparation by O. Munnich, the OG text of Daniel would have been worthy of a thesis in its own right.[22] On the other hand, the OG and Th texts of Daniel were ideal for the purposes of this research, so by establishing a preliminary critical text we should be able to achieve reasonably accurate results. Furthermore, the lack of a standard critical text allows us the freedom to work with the evidence unencumbered by someone else's presuppositions about what the text should read. At the same time, many of our text-critical decisions are not made in a vacuum. The editors of 967 and other scholars like Jeansonne and Albertz have already evaluated variant readings in the papyrus. In many cases they have provided more than adequate reason to adopt a reading as OG, and the reader is sometimes directed to one of their volumes for further discussion. Of course, in some cases our choice of reading does not agree.

In order to indicate the significance of 967 for the reconstruction of OG I will offer just one example. מה די להוא occurs four times in chapter 2: vv. 28, 29(2), 45. Th renders it in each instance with ἅ(τί) δεῖ γενέσθαι. OG uses ἃ δεῖ γενέσθαι in 2:28 and τὰ ἐσόμενα in 2:45, while the textual witnesses have variant readings for the two occurrences of the phrase in 2:29. The first occurrence in 2:29 is omitted in 88 due to homoioteleuton, and so Ziegler reconstructs πάντα ἃ δεῖ γενέσθαι from Syh; whereas 967 reads ὅσα δεῖ γενέσθαι. In the second, Ziegler again reads ἃ δεῖ γενέσθαι while 967 has ἃ μέλλει γίνεσθαι. Given the reading in 2:45 and the greater probability that the OG readings in 2:29 are represented by 967 which offers a variety of translation equivalents for the Aramaic מה די להוא, the readings of 88-

---

[22] The revised edition of Ziegler's text by O. Munnich is due for completion in the next few years.

Introduction   9

Syh are probably due to later scribal harmonization to the first reading in 2:28 or, more likely, Th influence.²³

Once the OG text is established and the textual critic encounters a passage, which, when retroverted, witnesses to a variant reading against MT, it has to be evaluated. There are three basic options: 1) Does the OG reflect a different *Vorlage* or a misunderstanding of the *Vorlage*?²⁴ 2) Is the reading merely a dynamic rendering or does it in some way reflect the TT of the translator? 3) Is there evidence of theological *Tendenz* on the part of the translator, which motivated the rendering? Only with a balanced assessment of the TT of the whole book/unit in question can the text-critic begin to evaluate each possible variant and whether it originates from a differing *Vorlage*. As Talshir states, "The scholar finds himself in a vicious circle of evaluating the character of the translator's source on the one hand, and his translation technique on the other."²⁵

There is an important caveat to be added to our cursory introduction to the process of evaluating texts, which is the third difficulty of using the LXX for textual criticism. The *Vorlage* from which an OG translation was made was not always the same as the majority text which

---

²³ See also 8:19; compare the remarks of F.F. Bruce who states that the use of ἃ δεῖ γενέσθαι (presupposing Ziegler's text) is an implicit "emphasis on apocalyptic necessity." F. F. Bruce, "The Oldest Greek Version of Daniel," *OTS* 20 (1977): 24. Even if the text did read as Bruce supposes, it would not justify his interpretation because the OG employs a variety of equivalents for the same Aramaic. It is Th who employs ἃ δεῖ γενέσθαι consistently. In fact, given the Th influence on the 2 uses in 2:29—which would remain unknown without 967—and the Th influence on all our witnesses to OG, it is probable that the reading of ἃ δεῖ γενέσθαι in v. 28 of OG stems from Th.

²⁴ Obviously, if a reading in the OG can be explained by the fact that the trans-lator possibly misread (*metathesis, parablepsis*) or misunderstood the *Vorlage* in any way, then the OG does not witness to a variant at all.

²⁵ Z. Talshir, "Linguistic Development and the Evaluation of Translation Technique in the Septuagint," *Scripta* 31 (1986): 301; J. H. Sailhamer, "The Translational Technique of the Greek Septuagint for the Hebrew Verbs and Participles in Psalms 3-41," (Ph.D. Dissertation, University of California, 1981) 6-7.

eventually emerged as MT.[26] In fact, the manuscripts discovered in Qumran prove that in some cases they were very different.[27] There are several theories to account for these discrepancies, but it is impossible to evaluate the merits of these theories here.[28] However, it is also impossible to avoid the issue of the *Vorlage* for OG because of chapters 4-6.

The presence of an alternative *Vorlage* in the OG of chapters 4-6 is assumed for the analysis of TT. However, it need not follow from the existence of an alternative *Vorlage* in chapters 4-6 that the *Vorlage* in chapters 1-3, and 7-12 also differed significantly from MT. Not only is this premise logical, but there are two additional factors to consider. First, and this anticipates our conclusions, the analysis of TT in OG supports Albertz' contention that chapters 4-6 originate from a different

---

[26] See *Text-Critical Use* by Tov, or any of several articles for brief introductions to some of the problems of using the LXX for textual criticism: Tov, "The Nature of the Hebrew Text Underlying the Septuagint. A Survey of the Problems," *JSOT* 7 (1978): 53-68; "The Original Shape of the Biblical Text," *VTSup* 43 (1991): 345-59; J. W. Wevers, "The Use of the Versions for Text Criticism: The Septuagint," *La Septuaginta en la Investigacion Contemporanea (V Congreso de la IOSCS)* (ed. N. F. Marcos; Madrid: Instituto Arias Montano, 1985) 15-24; N. Fernández Marcos, "The Use of the Septuagint in the Criticism of the Hebrew Bible," *Sef* 47 (1987): 60-72; *Scribes and Translators: Septuagint and Old Latin in the Books of Kings. VTSup* 54 (Leiden: Brill, 1994) 15-26. For an introduction to specific textual problems using the *DSS* and LXX see, J. H. Tigay, ed., *Empirical Models for Biblical Criticism* (Philadelphia: University of Pennsylvania Press, 1985).

[27] See for example, E. Ulrich, *The Qumran Text of Samuel and Josephus* (HSM 19; Chico: Scholars Press, 1978); J. G. Janzen, *Studies in the Text of Jeremiah* (HSM 6; Cambridge: Harvard University, 1973). S. Soderlund has attempted to overthrow Janzen's results in his work, *The Greek Text of Jeremiah* (JSOT 47; Sheffield: JSOT, 1985) 193-248; but see Janzen's review, "A Critique of Sven Soderlund's *The Greek Text of Jeremiah*," *BIOSCS* 22 (1989): 16-47.

[28] See F. M. Cross and S. Talmon, eds., *Qumran and the History of the Biblical Text* (Cambridge: Harvard University Press, 1975). For a good discussion and evaluation of the issues, see E. Tov, "A Modern Textual Outlook Based on the Qumran Scrolls," *HUCA* 53 (1983): 11-27; E. Tov, *Textual Criticism of the Hebrew Bible* (Minneapolis: Fortress, 1992) 155-197. See also the recent discussion between Tov and Cross, as well as the articles by E. Ulrich and B. Chiesa in J. T. Barrera and L. V. Montaner, eds., *The Madrid Qumran Congress* (2 vols.; Leiden: Brill, 1992).

translator.²⁹ Second, in the main, the OG text itself and the extant manuscripts from Qumran are very close to MT.³⁰ As Collins states in the latest commentary on Daniel, "On the whole, the Qumran discoveries provide powerful evidence of the antiquity of the textual tradition of the MT."³¹ For this reason, although the view that the OG translator was engaging in a type of wholesale theological reinterpretation of the text envisaged by McCrystall³² ought to be rejected, we cannot automatically assume that every difference between OG and MT necessarily points to an alternative *Vorlage*. The latter error is committed in a recent thesis by Wenthe.³³ It is true that the Dead Sea Scrolls have confirmed many retroverted readings and the existence of alternative literary editions. However, each variant has to be evaluated individually. We have to consider the corrupt condition of the OG text and then attempt to discern the TT as best as we are able in order to use

---

²⁹ See R. Albertz, *Der Gott des Daniel* (SBS 131; Stuttgart: Katholisches Bibelwerk, 1988).

³⁰ See also E. Ulrich, "The Canonical Process, Textual Criticism, and Latter Stages in the Composition of the Bible," *Sha'arei Talmon* (ed. M. Fishbane, E. Tov, and W. W. Fields; Winona Lake: Eisenbrauns, 1992) 284-285. See the preliminary edition of the Qumran fragments of Daniel from cave four by Ulrich, "Daniel Manuscripts from Qumran. Part 1: A Preliminary Edition of 4QDan^a," *BASOR* 268 (1987): 17-37; "Daniel Manuscripts from Qumran. Part 2: A Preliminary Edition of 4QDan^b and 4QDan^c," *BASOR* 274 (1989): 3-31.

³¹ J. J. Collins, *Daniel* (Minneapolis: Fortress, 1993) 3.

³² McCrystall's research of the Old Greek translation of Daniel was the first extensive examination of the OG since that of A. Bludau in 1897, and the first chapter offers (1-68) an excellent summary of the history of the investigation of the Old Greek of Daniel. However, his contention that the Book of Daniel underwent extensive revision at the hands of OG has been shown to be seriously flawed by Jeansonne, 118-123. See also my thesis "Translation Technique," 25-31.

³³ Wenthe basically accepts Ziegler's text as representing OG in chapters 1-6 and only rarely refers to the reading of 967. For example, Wenthe (55, 260-261) accepts as OG the texts of 1:20-21 as they are found in Ziegler and believes the pluses stem from an alternative *Vorlage*; but the text of 967 is very different. Wenthe also makes numerous references to Th's revision towards MT (54, 57, 61 *passim*), but does not evidence any careful analysis of the question. See McLay, "Translation Technique," 58.

this understanding for textual criticism of MT. Therefore, our working hypothesis is that the *Vorlage* of OG was very close to MT except in chapters 4-6 and the end of chapter 3 where OG has differences due to the long addition in the text.

I.3. The Book of Daniel and the OG and Th Versions

The co-existence of the OG and Th versions of Daniel inevitably leads to a discussion of how the two are related to one another. The third aim of this investigation is to determine whether Th is a translation or a recension of the OG and, if it is a recension, is it part of the *kaige* tradition?[34] Previous research on the recensions has been limited for the most part to lexical studies,[35] whereas this analysis of TT—primarily because we have access to two translations of the same text—offers the

---

[34] The best recent introductions to the text of the Septuagint and the recensions have been written by E. Tov and O. Munnich. See Tov, "Die griechischen Bibelübersetzungen," *ANRW* II.20.1 (1986): 121-89; G. Dorival, M. Harl, and O. Munnich, *La Bible Grecque des Septante* (Paris: Éditions du CERF, 1988) 129-200. See also S. Jellicoe, *The Septuagint and Modern Study* (Oxford: Clarendon, 1968). The terminology *kaige* tradition rather than recension is employed because there is no justification for treating the texts identified with *kaige* as a monolithic group. See J. W. Wevers, "Barthélemy and Proto-Septuagint Studies," *BIOSCS* 21 (1988): 33-34. See also the recent exhaustive treatment of the revisor of Job by Peter Gentry, "An Analysis of the Revisor's Text of the Greek Job," (Ph.D. Dissertation, University of Toronto, 1994) 411-484, 488.

[35] D. Barthélemy, *Les Devanciers D'Aquila: Première Publication Intégrale du Texte des Fragments du Dodécaprophéton* (*VTSup* 10; Leiden: E.J. Brill, 1963); K.G. O'Connell, *The Theodotionic Revision of the Book of Exodus* (*HSM* 3; Cambridge: Harvard University Press, 1972); E. Tov, *The Septuagint Translation of Jeremiah and Baruch* (*HSM* 8; Missoula: Scholars Press, 1976); W. Bodine, *The Greek Text of Judges* (*HSM* 23; Chico: Scholars Press, 1980); L.J. Greenspoon, *Textual Studies in the Book of Joshua* (*HSM* 28; Chico: Scholars Press, 1983). A notable exception to the above studies is the recent thesis by Gentry. Although his approach is different from the methodology that is employed here, he provides an exhaustive analysis of the Theodotionic material in the text of Job. Besides the lexical equivalency of all nouns in Theodotion Job, Gentry separately examines proper nouns, common nouns, differences in number, bound phrases, attributive phrases, and articulation. He then treats the translation of all pronouns, verbal forms, particles, prepositions, and conjunctions in separate categories.

Introduction   13

opportunity of providing a more complete description of the activity of Th. Most scholars would affirm that Th is a recension (or revision) of the OG,[36] but such an assessment has to be grounded in a detailed analysis.

Our purpose is to determine whether Th is a recension, but how do we distinguish between revision and translation? This is a difficult question, and has not been sufficiently addressed. With respect to Th the views of scholars seem more often to reflect a general opinion rather than a sustained examination employing a well-defined methodology. To our knowledge, Jeansonne is the only one who offers some statistics in support of her conclusion that Th is a revision. However, the fact that Th reads the same as OG in 40% of the passage she analyses (8:1-10), does not necessarily lead to the conclusion that in that portion of the passage " θretains the OG."[37] Jeansonne's analysis betrays a basic but misleading assumption that scholars have made, i.e. common readings prove dependence. However, verbal agreements may be explained without recourse to pseudo-theories of recensional activity.[38]

In order to determine whether Th is a revision of OG it is necessary to work with well-defined criteria. In previous research there have been two criteria proposed to determine whether a text is a revision of another text: 1) there must be a sufficient number of distinctive agreements between the texts to prove that one used the other as its

---

[36] Barthélemy, *Les Devanciers*, 43-44; 66-67; J.R. Busto Saiz, "El Texto Teodocionico de Daniel y la Traduccion de Simaco," *Sef* 40 (1980): 41-55; Tov, "Bibelübersetzungen," 177-178. A. Schmitt agrees Th is a recension, but believes it is not part of *kaige*. See A. Schmitt, "Stammt der sogennante Θ' Text bei Daniel wirklich von Theodotion?" *MSU* 9 (1966): 112.

[37] Jeansonne, 57.

[38] See also the recent article by L. L. Grabbe who does not accept common vocabulary as an indication of dependence in his examination of a portion of the Hexapla of the Psalms extant in the Mailand text. L. L. Grabbe, "The Translation Technique of the Greek Minor Versions: Translations or Revisions?" *Septuagint, Scrolls and Cognate Writings* (*SCS* 33; ed. G. J. Brooke and B. Lindars; Atlanta: Scholars Press, 1992) 505-56.

basis; 2) that the revisor worked in a certain way, i.e., in our case, towards the proto-MT.[39] The first criterion is more important than the second for two reasons. First, a translation may be closer to its *Vorlage* solely on the basis of the translator's methodology (i.e. formal equivalence). Therefore, a sufficient number of distinctive agreements are required between two texts in order to argue for dependence of one translator upon another. Second, without distinctive agreements the use of common readings is difficult to evaluate, because LXX translators could and (more often than not) did employ common and expected SEs for a significant percentage of the vocabulary in their Hebrew *Vorlagen*.

Unfortunately, even the criterion of distinctive agreements has to be applied cautiously, because agreements are sometimes due to textual corruption. Therefore, we have to add a third criterion to our list: distinctive disagreements. Distinctive disagreements are not mere inconsistencies in the work of the (presumed) revisor, but renditions that are totally independent of the text (presumably) being revised. In other words, distinctive disagreements are features that indicate the work of an independent translator. In a comparison of the texts of Th and OG in Daniel we will have to weigh very carefully evidence of agreements and disagreements in order to give us a balanced perspective of Th's text, especially when our witnesses to the text of the OG are so sparse. Even with the advent of 967 as a witness to the OG we will discover that there remains significant evidence that the text of OG has been corrupted through harmonization to MT and Th. Therefore, the task of determining the relationship that existed between the texts in their original composition is complex, and requires that the original OG text be disentangled as much as possible from the later corrupted form. In some passages this task is impossible.

---

[39] E. Tov, *Jeremiah*, 43; J.W. Wevers, "An Apologia for Septuagint Studies," *BIOSCS* 18 (1985): 29-33; L. J. McGregor, *The Greek Text of Ezekiel: An Examination of Its Homogeneity* (*SCS* 18; Atlanta: Scholars Press, 1985), 132-133.

There are at least three ways by which we could characterize Th's relation to OG. 1) It could be a completely independent translation. 2) It could be a recension in the way that it is generally understood. That is, Th had the OG and proto-MT before him and copied OG as long as it formally reproduced the *Vorlage*. In certain cases Th standardized the terminology, though not always consistently, and Th introduced corrections to the OG where it departed from his proto-MT *Vorlage*. These corrections may have resulted from Th's perception that OG translated incorrectly or too freely.[40] 3) Another way to view their relationship is that Th did have both proto-MT and OG (or may have been familiar with OG), but that Th translated his *Vorlage* more or less independently and employed OG occasionally or when confronted with difficult passages.

Ideally, as we begin the investigation we should allow the evidence to speak for itself and for the possibility that any one of the three options provides the closest approximation to Th's methodology. However, given the fact that most readers assume that Th is a recension (option #2), the argument will usually take this assumption as its point of reference and challenge it. I will argue that the available evidence supports the last of these three options, though it is probable that Th is a completely independent translation. The analysis of the texts will provide the reader with an opportunity to draw his/her own conclusion regarding this issue.

Finally, an examination of the OG and Th texts of Daniel cannot be separated from the question of whether Th is related to the so-called *kaige* texts or *kaige*-Theodotion. This is so for two reasons: 1) most scholars assume that Th is a recension of OG; 2) most scholars assume that Th is part of *kaige*. Following our examination of the TT in OG

---

[40] See S. P. Brock, "To Revise or Not to Revise: Attitudes to Jewish Biblical Translation," *Septuagint, Scrolls and Cognate Writings* (*SCS* 33; ed. G. J. Brooke and B. Lindars; Atlanta: Scholars Press, 1992) 301-38. L. Greenspoon suggests an interesting modern analogy to "Theodotion's" activity in, "Biblical Translators in Antiquity and in the Modern World," *HUCA* 60 (1989): 91-113.

and Th we will investigate Th's relationship to the *kaige* tradition based on the list of *kaige* characteristics that have been proposed by various writers.[41]

I.4. The Methodology for the Analysis of TT

In brief, the model of TT upon which this research is based postulates that the description of the TT of a unit of translation requires the comparison of the translation equivalents employed in the target text with the elements of the source text from which they were derived.[42] The model is based upon two key linguistic presuppositions: 1) each language has its own structure; 2) there is a distinction in language between *langue* and *parole*.[43]

The emphasis on *structuralism* in linguistics originated with Ferdinand de Saussure. The thesis of structuralism is:

> . . . that every language is a unique relational structure, or system, and that the units which we identify, or postulate as theoretical constructs, in analysing the sentence of a particular language (sounds, words, meanings, etc.) derive both their essence and their existence from their relationships with other units in the same language-system. We cannot first identify the units and then, at a subsequent stage of

---

[41] A list is provided by Greenspoon, *Joshua*, 270-273; Gentry, 400-405.

[42] For works dealing with methodology for the analysis of TT, see Soisalon-Soininen, *Die Infinitive*; "Beobactungen zur Arbeitsweise der Septuaginta-Übersetzer," *Isac Leo Seeligmann Volume* (ed. A. Rofé and Y. Zakovitch; Jerusalem: Magnes, 1983) 319-29; "Methodologische Fragen der Erforschung der Septuaginta-Syntax," *VI Congress of the IOSCS* (ed. C. Cox; Atlanta: Scholars Press, 1986) 425-44; A. Aejmelaeus, "Translation Technique and the Intention of the Translator," *VII Congress of the IOSCS* (SCS 31; ed. C. Cox (Atlanta: Scholars Press, 1991) 23-36.

[43] A more detailed introduction to the linguistic presuppositions upon which this research is based is given in my thesis, "Translation Technique," 123-172. For an introduction to basic linguistic concepts and terminology, see S. E. Porter, "Studying Ancient Languages from a Modern Linguistic Perspective: Essential Terms and Terminology," *FN* 2 (1989): 147-72.

Introduction   17

   the analysis, enquire what combinatorial or other relations hold
   between them: we simultaneously identify both the units and their
   interrelations.[44]

   Each language, then, has its own way of combining linguistic elements together to convey meaning. The connection between the structure of the language system and semantic information conveyed is critical for the analysis of TT, because the structure of two different languages will inevitably reveal differences. In the process of translating the translator is immediately confronted with the clash between structure and meaning. That is, if the translator attempts to render the source text using the same surface structures in the target language (*formal equivalence*), then there is liable to be some loss of meaning. Loss of meaning occurs because the surface structures of the target language do not convey meaning in the same way as the surface structures of the source language.[45] Conversely, the decision to render the meaning of the *Vorlage* will often require the choice of different surface structures in the target language (*dynamic equivalence*).[46] In the LXX the translators were able to reproduce the formal structure of their semitic *Vorlage* largely because of the freedom allowed in Greek word order. This

---

[44] J. Lyons, *Semantics* (2 vols.; Cambridge: University Press, 1977) I.231-232.

[45] Soisalon-Soininen ("Methodologische Fragen," 426) states, " . . . der Character der Übersetzung wird von zwei ganz verschiedenen Faktoren bestimmt: erstens vom Stil des hebräischen Urtextes, der in den verschiedenen Büchern des ATs sehr unterschiedlich ist, zweitens von der unterschiedlichen Arbeitsweise der Übersetzer."

[46] E. Nida, *Toward a Science of Translating* (Leiden: E.J. Brill, 1964) 159-176. For the most part we only have to be concerned with the surface (as opposed to deep) structure of grammar because the LXX translators reproduced so much of the formal structure of their source. However, occasions where the translators made additions to the text to make an element explicit that was only implicit in the source text, or made transformations (eg. changed an active verb to a passive) do reflect their understanding of deep structure. For explanations of deep structure (transformational) grammar, see J. Lyons, *Chomsky* (London: Fontana, 1970); A. Radford, *Transformational Syntax: A student's guide to extended standard theory* (Cambridge: University Press, 1981).

ability to mimic the semitic text resulted in unusual, but rarely "grammatically incorrect" Greek. More often is the case that grammatically correct Greek is found, but certain constructions occur with unusual frequency; and/or typical Greek idioms are not encountered as frequently as would otherwise be expected.[47] However, in the midst of the basically formal approach there is relevance in the variations that we do find.

Another distinction made by Saussure was that between *langue* and *parole* (there are no generally accepted translation equivalents in English). *Langue* refers to language as an abstract system, which is common to all speakers of a language community, while *parole* refers to the actual discourse of individuals within the community.[48] Both of these aspects of language play an important role in the study of TT. We could visualize the process of translation and the perspective of the one engaged in the study of TT as we have it in the diagram below.

---

[47] See Soisalon-Soininen's discussion of what constitutes a Hebraism and the importance of determining Hebraizing tendencies in the analysis of TT in "Zurück zur Hebraismenfrage," *Studien zur Septuaginta - Robert Hanhart zu Ehren* (*MSU* 20; ed. D. Fraenkel, U. Quast, and J. Wevers Göttingen: Vandenhoeck & Ruprecht, 1990) 39-43. The translators' reverence for the text is evident in the desire to follow the word order and represent the various elements of the words in the source, but they were able to do this while faithfully attempting to translate the *meaning* of the text as they understood it. See H. M. Orlinsky, "The Septuagint as Holy Writ and the Philosophy of the Translators," *HUCA* 46 (1975): 89-114. That the translators regarded the LXX as authoritative; therefore, they were concerned with accuracy is discussed in J. W. Wevers, "A Study in the Narrative Portions of the Greek Exodus" *Scripta Signa Vocis* (ed. H. L. J. Vanstiphout et al.; Groningen: Egbert Forsten, 1986) 295-303.

[48] Lyons, *Semantics* 1.239.

Introduction

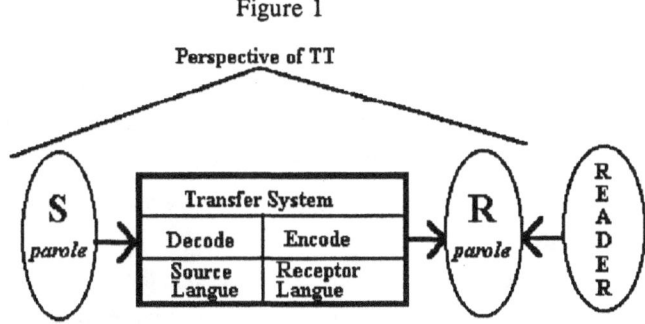

Figure 1

In our diagram the S stands for the source text while the R stands for the receptor text. The Transfer System is the translator. There are other factors which enter into the process of decoding the meaning of the source text (eg. translator's knowledge of vocabulary and cultural differences; textual difficulties), but the present focus is the interplay of *langue* and *parole* for the translator who acts as the medium of transferring the source text into the target language. In the act of translation the original translator has to read the source text (which as a written document is an example of *parole*), and attempts to decode the meaning of that text on the basis of his/her knowledge of the grammar of the source language (*langue*). The translator then has to encode the message of the source text in the receptor language (*parole*) based on his/her knowledge of the grammar of that language (*langue*).[49] These are the minimum requirements for what the translator does though we cannot be

---

[49] As a point of interest the reader of the receptor text has been included in the diagram in order to point out that s/he has no access to the original text or the translation process.

absolutely sure how the neurological process takes place.[50] As the translator encodes the message in the target language s/he must make adjustments in the formal structure of the message due to the different linguistic structures of the two languages. The number of adjustments will largely depend upon the inherent differences in the two languages and how closely the translator attempts to maintain formal correspondence with the source text.[51]

The above diagram also makes clear that the analyst of TT stands above the source and receptor texts, able to view both simultaneously and, therefore, is in a position to describe how the translator (Transfer System) went about the task of translation. Ideally—though this is never the case—the analyst of TT would be omniscient regarding the language, time and place in which both texts were produced and would have both texts in their original form. The analyst is also in a position to see the effect on the meaning of the structure that has passed through the transfer system. Is it basically synonymous, or has some alteration taken place? On the basis of the analysis of TT, the analyst can often suggest why a change has taken place.

---

[50] Chomsky has argued that the faculty for language is genetically encoded in the brain; but, even if this is true, we do not know how the process takes place. See N. Chomsky, *Rules and Representations* (Oxford: Basil Blackwell, 1980), 3-87, 185-216; Lyons provides a useful overview in *Language, Meaning and Context* (Suffolk: Fontana, 1981) 248-257.

[51] For a discussion of the differences between the Hebrew and Greek languages, see J. W. Wevers, "Use of the Versions," 16-19. For example, Greek inflects nouns in five cases, three genders, and two numbers whereas Hebrew has three numbers (dual), two genders, and no case system, though it does inflect for state. Works specifically treating the translation of verbs include J. Barr, "Translators' Handling of Verbs in Semantically Ambiguous Contexts," *VI Congress of the IOSCS* (ed. C. Cox; Atlanta: Scholars Press, 1986) 381-403; Soisalon-Soininen, *Infinitive*; "Die Konstruktion des Verbs bei einem Neutrum Plural im griechischen Pentateuch," *VT* 29 (1979): 189-199; R. Sollamo, "The LXX Renderings of the Infinitive Absolute Used with a Paronymous Finite Verb in the Pentateuch," *La Septuaginta en la Investigacion Contemporanea (V Congreso de la IOSCS)* (ed. N. F. Marcos; Madrid: Instituto Arias Montano, 1985) 101-113; A. Aejmelaeus, "*Participium Coniunctum* as a Criterion of Translation Technique," *VT* 32 (1982): 385-93. See also the detailed analysis of the translation of the verb in Theodotion Job by Gentry, 170-241.

Introduction   21

It must be emphasized that TT is primarily concerned to describe what the translator did regardless of why it was done or the effect of the adjustments on the meaning of the text. Meaning is important for the determination of how the translator understood the text, and, therefore, the translation equivalents that s/he chooses to render the *Vorlage*. However, if we are going to conceptualize translation as a process, then it is more appropriate to isolate semantic considerations of the actual choice of renderings to the transfer system. This distinction between the encoding process in the transfer system and the formal surface structure chosen to be employed in the translation is based on the recognition of a clear distinction between the meaning (semantic structure) one is attempting to communicate and how that meaning is converted into a surface structure in a written text.[52] It is by means of this formal comparison of the source and target texts that differences are discovered that were introduced by the transfer system (the translator). Therefore, it is only after this initial formal comparison of linguistic elements that the analyst can begin to formulate answers to the questions about the transfer system, i.e. how the translator made changes (Adjustment), why the changes were made (Motivation), and finally the effect that these changes had on meaning.[53]

Our analysis of TT assumes there are three structural elements that are necessary to analyze and compare in the source and receptor texts: Morphology, Syntax, and Lexicology.[54] In this way all the elements

---

[52] See W. L. Chafe, *Meaning and the Structure of Language* (Chicago: Univ. of Chicago, 1970) 15-91.

[53] Element of Translation, Adjustment, Motivation, and Effect on Meaning are the terms employed by Szpek, 13.

[54] So also Sollamo, who refers to "vocabulary, morphology, and syntax." See R. Sollamo, "Some "improper" prepositions, such as ENΩΠION, ENANTION, ENANTI etc., in the Septuagint and early koine Greek," *VT* 28 (1975): 775. It is in the formal classification of the elements to be analyzed that Szpek's model and the one proposed by myself exhibit considerable differences. The issues are explained in detail in my thesis, "Translation Technique," 151-155.

of the translation can be consistently classified and systematically analyzed as to how they have been employed to translate the elements found in the source text. In the end, every relationship between two texts, both the similarities and differences, can be described as additions, omissions, or substitutions in the forms of the words, the choice of particular words, or in how the words are put together to form larger meaningful units of discourse.

I.5. *Introduction to the Analysis*

Chapters 2-6 consist of an analysis of five passages from the book of Daniel: 1:1-10, 2:1-10, 3:11-20, 8:1-10, 12:1-13. Each passage begins with annotated texts of Th, MT, and OG, which are arranged vertically in parallel alignment. The texts represent both the Hebrew and Aramaic sections of Daniel, and, except for two passages, were chosen at random. The first section, chapter 1:1-10, was chosen because it offered few difficulties, and, therefore, was a suitable means for the reader to become acquainted with the analysis. Chapter 8:1-10 was analyzed because in her examination of the passage Jeansonne concluded that Th is a recension of OG.

The texts for each passage have been aligned in an attempt to maximize readability and facilitate the analysis. As we would expect, however, there are numerous occasions where the wording of OG does not formally correspond to the HA on the same line. The procedure followed for the annotation of the text is described below, and a portion from 1:10 is included as an illustration in Figure 2.

Figure 2

98 τὰ πρόσωπα ὑμῶν	אֶת־פְּנֵיכֶם	^{M}τὸ πρόσωπον ὑμῶν
99 (σκυθρωπὰ)	זֹעֲפִים	διατετραμμένον
100		+καὶ ἀσθενές

There are four columns. Each line is numbered consecutively in the left hand column to provide a more specific point of reference for the discussions that follow. The second and fourth columns contain annotated texts of Th and OG respectively, while the third column has MT. The OG is annotated in four ways. First, the text is annotated numerically to indicate where our text differs from the critical edition of Ziegler. The text critical notes are discussed immediately following the passage.[55] Second, the text is annotated with letters (eg. ^{M} in l. 98) corresponding to the three areas of linguistics for the analysis of TT: ^{M}=Morphology, ^{S}=Syntax, and ^{L}=Lexicology. Third, square brackets [ ] are used to enclose words whose originality is questioned. Fourth, possible pluses and omissions of words in OG are designated by the signs + and - (see l. 100). Most pluses and minuses have been isolated to their own line, but that has not always been possible. Therefore, a + at the beginning of a line designates that the whole line may be a plus, while - - marks omissions in a line of OG compared to MT. If a word (or words) occurs as a plus in a line with word(s) that translate the presumed *Vorlage*, the + occurs immediately before and after the plus. Omissions of some elements, which usually occur as bound morphemes in HA (suffixes, the definite article, the conjunction ו, directive ה, interrogative ה), but in Greek as free morphemes (words), are not normally marked by -. In keeping with the linguistic approach, these items are normally considered in the discussion of TT. The same

---

[55] Several decisions were made regarding the presentation of the text-critical notes in order to avoid unnecessary detail: 1) We have focussed primarily on those instances where the reading of 967 should be accepted over Ziegler's text. 2) In the case of a few minor variants such as prepositions we have retained Ziegler's text even where we believe 967 is superior, if the variant is inconsequntial to the main argument. 3) A few orthographical changes are accepted into our text without comment. For example, 967 consistently employs final ν (112x against 88 in our texts) and there is only one occurrence in 967 in which the ν is omitted against 88. There are 13x where 967 has the final ν on nouns and adjectives against 88 as well. Since the ν dropped out before consonants in later usage (see Thackeray §9.7), it is more probable that we should retain it in all cases where it is attested. Therefore, we will employ the ν where it is found in 967.

principle applies to words such as personal and relative pronouns, the *nota accusativi* את(־את), and inseparable prepositions. Likewise, the appearance of minor morphological elements in the OG, which could be retroverted into HA, are not normally marked by +.

Apart from the numeric citations indicating text-critical notes, the same markings are in Th as in OG, but they are employed differently. First, the use of superscript letters is more sparing than in the case of OG and often highlights features that distinguish the TT of Th from OG. This approach is justified on the basis of the close formal correspondence of Th to MT. Second, due to the close formal relationship between Th and MT, Th is more frequently marked with a + or - for minor morphemes. The omission of minor morphemes in Th, which are usually unmarked in OG, will often be indicated by only one -. Th is marked in a fourth way as well. <u>Underlining</u> marks portions of Th that may indicate dependence on OG. Round brackets (l. 100) are used to indicate places where Th demonstrates significant independence in translation. This marking is for the purpose of determining whether Th is a recension of OG.

The analysis that follows the text will be divided into three sections, each of which addresses one of the major issues of this research. Immediately following the passage we evaluate the TT of OG and Th.[56] The discussion will proceed according to the major headings: morphology, syntax, and lexicology. Sometimes the frequency with which a Greek word renders a HA word in the *Vorlage* is indicated in brackets separated by a slash (/). The frequency of words that are rare in Daniel and the OT are also indicated in round brackets, but are separated by a dash (-). The first number indicates the frequency in Daniel, the second in the LXX.[57] The frequency in OG and Th will

---

[56] The OG reading in all cases assumes the critical text which we have reconstructed.

[57] It should be noted that HR is the source for the frequencies for the LXX, and the time has not always been taken to verify the accuracy of HR with the Göttingen critical editions. The OG of Daniel is an excellent example of the care that must be

usually be inclusive, i.e. they are not counted as separate works. However, if a word is referred to as a HL or a frequency such as 1-10 is given, then that is the only occurrence of that word including both Greek texts. The discussion will always clarify any ambiguous cases. The analysis of the passage will conclude with a summary.

Following the TT analysis there will be a preliminary discussion of the relationship of Th to OG, which is indicated in that particular passage. In the comparison of OG and Th, passages of Th will not be underlined that agree with OG, *if* they can easily be explained as derivative from MT. Neither does the fact that a word(s) is underlined indicate that Th necessarily borrowed from the OG. Underlining only indicates the *possibility* that Th is dependent on the OG or that they share a common reading. Inevitably, there is a subjective element to our discussion, but that cannot be avoided. However, by focusing on instances where Th seems to have borrowed from OG and those where it seems to be independent, it will be possible to arrive at a clearer understanding of their relationship.

We will conclude the investigation of each passage with a discussion of textual variants between OG, Th, and MT. The evaluation of readings will be guided by our understanding of the TT in the OG and Th. We will also consider the witness of the Qumran mss., as well as the Peshitta and Vulgate.

I.6. *Texts and Witnesses Consulted*

The HA text for this study is the fourth edition of *Biblia Hebraica Stuttgartensia* (BHS), which is based on the Leningrad Codex of the Masoretic Text.[58] Reference is also made to the manuscript fragments

---

taken with the use of HR.

[58] K. Elliger and W. Rudolph, *Biblia Hebraica Stuttgartensia* (Stuttgart: Deutsche Bibelstiftung, 1977).

from Qumran, particularly 4QDan^{a,b,c}.⁵⁹ The fragments from caves 1 and 6 do not witness any significant variants from MT, though 1QDan^a does preserve the beginning of the Aramaic section in 2:4b.⁶⁰

The main text for the Th version of Daniel is the critical text by Ziegler. As stated earlier, we will have to reconstruct a critical text for OG in those passages for which papyrus 967 was unavailable to Ziegler.

Occasional reference is also made to the standard critical editions of the Peshitta and Vulgate versions of Daniel.⁶¹

I.7. *Computers and the Analysis of TT*

It is important to acknowledge the significance that modern technology played in the completion of this research. I am grateful to Dr. Robert A. Kraft who made available the files of Daniel from the CATSS project for use in my research. There are three main parts to the CATSS database.⁶² First, there is the morphological analysis of the LXX/OG.⁶³ Second, there is a parallel alignment of the LXX/OG and

---

⁵⁹ See n. 30 above.

⁶⁰ Jeansonne, 6, n. 3.

⁶¹ T. Sprey and The Peshitta Institute, eds., *The Old Testament According to the Peshitta Version: Daniel and Bel and the Dragon* (Leiden: Brill, 1980); R. Weber et al., eds., *Biblia Sacra Iuxta Vulgatam Versionem* (2 vols.; Stuttgart: Deutsche Bibelgesellschaft, 1983). For an extensive study of the Peshitta of Daniel see R. Taylor, *The Peshitta of Daniel* (Leiden: Brill, 1994).

⁶² For a discussion of the philosophy behind the database and the apparatus used see J.R. Abercrombie et al, *Computer Assisted Tools for Septuagint Studies: Volume 1, Ruth* (*SCS* 20; Atlanta: Scholars Press, 1984). For the most recent progress report on the project and a bibliography of published studies which have used the database, see E. Tov, "The CATSS Project: A Progress Report," *VII Congress of the IOSCS* (ed. C. Cox; *SCS* 31; Atlanta: Scholars Press, 1991) 157-163.

⁶³ It should be noted that we use LXX/OG because critical editions of the OG for each book of the LXX have not yet been written. The text of Rahlfs' has been adopted for the data in such cases, but the database itself is continually updated with advances in research.

Introduction 27

MT. Third, there are the textual variants for the LXX/OG.[64] All of the Daniel files proved useful in the present research, though the morphologically analyzed OG along with the morphologically analyzed MT were of prime importance.[65] These texts were searched in order to isolate specific words, morphemes, or syntactical constructions for the purpose of comparison. The programs LBASE and Bible Windows[66] were used to read, search, and retrieve the data from the Biblical texts. LBASE could not use the parallel alignment and morphological files interactively,[67] so the actual comparison and analysis of the data was done manually.

I.8. *A Note on the Citation of the Texts of Daniel*

Most readers are familiar with the fact that the chapter and verse divisions are different in MT and the critical edition of the Greek texts in Ziegler. However, these discrepancies are confined primarily to chapters 3, 4, and 6. In an effort to be as inclusive as possible, passages in Daniel will be cited as follows. The cited text will always be MT in the first instance, while any deviations will follow in round ( ) brackets. For example, the passage corresponding to 3:24 in MT is 3:91 in OG and Th, so it will be cited as 3:24(91). The basic rule is that there is a difference of three verses in chapter 4 and one verse in chapter 6.

---

[64] See B. A. Taylor, "The CATSS Variant Database: An Evaluation," *BIOSCS* 25 (1992): 28-37.

[65] The morphologically tagged MT is distributed by Westminister Theological Seminary.

[66] Developed by John Baima and distributed through Silver Mountain Software, Texas.

[67] Compare the software developed for a different computer system by G. Marquis in "Computer Assisted Tools for Septuagint and Bible Study for ALL—Transcript of a Demonstration," *VII Congress of the IOSCS* (ed. C. Cox, *SCS* 31; Atlanta: Scholars Press, 1991) 165-203; the procedure of Wright, *Difference*, 259-260.

Furthermore, the differences between the HA and Greek texts of Daniel means that in many cases OG has a plus or minus compared to MT. Therefore, in our discussion of translation equivalents it will be noted when there is no corresponding *Vorlage* (eg. MT=0).

I.9. *Plan of Study*

Chapters 2-6 are an investigation of the translation technique of selected texts in the book of Daniel: 1:1-10; 2:1-10; 3:11-20; 8:1-10; 12:1-13. The analysis of 8:1-10 in Chapter 5 will be different because this passage has been examined by Sharon Pace Jeansonne.[68] Our sole concern in that chapter will be to determine whether her claim that Th is a recension based on her analysis of 8:1-10 can be substantiated. Chapter 7 will summarize the conclusions from our analysis of TT. A final chapter will examine the relationship of Th with the so-called *kaige* texts.

---

[68] Jeansonne, 32-57.

Chapter II

Daniel 1:1-10

The first passage for examination is 1:1-10. This passage was chosen because it opens the book and it offers few textual difficulties. The separate discussion of the relationship between OG and Th will be lengthier in this opening section in order to help clarify the issues involved. In the following sections more of the discussion of their relationship will take place within the analysis of TT, because the two are naturally considered together.

The OG and Th Versions of Daniel

Table 1

	1:1 Th	1:1 MT	1:1 OG
1	Ἐν ἔτει τρίτῳ	בִּשְׁנַת שָׁלוֹשׁ	ᶳἘπὶ βασιλέως Ιωακιμ
2	τῆς βασιλείας	לְמַלְכוּת	τῆς Ιουδαίας
3	Ιωακιμ	יְהוֹיָקִים	ἔτους τρίτου
4	βασιλέως Ιουδα	מֶלֶךְ־יְהוּדָה	ᴸπαραγενόμενοςˢ
5	ἦλθε Ναβουχοδονοσορ	בָּא נְבוּכַדְנֶאצַּר	Ναβουχοδονοσορ
6	βασιλεὺς Βαβυλῶνος	מֶלֶךְ־בָּבֶל	βασιλεὺς Βαβυλῶνος
7	†εἰς Ιερουσαλημ	יְרוּשָׁלַםִ	εἰς Ιερουσαλημ
8	καὶ ἐπολιόρκει αὐτήν	וַיָּצַר עָלֶיהָ	ˢᴸἐπολιόρκει ˢαὐτήν
	1:2	1:2	1:2
9	καὶ ᴸἔδωκε κύριος	וַיִּתֵּן אֲדֹנָי	καὶ ᴸπαρέδωκεν αὐτὴνᴹ
10	ἐν χειρὶ αὐτοῦ	בְּיָדוֹ	κύριος εἰς χεῖρας αὐτοῦ
11	τὸν Ιωακιμ	אֶת־יְהוֹיָקִים	ˢκαὶ Ιωακιμ
12	βασιλέα Ιουδα	מֶלֶךְ־יְהוּדָה	τὸν βασιλέα τῆς Ιουδαίας

Chapter 1:1-10

13	καὶ ἀπὸ μέρους	הַמִּקְצָת	καὶ ᴸˢμέρος τι
14	τῶν σκευῶν	כְּלֵי	τῶν ᴸˢἱερῶν σκευῶν
15	οἴκου τοῦ θεοῦ	בֵית־הָאֱלֹהִים	τοῦ κυρίου
16	καὶ ᴸἤνεγκεν αὐτὰ	וַיְבִיאֵם	καὶ ˢᴸἀπήνεγκας¹ αὐτὰ
17	εἰς γῆν ᴸΣενναα̣ρ	אֶרֶץ־שִׁנְעָר	ˢεἰς Βαβυλῶνα²
18	οἴκον τοῦ θεοῦ αὐτοῦ	בֵית אֱלֹהָיו	- -
19	καὶ τὰ σκεύη	וְאֶת־הַכֵלִים	- -
20	ᴸεἰσήνεγκεν	הֵבִיא	ᴸἀπηρείσατο³
21	ˢεἰς τὸν οἶκον θησαυροῦ	בֵית אוֹצַר	- -
22	τοῦ θεοῦ αὐτοῦ	אֱלֹהָיו	ἐν τῷ ᴸεἰδωλείῳ αὐτοῦ
	1:3		1:3
23	καὶ εἶπεν ὁ βασιλεὺς	וַיֹּאמֶר הַמֶּלֶךְ	καὶ εἶπεν ὁ βασιλεὺς
24	Ασφανεζ	לְאַשְׁפְּנַז	Αβιεσδρι
25	τῷ ᴸἀρχιευνούχῳ αὐτοῦ	רַב סָרִיסָיו	τῷ ᴹἑαυτοῦ ᴸἀρχιευνούχῳ
26	ᴸᴹεἰσαγαγεῖν	לְהָבִיא	ᴸἀγαγεῖν⁴
27	ἀπὸ τῶν υἱῶν	מִבְּנֵי	ἐκ τῶν υἱῶν
28	+τῆς αἰχμαλωσίας		+τῶν μεγιστάνων

The OG and Th Versions of Daniel

32				
29	- Ισραηλ	יִשְׂרָאֵ֑ל		τοῦ Ισραηλ
30	καὶ ἀπὸ τοῦ σπέρματος	וּמִזֶּ֥רַע		καὶ ἐκ τοῦ ᴹβασιλικοῦ
31	τῆς βασιλείας	הַמְּלוּכָ֖ה		γένους
32	καὶ ἀπὸ τῶν ᴸ(φορθομμιν)	וּמִן־הַֽפַּרְתְּמִֽים׃		καὶ ἐκ τῶν ᴸἐπιλέκτων
	1:4		1:4	1:4
33	ᴸνεανίσκους οἷς	יְלָדִ֣ים אֲשֶׁ֣ר		ᴸνεανίσκους
34	οὐκ ἔστιν ἐν αὐτοῖς	אֵין־בָּהֶ֣ם		
35	-μῶμ-	כָּל־מאוּם֒		ˢἀμώμους
36	καὶ καλοὺς τῇ ᴸὄψει	וְטוֹבֵ֣י מַרְאֶ֗ה		καὶ ᴹεὐειδεῖς
37	καὶ ᴸ(συνιέντας)	וּמַשְׂכִּילִ֤ים		καὶ ᴸἐπιστήμονας
38	ἐν πάσῃ ᴸσοφίᾳ	בְּכָל־חָכְמָה֙		ἐν πάσῃ ᴸσοφίᾳ
39	καὶ γιγνώσκοντας ᴸγνῶσιν	וְיֹ֣דְעֵי דַ֔עַת		καὶ ᴹγραμματικοὺς⁵
40	καὶ ᴸδιανοουμένους	וּמְבִינֵ֣י		καὶ ᴹᴸσοφοὺς
41	ᴸ(φρόνησιν)	מַדָּ֔ע		
42	καὶ ˢοἷς ἔστιν ἰσχὺς	וַאֲשֶׁר֙ כֹּ֣חַ בָּהֶ֔ם		καὶ ˢἰσχύοντας
43	ἐν αὐτοῖς ᴹἑστάναι	לַעֲמֹ֖ד		ˢὥστε ᴸεἶναι⁶
44	ἐν τῷ ᴸοἴκῳ τοῦ βασιλέως	בְּהֵיכַ֣ל הַמֶּ֑לֶךְ		ἐν τῷ οἴκῳ τοῦ βασιλέως

Chapter 1:1-10

45	καὶ ^Mδιδάξαι αὐτοὺς		ולימדם	καὶ διδάξαι αὐτοὺς
46	γράμματα καὶ γλῶσσαν		ספר ולשון	γράμματα καὶ διάλεκτον
47	Χαλδαίων		כשדים	Χαλδαϊκήν
	1:5	1:5		1:5
48	καὶ ^L(διέταξεν) αὐτοῖς		וימן להם	καὶ ^{LM}διδοσθαι αὐτοῖς
49	ὁ βασιλεὺς		המלך	^s+ἔκθεσιν ⁷παρὰ τοῦ βασιλέως
50	τὸ τῆς ἡμέρας καθ'		דבר יום	καθ' ἑκάστην
51	ἡμέραν		ביומו	ἡμέραν⁸
52	ἀπὸ τῆς ^Lτραπέζης		מפתבג	ἀπὸ τῆς ^Mβασιλικῆς
53	τοῦ βασιλέως		המלך	^Lτραπέζης
54	καὶ ἀπὸ τοῦ οἴνου		ומיין	καὶ⁹ ^sτοῦ οἴνου
55	τοῦ ^Lπότου αὐτοῦ		משתיו	^sοὗ ^{LM}πίνει ὁ βασιλεύς
56	καὶ ^{LM}(θρέψαι) αὐτοὺς		ולגדלם	καὶ ^Lἐκπαιδεῦσαι αὐτοὺς
57	ἔτη τρία καὶ ^Lμετὰ ταῦτα		שנים שלוש ומקצתם	ἔτη τρία καὶ
58	^Mστῆναι		יעמדו	^Lἐκ τούτων ^Mστῆναι
59	^Lἐνώπιον τοῦ βασιλέως		לפני המלך	ἐπιφοραῖς τοῦ βασιλέως
	1:6	1:6		1:6

60	καὶ ἐγένετο ἐν αὐτοῖς		καὶ ἦσαν ¹⁰ἐκ τούτων
61	ἐκ τῶν υἱῶν Ιουδα		ἀπὸ τῶν υἱῶν
62			τῆς Ιουδαίας
63	Δανιηλ ˢ+καὶ+ Ανανιας		Δανιηλ Ανανιας
64	+καὶ Μισαηλ καὶ Αζαριας		Μισαηλ ˢΑζαριας
	1:7	1:7	1:7
65	καὶ ᴸἐπέθηκεν αὐτοῖς		καὶ ἐπέθηκεν αὐτοῖς
66	ὁ ᴸἀρχιευνοῦχος ὀνόματα		ὁ ᴸἀρχιευνοῦχος ὀνόματα
67	- τῷ		ˢ_ - τῷ
68	Δανιηλ ᴸΒαλτασαρ		ˢμὲν Δανιηλ ᴸΒαλτασαρ
69	καὶ τῷ Ανανια Σεδραχ		τῷ δὲ Ανανια Σεδραχ
70	καὶ τῷ Μισαηλ Μισαχ		καὶ τῷ Μισαηλ Μισαχ
71	καὶ τῷ Αζαρια Αβδεναγω		καὶ τῷ Αζαρια Αβδεναγω
	1:8	1:8	1:8
72	καὶ ἔθετο Δανιηλ		καὶ ᴸἐνεθυμήθη Δανιηλ
73	ἐπὶ τὴν καρδίαν αὐτοῦ		ἐν τῇ καρδίᾳᴹ
74	ˢὡς οὐ μὴ (ἀλισγηθῇ)		ˢὅπως μὴ ᴸἀλισσθῇ¹¹

Chapter 1:1-10

75	ἐν τῇ ᴸτραπέζῃ	ܒܦܬܘܪܗ	ἐν τῷ ᴸδείπνῳ
76	τοῦ βασιλέως	ܕܡܠܟܐ	τοῦ βασιλέως
77	καὶ ἐν τῷ οἴνῳ	ܘܒܚܡܪܐ	καὶ ἐν ˢᾧ
78	τοῦ ᴸπότου αὐτοῦ	ܕܡܫܬܝܗ	ᴸᴹπίνει οἶνῳ
79	καὶ ἠξίωσε	ܘܒܥܐ	καὶ ᴸˢἠξίωσεν
80	-τὸν ᴸἀρχιευνοῦχον	ܡܢ ܪܒ ܡܗܝܡܢܐ	τὸν ᴸἀρχιευνοῦχον
81	ˢὡς οὐ μὴ (ἀλισγηθῇ)	ܐܝܟ ܕܠܐ ܢܬܛܢܦ	ˢἵνα μὴ ᴸσυμμολυνθῇ
	1:9		1:9
82	καὶ ᴸἔδωκεν ὁ θεός	ܘܝܗܒ ܐܠܗܐ	καὶ ᴸἔδωκεν κύριος
83	τὸν Δανιηλ	ܠܕܢܝܐܝܠ	τῷ Δανιηλ
84	εἰς ἔλεον	ܠܪܚܡܐ	ᴸτιμὴν
85	καὶ εἰς οἰκτιρμὸν	ܘܠܪܚܡܬܐ	καὶ ᴸˢχάριν
86	ᴸἐνώπιον	ܩܕܡ	ἐναντίον
87	τοῦ ᴸἀρχιευνούχου	ܪܒ ܡܗܝܡܢܐ	τοῦ ᴸἀρχιευνούχου
	1:10		1:10
88	καὶ εἶπεν	ܘܐܡܪ	καὶ εἶπεν
89	ὁ ᴸἀρχιευνοῦχος	ܪܒ ܡܗܝܡܢܐ	ὁ ᴸἀρχιευνοῦχος

90	τῷ Δανιηλ	לדניאל	τῷ Δανιηλ
91	Φοβοῦμαι ἐγὼ	אני ירא	Ἀγωνιῶ
92	τὸν κύριόν μου	את אדני	τὸν κύριόν μου
93	τὸν βασιλέα	המלך	τὸν βασιλέα
94	τὸν ᴸἐκτάξαντα	אשר מנה	τὸν ᴸἐκτάξαντα
95	τὴν βρῶσιν ὑμῶν	את מאכלכם	τὴν βρῶσιν ὑμῶν
96	καὶ τὴν ᴸπόσιν ὑμῶν	ואת משתיכם	καὶ τὴν ᴸᴹπόσιν¹²
97	μήποτε ἴδῃ	אשר למה יראה	ˢἵνα μὴ ¹³ἐὰν ἴδῃ
98	τὰ πρόσωπα ὑμῶν	את פניכם	ᴹτὸ¹⁴ πρόσωπον ὑμῶν
99	ᴸ(σκυθρωπὰ)₁	זעפים	ˢˢνοσηθροδαιος
100			ˢπαρὰ τοὺς
101	παρὰ τὰ ᴸ(παιδάρια)	מן הילדים	ˢᴸσυντρεφομένους ὑμῖν
102	τὰ ᴸ(συνήλικα)₁	כגילכם	ᴸνεανίσκους¹⁵
103			+ˢτῶν ἀλλογενῶν+
104			
105	καὶ ᴸ(καταδικάσητε)	וחיבתם	καὶ ᴸκινδυνεύσω τῷ ἰδίῳ
106	τὴν κεφαλήν μου	את ראשי	τραχήλῳ

Chapter 1:1-10

107 τῷ βασιλεῖ   לַמֶּלֶךְ   - -

II.1. Textual Notes

1. ἀπήνεγκεν] ἀπενέγκας 967 has the participle for the finite verb also 2x in 4:16(19). The participle is better Greek style while 88-Syh has been influenced by MT. See also Hamm, *I-II*, 83.

2. Βαβυλωνίαν] >καί The omission of the conjunction is based on our acceptance of the participle in note 1.

3. ἀπηρείσατο] >αὐτά The addition of the pronoun in 88-Syh is most likely under the influence of MT. See Hamm, *I-II*, 85; Bludau, 54.

4. ἀγαγεῖν] >αὐτῷ The omission of the pronoun in 967 agrees with MT and Th. In this case, it might be that the pronoun was added in 88-Syh because it was present in a *Vorlage* at some stage in the copying process.

5. >καὶ συνετούς The omission may be a scribal error, but given the fact that OG tends to shorten MT, it is more likely that either καὶ γραμματικούς or καὶ συνετούς is a doublet. Both words appear 1x elsewhere in OG (γραμματικῇ 1:17; συνετός 6:3[4]), but since we believe chapters 4-6 derive from a different translator it is our opinion that καὶ συνετούς is the doublet.

6. στῆναι] εἶναι Ziegler's reading (στῆναι) is actually a conjecture, while 967 agrees with 88-Syh. εἶναι should be retained as OG because the "free" translation is in keeping with the style OG employed elsewhere and the reading is found in all of our manuscripts.

7. ἐκ τοῦ οἴκου (+παρά=Syh) τοῦ βασιλέως] παρὰ τοῦ βασιλέως Although ἐκ τοῦ οἴκου in 88 sounds better (Hamm, *I-II*, 89), Syh preserves the reading as it is found in 967.[1] It is probable that the awkward OG reading preserved in 967 was fixed by harmonization with l. 44 in 88 (ἐν τῷ οἴκῳ τοῦ βασιλέως) and that Syh preserves a conflation of the two.

---

[1] In my research, there were 11x that Syh or its marginal reading agreed with 967 to preserve original readings against 88 (2:12[2x], 44; 3:3, 21, 95[28]; 4:30[33]; 5:31[6:1]; 6:10[11], 28[29]; 9:25).

8. ἡμέραν] > καὶ The conjunction in 88-Syh is an addition against MT, but may stem from an alternative *Vorlage* with ומן (or ומך, see Bludau, 46).
9. τραπέζης καὶ] > ἀπὸ The repetition of the preposition is a Hebraism which OG occasionally avoids (see also 11:38, 44).
10. ἐκ τοῦ γένους τῶν υἱῶν Ισραηλ τῶν ἀπὸ τῆς 'Ιουδαίας] ἐκ τούτων ἀπὸ τῶν υἱῶν τῆς 'Ιουδαίας The reading of 88-Syh is obviously a conflation of at least two readings (see Hamm, *I-II*, 91), while 967 is shorter and not too literal to be described as a reading harmonized to MT.
11. ἀλισγηθῇ] ἀλ{ε}ισθῇ 88-Syh=Th יתגאל appears only twice in Daniel, both times in this verse. The fact that OG has a HL for the second occurrence whereas Th employs ἀλισγηθῇ in both instances suggests that OG was corrected toward Th on the assumption that ἀλισθῇ was an error. O. Munnich has also recently argued that OG's reading stems from ἀλίζω being employed as a military metaphor and that Daniel did not want to be "recruited" into the king's service. The reading ἀλισγηθῇ is the result of pre-hexaplaric correction toward Th.[2]
12. πόσιν] > ὑμῶν The second personal pronoun is unnecessary in Greek and is often omitted in OG.
13. μὴ] +ἐάν See also 1:13: 2:9. The particle was omitted in 88-Syh accidently or due to harmonization toward MT.
14. τὰ πρόσωπα κ.τ.λ.] τὸ πρόσωπον ὑμῶν διατετραμμένον καὶ ἀσθενές παρὰ τοὺς συντρεφομένους Given the predominant use of פני(ם) in idioms and semi-prepositions it is not unexpected that OG always has the singular elsewhere in Daniel where פני(ם) is rendered by προσώπον,[3] but OG also employs προσώπον in all other cases as well.[4]

---

[2] O. Munnich, "Origène, éditeur de la *Septante* de *Daniel*," *Studien zur Septuaginta - Robert Hanhart zu Ehren* (*MSU* 20; ed. D. Fraenkel, U. Quast, and J. Wevers; Göttingen: Vandenhoeck & Ruprecht, 1990) 188; see also p. 52 below.

[3] 8:5, 17, 18, 23; 9:3, 7, 8, 13, 17; 10:6, 9, 15; 11:17, 18, 19, 22.

[4] 3:19, 41; 4:19(22), 30(33); 6:11(10), 13(12), 14(13); 7:10; 10:12.

This is the only instance in Daniel where a plural would be suitable in Greek, but see 1:13, 15 where OG has the singular ὄψις.
15. νεανίας] νεανίσκους Hamm, *I-II*, 99 prefers 88 because he presupposes the "freer" rendering is original. On the other hand, OG employs νεανίσκος in all other instances (1:4, 13, 15, 17), so 88 may just be an error.

II.2. *Analysis of 1:1-10*

II.2.i. *Morphology*

l. 9, 73, 96-OG sometimes adds a personal pronoun against MT (l. 9), though it could be a later harmonization to l. 8. On the other hand, in l. 73, 96 OG omits the pronoun, which is unnecessary to the Greek.
l. 25-OG renders the Hebrew 3 masculine singular suffix with a reflexive pronoun and also alters the order by putting the pronoun in the attributive position.
l. 26, 43, 45, 56, 58-Th does not employ an article as a formal equivalent for ל as a marker of the infinitive construct.
l. 30, 52-In both instances OG substitutes an adjective in the attributive position for a genitive. This change also affects the word order.
l. 36, 39, 40-OG substitutes a plural accusative for the noun + genitive construct.
l. 48-OG substitutes an infinitive for the finite verb due to harmonization with the infinitive in l. 43 and 45.
l. 55, 78-OG substitutes a verb for the genitive construct, which makes explicit the consumption of the wine. Quite possibly the motivation was that the translator did not understand the text and made a contextual guess. See the discussion of Th and OG on p. 59.

---

[4] 3:19, 41; 4:19(22), 30(33); 6:11(10), 13(12), 14(13); 7:10; 10:12.

l. 58-OG and Th render the jussive with the aorist active infinitive to indicate the final clause.

l. 98-OG substitutes singular for plural. See the discussion in the textual notes above.

II.2.ii. *Syntax*

l. 1-3-OG characteristically uses a genitive for dating (3:1; 4:1; 7:1; 8:1; 9:1)[5] and transposes the information regarding the king prior to the adverbial phrase, which omits מלך as unnecessary.

l. 4, 16-OG substitutes the parataxis of MT with a hypotactic construction, participle + verb.

l. 7, 17-The preposition is added in keeping with Greek idiom, though in l. 21 it is unnecessary in Th.

l. 8-The preposition is omitted as redundant.

l. 11-OG chooses to substitute the conjunction for the sign of the accusative, which results in a καὶ . . . καὶ (both/and) construction. It removes any ambiguity that might exist in the Hebrew concerning the removal of Jehoiakim.[6]

l. 13, 54, 85-OG omits the preposition as redundant.

l. 14-OG substitutes an attributive adjective for the genitive construct.

l. 17-OG omits redundant material in l. 18-22 (see *Text-Critical*), but no information is lost.[7]

---

[5] The exceptions are 2:1 and 10:1, both of which mirror the text of Th quite closely. It cannot be proven from our textual witnesses, but it is possible that we should read genitives in both of these verses.

[6] See R. H. Charles, *A Critical and Exegetical Commentary on the Book of Daniel* (Oxford: Clarendon, 1929) 4-5; J. A. Montgomery, *A Critical and Exegetical Commentary on the Book of Daniel* (ICC; New York: Charles Scribner's Sons, 1927) 113-115.

[7] 88-Syh correctly mark the asterisked addition that conforms to MT in l. 18-19.

l. 42-OG substitutes an accusative participle for the relative phrase, which renders בהם redundant. Th follows MT but adds the 3 singular verb that is implicit in the Hebrew.

l. 43-OG employs ὥστε (reading against 967) and this makes it explicit that the ל on the infinitive construct signifies consequence.

l. 49-ἔχθεσιν is a substitution for רבר in order to make the meaning of the term explicit and the prepositional phrase is added for clarification.

l. 55, 77-OG substitutes a relative clause (see *Morphology*) for the genitive construct.

l. 63-64, 68-71-OG omits the conjunction in l. 64 in harmony with the previous omission, whereas in l. 68-69 OG seems to have employed the Greek μὲν/δὲ,[8] followed in l. 70-71 by coordination with καί. There are no grounds to question whether the *Vorlage* was different in OG. Th coordinates the names with καί also in 1:19.

l. 67-The verb שׂים probably was not in the *Vorlage*. See the discussion of these lines below in *The Relationship Between OG and Th*.

l. 74, 81-Th employs the same equivalent (ἀλισγηθῇ) for יתגאל while OG uses variety.

l. 79-ἀξιόω + accusative + ἵνα is an idiom (BAG, 78), so we would not expect the Hebrew preposition to be represented.

l. 97-OG and Th both substitute more appropriate Greek usage. However, OG uses ἵνα + subjunctive in a consecutive clause, while Th has a more idiomatic rendering with μήποτε (see BDF §370.2).

l. 99 to 100-OG requires the addition of the noun in l. 100 to the participle διατρέπω (1-4) in order to render the sense of the Hebrew.

1. 101-OG and Th employ παρά + accusative for the comparative. Comparative מן occurs 5x elsewhere: 1:15 OG has κρείσσων + geni-

---

[8] See the discussion of μὲν/δὲ in 3:11-20, Syntax, l. 51.

tive, Th ὑπέρ + accusative; 2:30 OG ὑπέρ + accusative, Th παρά + accusative; 7:19 OG παρά + accusative, Th genitive participle!; 7:23 OG παρά + accusative, Th finite verb!; 8:3 OG ὑψηλότερον, Th ὑψηλότερον + genitive. The comparative + genitive and the positive with παρά/ὑπέρ + accusative are common equivalents in the LXX.[9] Therefore, the agreement in 1:10 is not particularly striking, especially when we consider the OG and Th choices elsewhere. 7:19, 23 both involve the verb שׂנא + מן and it is Th who has the dynamic renderings.

l. 102-OG renders the relative phrase with the accusative participle. Th employs a complementary accusative in order to provide good Greek and follow the word order of the Hebrew.

l. 104-Added by OG for clarification of the identity of the other youths in training.

II.2.iii. *Lexicology*

l. 4-παραγίγνομαι is 2/2 for בוא in OG (also 2:2), never in Th.

l. 8-πολιορκέω for צור (both HL in Daniel) is a fairly common equivalent in the later literature of the LXX (8-30, as well as 7x in Pentateuch).

l. 9, 82-δίδωμι and its compound form with παρά is an expected SE in Th for נתן (21/21)[10] and יהב (20/20).[11] There are 6 other instances

---

[9] See I. Soisalon-Soininen, "Renderings of Hebrew Comparative Expressions with MIN in the Pentateuch," *BIOSCS* 12 (1979): 27-42.

[10] 1:2, 9, 12, 16, 17; 2:16; 4:14(17), 22(25), 29(32); 8:12, 13; 9:3, 10; 10:12, 15 11:6, 11, 17, 21, 31; 12:11. Th has παραδίδωμι in 11:6, 11.

[11] 2:21, 23, 37, 38, 48; 3:28(95); 4:13(16); 5:17, 18, 19, 28; 6:3(2); 7:4, 6, 11, 12, 14, 22, 25, 27. Th has παραδίδωμι (=OG) in 3:28(95) and ἀποδίδωμι in 6:3.

of δίδωμι or one of its compounds in Th. There is no available *Vorlage* in 3:32(=OG) and 34(=OG). In 10:1 the verb is an addition that makes the meaning of the Hebrew explicit, and in 9:27 both Th and OG read the 3 feminine singular qal imperfect of נתן for תתך (HL).[12] Finally, the simple form is found twice in 5:21. In the first instance it is a contextual guess for the rare verb שוה, which is only found twice in Daniel.[13] In the second case, Th evidently read יחקים as יהב due to influence from 4:14(17), 22(25), 29(32). The texts read as follows:

4:14(17), etc.   ולמן־די יצבא יתננה
5:21   ולמן־די יצבא יהקים עליה

Th reads καὶ ᾧ ἐὰν δόξῃ δώσει αὐτήν in all four cases.

OG is similar to Th in his extensive use of δίδωμι and its compound forms for נתן (16/18)[14] and יהב (13/15),[15] but exhibits greater variety in his employment of the compounds and uses them more frequently to render a greater variety of verbs in MT. On seven occasions OG relies on the general meaning of δίδωμι to translate the

---

[11] 2:21, 23, 37, 38, 48; 3:28(95); 4:13(16); 5:17, 18, 19, 28; 6:3(2); 7:4, 6, 11, 12, 14, 22, 25, 27. Th has παραδίδωμι (=OG) in 3:28(95) and ἀποδίδωμι in 6:3.

[12] The reading of the verb δοθήσεται is a distinctive agreement, but it also falls within a portion where there is extensive agreement between Th and OG: ἕως συντελείας (+καιρου 967) καὶ συντέλεια δοθέσεται ἐπὶ τὴν ἐρήμωσιν. There is no doubt that 9:24-27 has undergone extensive revision in OG (see P. David, 280-356), so it is quite possible that the agreement is due to Th influence. Although this suggestion may seem premature to the reader at this point in the discussion, it will gain credibility in the light of our entire argument. Geissen, 221, also considers the possibility that συντέλεια δοθέσεται ἐπὶ τὴν ἐρήμωσιν is a doublet to βδέλυγμα τῶν ἐρημώσεων ἔσται ἕως συντελείας [+ καιροῦ]. He does not pursue this line of inquiry, however, perhaps because he does not recognize the extent of the influence of Th on OG.

[13] It is untranslated by Th in 3:29(96).

[14] OG has παραδίδωμι in 1:2; 11:11; ἀντιδίδωμι in 1:16; γίνομαι in 8:12 (textual difficulty); ναρκάω? (1-5) in 11:6. OG=0 in 4:14(14), 22(25), 29(32).

[15] OG=0 in 4:13(16); 5:17, 18, 19; 6:3(2) and παραδίδωμι in 2:38; 3:28(95).

Chapter 1:1-10   45

sense of the *Vorlage*. This is the case for וימן in 1:5, משה in 7:22, ישבר in 8:25, להביא in 9:24, and נגלה in 10:1.[16] 11:17 and 18 both read δώσει, which is interesting because there is a difference in the *Kethib-Qere* in verse 18.[17] OG reflects the reading of the Q=וישם (K=וישב). On one occasion the translator uses the verb when making a contextual guess. In 11:24 the translator did not understand the 3 masculine singular qal imperfect of בזר (1-2), which is otherwise found only in Ps 68:31.

l. 13, 58-The OG translation is somewhat surprising in l. 57 when we consider that elsewhere קצת (7x) is rendered well.[18] OG seems to take the masculine plural suffix of the noun to refer to the feminine ἔτη, but gives a very literal "Theodotionic" type of rendering without including τέλος to get the sense that it is "at the end of" the 3 years. Th's rendering using μετά + accusative is more idiomatic.

l. 14-The adjective of OG gives greater specificity than the genitive construct it replaces. Th's choice represents incomplete lexical levelling (see l. 44).

---

[16] There is a textual variant in 10:1: ἐδείχθη (88-Syh) ἐδόθη (967). ἐδείχθη would be a HL in OG (never in Th) and would render the meaning. However, the choice would not conform to OG's TT. In six other occurrences of נלה OG employs ἐκφαίνω or ἀνακαλύπτω (2:19, 22, 28, 29, 30, 47). Also OG uses only compounds of δεικνύω in 17 other places: ἀποδεικνύω in 1:11, 20: 2:48; 4:34c; ἐνδεικνύω in 3:44; ὑποδεικνύω in 2:17; 4:15(18), 34c; 5:7, 9, 12, 16; 9:22, 23; 10:14, 21; 11:2. Therefore, if OG were going to employ δεικνύω, it would more likely appear in the compound ὑποδεικνύω. 967 has the OG, which employed a favourite verb (over 40x) to render the meaning of the *Vorlage*. This was later revised closer to MT by the changing of a few letters, on the assumption of scribal error. Presumably, OG employed the more general term as an adequate equivalent.

[17] 11:17 MT begins וישם and v. 19 וישב. In v. 18 the *Qere* has the former while the *Kethib* has the latter. Th reads with the *Kethib*.

[18] Also 1:15, 18; 2:42; 4:26(29), 31(34). In 4:31 OG=0. OG and Th share the reading μέρος τι for מן־קצת in 2:42.

l. 16, 20, 26-In all three cases of בוא (hiphil) OG chooses a different verb. ἀπερείδω in l. 20 of OG is fairly rare (1-9) in the LXX. Th uses a form of φέρω for בוא in the first two instances, but also gives good renditions.[19]

l. 17, 32-Th (also P) transliterates. OG's use of ἐπίλεκτος (1-16) for פרתמים (1-3) "nobility" (BDB, 832) in l. 32 is most likely an exegetical rendering based on the parallel with ומזרע המלכה, but OG manages to convey that the trainees are to be chosen from the cream of (Israelite) society.[20]

l. 22-OG uses a more specific term to make the meaning explicit. OG also employs εἴδωλον 3x to render אלוה (אלוהים) when the referent is the "idol" of the king as opposed to Israel's God (3:18; 5:4, 23; 6:28[27] where MT=0).

l. 25, 66, 80, 87, 89-OG and Th share a common loan translation. Also 1:11, 18.

l. 33, 101, 103-(ה)ילדים appears 5x in chapter 1 and OG translates consistently with νεανίσκους,[21] whereas Th prefers παιδάρια (4/5). Th's agreement with OG in l. 33 is a common reading, though it could be due to textual corruption.

---

[19] MT has בוא in the hiphil 10x. The OG equivalences elsewhere are ἄγω in 1:18(2); ἐπάγω in 9:12, 14; δίδωμι in 9:24; a textual problem in 11:6; ἀποφέρω in 11:8. Th has common readings in 9:12, 14. Th has εἰσάγω in 1:18(2); ἄγω in 9:24; φέρω in 11:6, 8.

[20] Here we are taking the first conjunctive in ומזרע המלכה as explicative. This position is argued in detail in the forthcoming thesis of R.G. Wooden at St. Andrews. Also Taylor, *Peshitta*, 43.

[21] OG has νεανίσκος 5/5 in 1:4, 10 (88=νεανίας), 13, 15, 17. 11:6=0? Th has νεᾶνις in 11:6.

Chapter 1:1-10   47

1. 36-Th has ὄψις also in 3:19, whereas OG employs it in 1:13, 15 for מראה. See *Lexicology* in 3:11-20.

1. 37-The hiphil substantive participle מַשְׂכִּלִים occurs 5x. OG has several equivalents: ἐπιστήμων (1-12, 1. 37), ἐννοέω (1-9, 11:33; see Th in 9:23), συνίημι (11:35; 12:3), διανοέομαι (12:10). Th employs συνίημι 3/5 and prefers to render all words related to √שׂכל with σύνεσις or its cognates. In 11:33 Th employs συνετός for המשׂכלים and in 12:10 he employs νοήμονες (1-10 in LXX). σύνεσις also renders all three occurrences of שׂכלתנו (5:11, 12, 14) and συνίημι is usually the equivalent for the verb שׂכל (3/5).²² In 8:25 the noun שׂכל occurs in a difficult passage to refer to Antiochus' insight. There are then five instances where Th does not render √שׂכל with σύνεσις or a related word, but it is possible to provide a reason for this in each case.

In 7:8 (hithpael) and 8:25 there is not the same specific emphasis on the quality of wisdom, so Th uses alternative renderings.²³ However, the differences in 9:22, 12:10, and 11:33 are due to Th's TT and may be explained on the basis of the syntagmatic relations that exist between words. The theory of syntagmatic relations emphasizes the meaningful relationships that exist between particular combinations of words in a syntagm. For example, Porzig points to the relationship between biting and teeth; barking and dog; blonde and hair.²⁴ The most significant aspect of the syntagmatic relationship between words is

---

²² 1:17; 7:8; 9:13, 22, 25. For our purposes we include only 7:8 and 9:22 as instances where Th fails to make the equivalent συνίημι=שׂכל. According to Ziegler, in 1:17 Th has σύνεσιν καὶ φρόνησιν for מרע והשׂכל which is the opposite of the normal translation equivalents used by Th (see 1:4). However, the 4th century Sahidic ms. 925 does transpose the terms and it is quite possible that it contains the original Th reading.

²³ As we have mentioned, in 8:25 it is Antiochus who has insight, while in 7:8 προσενόουν (1-8, never in OG) "I was thinking about" is an adequate translation of the sense.

²⁴ W. Porzig, *Das Wunder der Sprache* (Bern: Francke, 1950) 68.

that it limits or defines the paradigmatic choices in any given context. Blonde is only used as a description of hair. Biting is only done with teeth. Syntagmatic relations between words are also referred to as the study of their collocations.[25] For example, the words strong and powerful may be used to describe a person, but strong would not be used in collocation with car though powerful could. Likewise, we refer to tea being strong but not powerful.[26]

The understanding of syntagmatic relationships has obvious implications for the analysis of TT. In general, the choices of many translation equivalents in the LXX were defined by previous translators who established certain SEs. Each individual translator often established his own set of equivalents as well. However, there were times when the established sets of equivalents would conflict. For example, in 9:22 the hiphil infinitive construct שׂכל occurs together with בינה, and in the case of these terms with similar meanings Th has an even higher preference for σύνεσις to translate בינה (4/5).[27] Therefore, Th chose a different verb for the infinitive construct of שׂכל. In this case Th chose the fairly rare term συμβιβάζω (1-10 in LXX). The same phenomenon accounts for 12:10, except in this case משׂכילים is the subject of יבינו. In this instance Th uses νοήμονες for המשׂכילים because Th prefers to translate the verb with the 3 active indicative of συνίημι. Even though συνετός is also cognate with σύνεσις, we can see that Th employed it for משׂכילים in 11:33 for the same reason that he made a change in 12:10, משׂכילים was the subject of יבינו.

In each of the three cases above (9:22; 11:33; 12:10) Th was forced to make a choice where one Greek word group was normally used

---

[25] "Collocations refers to the combination of words that have a certain mutual expectancy." See H. Jackson, *Words and Their Meanings* (New York: Longman, 1988) 96.

[26] Example from M.A.K. Halliday, "Lexis as a linguistic level," *In Memory of J.R. Firth* (ed. C. E. Bazell et al.; London: Longmans, 1966) 150-151.

[27] See 2:21; 8:15; 10:1. The exception is 1:20 where Th uses ἐπιστήμης. This is another HL (1-59 in LXX) for Th that is not found in OG.

Chapter 1:1-10   49

to render 2 different Hebrew words that occurred in a syntagm.[28] These examples combined with Th's use of no less than four HL (νοήμονες, ἐπιστήμης, προσνόουν, συμβιβάσαι) to render vocabulary in the domain of knowing that are not even found in OG indicate that Th was working to his own agenda.

l. 38-OG (5/7) and Th (8/8) both employ σοφία as a SE for חכמה.[29] There are two additional uses of the noun in 5:11, but the omission by both OG and Th as well as the content of the saying (וחכמה כחכמת־ אלהין) indicates that this is a later insertion in MT.

l. 39-γνῶσις is a SE (2/2) for דעת in Th (see also 12:4).

l. 40-This is the only place where Th employs διανοέομαι for בין. It is usually the common equivalent employed by OG, but OG has rendered the syntagm with a dynamic equivalent (see below).[30]

l. 41-מדע is only here and 1:17. OG employs the accusative plural of σοφός to render ומביני מדע in 1:4, but has a more formal approach with ἐπιστήμη in 1:17. Th possibly has φρόνησις in both cases.[31] The related term מנדע also appears in 2:21, 4:31(34), 33(36); 5:12. Th

---

[28] Another main way that syntagmatic relationships affect TT is occasions where one language uses a syntagm while the other language may only require a single lexeme to render roughly the same meaning. For example, see Dan 2:13 where OG translates דתא נפקת "a decree went out" with ἐδογματίσθη "it was decreed" and in 1:4 where וידעי דעת ומביני מדע ... ומובי מראה is translated καὶ εὐειδεῖς . . . καὶ γραμματικοὺς καὶ σοφούς. Other syntagmatic features to consider are the construct genitive relation in HA or infinitive absolutes modifying another verb; Greek verbs that are followed by a particular case, infinitive, or object clause; and prepositions because they require a certain case.

[29] OG and Th in 1:4; 2:20, 21, 23, 30. 1:17 OG has σύνεσις; 1:20=free; OG=0 in 5:14.

[30] For a detailed discussion of the renderings for בין, see the chapter on 8:1-10, v. 5.

[31] For the reading of σύνεσιν and φρόνησιν in 1:17, see n. 22 above.

employs φρήν in chapter 4 while φρόνησις is found in 2:21; 5:12. OG only has an equivalent in 2:21, σύνεσις.

l. 43-OG employs the more general εἶναι, but the meaning has been retained.

l. 44-One might argue that Th's choice of οἴκῳ for היכל is due to OG influence, but Th offers the same renderings in 5:5=OG and 6:19(18). For the most part, Th prefers οἶκος for both בית (11/12)[32] and היכל (3/7),[33] and we can account for why Th does not render 3 of the other 4 with οἶκος. Both terms occur in 4:1 and Th chooses to omit היכל as redundant; or it was not in his *Vorlage*. In 5:2 the context required a more specific word (ναός) as opposed to the more general term. Now, we might ask why οἶκος is not appropriate in 5:2 when the referent is the same as 1:4? The difference is easily explained. Th could say that Nebuchadnezzar took some of the holy vessels from "the house of God," (1:4) but it could not be said that he had brought them from "the house in Jerusalem," (5:2). Both of the Hebrew terms occur together again in 5:3 but neither one appears in the OG. The repetition of ναοῦ in 5:3 and the non-translation of בית could be due to harmonization with the previous verse. On the other hand, די־בית has the air of a gloss and this impression is supported by the witness of the versions (see BHS).[34] The remaining passage is 4:26(29) where the OG has the king walking ἐπὶ τῶν τειχῶν τῆς πόλεως and Th again employs ναός.

---

[32] 1:2(3); 2:5, 17; 3:29(96); 4:1(4), 27(30); 5:3, 10, 23; 6:11(10).

[33] 1:4; 4:1(4), 26(29); 5:2, 3, 5; 6:19(18).

[34] Contrast the recent argument that the phrase די־בית אלהא is the point of emphasis in the clause which is virtually verbatim from v. 2. See B.T. Arnold, "Wordplay and Narrative Techniques in Daniel 5 and 6," JBL 112 (1993): 481. However, the question is whether this emphasis was in the original text or was it introduced by a later scribe?

Chapter 1:1-10   51

l. 48, 94-Elsewhere Th renders מנה (4/5) with καθίστημι where it has the sense "to appoint someone."³⁵ Both διέταξεν (1-21, not in OG) and ἐκτάξαντα (1-6) (√τασσειν) are fairly rare in the LXX. Both OG (16x) and Th (11x) employ √τασσειν frequently, but their only common use is l. 94. OG prefers to use the compound forms προστάσσω (6x)³⁶ and ἐπιτάσσειν (6x),³⁷ while Th only employs ἐπιτασσω in 6:10(9), and prefers to use ἐντάσσω.³⁸

l. 52, 53, 75-OG and Th have a common reading of τραπέζης but both τράπεζα and δεῖπνον represent good renditions for the difficult פתבג (see BDB, 834). OG has δεῖπνον 4/6 (see 1:13, 15, 16) while Th prefers τράπεζα 4/6 (Th=OG in 1:15).³⁹

l. 55, 78, 96-Th and OG translate משתה with πόσιν (HL in LXX!) in l. 96. The choice of πόσιν could have been motivated by the similar sound of βρῶσιν in l. 95, but it is a distinctive agreement. Elsewhere Th translates משתה with πότος (see l. 55, 78) and πόμα (1-4) in 1:16. OG has the verb πινέω in l. 55, 78 and omits in 1:16.

---

³⁵ See 1:11; 2:24, 2:49; 3:12. OG also has καθίστημι in 2:24, 49; 3:12, though only in 3:12 do OG and Th have a common form (κατέστησας). In 5:26 מנה is rendered by ἀριθμέω in OG and μετρέω in Th. In 1:11 OG has ἀποδεικνύω.

³⁶ See 2:9, 12, 14; 3:10, 13; 4:11(14).

³⁷ See 1:18; 2:2, 46, 3:19, 20, 24. συντάσσω (aorist participle) is a dynamic rendering in 11:23. ὑποτάσσω for פלה in 7:27 is a unique reading and the verb occurs as part of a plus in 11:37.

³⁸ 5:24, 25; 6:11(10), 13(12), 14(13); 10:21. ὑποτάσσω is employed in 6:14(13) where Th has an omission and is also employed as a dynamic rendering for the hiphil of משל in 11:39 (contrast the more literal rendering in OG). Elsewhere Th always employs κυριεύω for משל (11:3, 4, 5, 43). The simple form of τάσσω occurs in Th 6:13(12) and 11:17.

³⁹ The remaining reference is 11:26 where Th guesses with δέω (feminine singular accusative participle) "his wants (reading צרך?) will devour him" and OG with μέριμνα "his thoughts (reading צרה?) will waste him." See Collins, *Daniel*, 366. Once again, the distinct choices show independant work.

l. 56-OG (HL) and Th employ good as well as distinct renderings for the verb. Th also employs τρέφω as a good rendition for the ithpeal יחזי (HL, see BDB, 1091) in 4:9(12).

l. 59, 86-Th prefers to restrict the rendering of ἐνώπιον to לפני (9/15), particularly in the opening Hebrew section (5/6), whereas OG uses a variety of equivalents throughout the book.[40] The same is true in the Aramaic section of Daniel where Th prefers ἐνώπιον for קדם (19/41). At the same time, Th does not rely on OG nor is Th exceedingly literal. For example, of the 57x לפני and קדם occur in MT, Th has a common rendering with OG in only 5 instances.[41]

l. 65, 67-See the discussion of Th's relationship to OG.

l. 68-OG and Th have a common transliteration of the name that agrees with the transliteration of the name of the king elsewhere in the book (see Appendix for references).

l. 74, 81-Th standardizes the translation of the verb whereas OG uses variety. These are the only two occurrences of the verb יתגאל (2-11),[42] in Daniel, but 2 forms of the piel and 1 pual are found together in Mal 1:7(2x), 12 in which the topic is the desecration of the Lord because of the food which the priests offer. Not only is there similarity in the themes—the priests polluting the alter, Daniel not wanting to defile

---

[40] See 1:5, 9, 13, 18, 19; 2:2; 8:3, 4, 6, 7; 9:10, 18, 20; 10:12. Th has ἔναντιον in 1:18; 9:20; 10:12; πρό in 8:3; the more literal κατὰ πρόσωπον αὐτοῦ in 9:10; 11:16. The preposition ἐνώπιον only occurs in three other places in Th, but is a good rendering in each: 3:3 for לקבל, 3:40 MT=0, and 8:15 for לנגדי.

OG has ἔμπροσθεν in 1:5; ἐναντίον in 1:9; 9:20; 10:12; 11:16; ὄψις ἡμῶν! in 1:13; πρός in 1:18; παρά in 1:19; 2:2; ἀπέναντι in 8:3; ἐν in 8:6; κατέναντι in 8:7; ἐνώπιον in 8:4; 9:10, 18.

[41] ἔμπροσθεν in 6:11(10); ἐνώπιον in 8:4; 9:18; ἐναντίον in 9:20; ἀπὸ προσώπου αὐτοῦ (for מלפניו) in 11:22. The last case is a distinctive agreement, but note that it is Th who has the literal reading κατὰ πρόσωπον αὐτοῦ in the previous use of לפני in 11:16.

[42] A weakened form of √געל, see Montgomery, 133; KB, 163.

himself—but the Greek verb found in Mal is ἁλισγεῖν. There is only one other occurrence in the LXX (Sir 40:29). Therefore, the rendering in Th most likely has been influenced by Mal. συνμολυνθῇ in l. 81 is a HL. 88-Syh read with Th in l. 74, but 967 has the OG reading with another HL ἁλι(ε)σθῇ.

l. 79-Th and OG have the same rendition of the Hebrew verb (see LEH, 43 and *Syntax*). An equivalent translation is found for the Aramaic בעא in OG and Th,[43] though elsewhere they give other renderings (1:20; 8:15; 9:3).

l. 84, 85-Two words from the semantic domain of mercy/compassion are employed in l. 84 and 85: חסד and רחמים, and in both cases OG has unusual equivalents. חסד appears 2x in Daniel, 1:9 and 9:4. In 9:4 OG employs ἔλεος for חסד, which offers a closer formal correspondence to חסד (Th uses ἔλεος in both 1:9 and 9:4). OG's choice of τιμὴν in l. 84 is unusual and involves some innovation with respect to how Daniel was viewed by the chief steward (honourably, as opposed to mercifully), but the overall sense of the passage is conveyed.

OG employs τιμή only 3x (see also 2:37 and 4:27[30] =Th) while in Th it is a SE (7/8) for יקר.[44] However, we should note that in 11:38 OG employs the verb τιμήσει for יכבד and gives a dynamic rendition of the clause. The non-translation of יקר in this verse seems to be due to the fact that OG did not know the meaning of יכבד and so offers a contextual translation (motivated by the connection of τιμή for יקר) with the verb τιμήσει. The only other occurrence of יכבד in MT is earlier in 11:38 where OG's contextual guess is not quite so successful.

---

[43] See OG-2:16, 23, 49; 4:30a?; 6:5(4), 8(7), 13(12); Th-2:16, 23; 6:12(11).

[44] See also 2:6; 7:14; 11:38. 4:33(36); 5:18, 20, OG=0. 7:14 may involve a textual variant. On one occasion Th uses ἔντιμον (2:37).

√רחם is found 4x in Daniel. Once again, OG's choice of χάριν in l. 85 is dynamic and OG also has a very free rendition of the term in 2:18, though the overall meaning is transferred.[45] In 9:9 and 18 OG uses a word whose range of meaning is closer—ἔλεος. So, OG can use ἔλεος to translate both חסד and רחמים, but OG does not use it for either in 1:9. Th's οἰκτιρμός for רחמים is a SE (4/4). Unfortunately, in this instance, we cannot discern an apparent motive to explain why the OG translator did not use ἔλεος for either term in 1:9, other than to regard his choice as a reflection of his understanding of the meaning of the semitic text.

l. 99-זעף is a rare term (1-5, see BDB, 277). Th gives a good dynamic rendering with σκυθρωπά (1-4, see BAG, 758). OG, see l. 99-100, *Syntax*.

l. 102-גיל is a HL in MT.[46] OG (1/3, see 4 Macc 13:21, 24) offers a conjecture συντρέφω (see LSJ). Th uses συνῆλιξ (1-3), which is a good translation of the Hebrew.

l. 105-חוב is rare in MT (1-2?, see BDB, 295). The rare and distinct vocabulary employed by OG, κινδυνεύω (1-7), and Th, καταδικάζω (1-10), illusstrates the independance of their translations. The OG rendering catches the emotion slightly better. We might translate, "And I would lose my neck!"

II.2.iv. *Summary*

In 1:1-10 OG gives a faithful translation of a *Vorlage* that is generally very similar to, if not, identical with MT. OG exhibits characteristics of formal equivalence because OG generally follows the

---

[45] In 2:18 the translator offers a good example of how the same message can be communicated by choosing alternative words and combining them differently.

[46] Bevan, 61, identifies this and the following term as Aramaic loan-words.

word order and represents most of the lexemes and morphemes in MT. However, OG does avoid some of the parataxis of MT by employing two hypotactic constructions with participle (1. 4, 16), and on one occasion OG uses a postpositive conjunction (δὲ in l. 69). OG's dynamic approach to translation is evident in various ways. On several occasions he makes appropriate changes to a semitic relative clause in order to render the semantic content (1. 42, 74, 81, 97) and omits elements that are redundant (1. 1-4, 16-22, 107). OG also introduces shorter readings by employing one lexeme to render the meaning of two in the parent text (1. 35-37, 39-40). However, in two cases he adds elements to clarify MT or to make it explicit (1. 49-50, 104). The most significant indication of OG's dynamic approach is the variety in his lexical choices (1. 4, 72, 74, 81, 84, 85, 105, 106), though a couple resulted from guesses (1. 99, 102).

Th's TT exhibits a high degree of formal correspondence to his *Vorlage*, but always with the intention of presenting the meaning of the parent text within the linguistic boundaries of the target language. Therefore, there are minor omissions or additions of morphemes and slight changes in the syntax to preserve the semantic content (1. 74, 79-81, 97, 102). On two occasions Th employs transliterations (1. 17, 32), and, generally speaking, Th exhibits his own pattern of translating MT.

II.3. *The Relationship Between OG and Th*

As an opening to our discussion of whether or not Th is a recension we will examine verse 8 in which there appears to be a high degree of verbal agreement between Th and OG. The argument that Th is a recension would go something like this: 1. Th has borrowed from OG in l. 79 (see *Lexicology*). 2. Th has borrowed the rendering of the verb in l. 74 from OG (1/2-5); therefore, l. 81 is also dependent on OG, because Th tends to standardize (see l. 74-*Syntax*).[47] 3. Th follows the loan translation of שׂר הסריסים. 4. Th has merely changed the preposition in l. 73 and standardized terms in l. 72, 75-78. On this analysis Th retains OG for 16 words, follows 1 omission, and is dependent upon OG for at least 2 more. There are 31 words in Th, but l. 82 repeats l. 74 and each time Th has one more word than OG. We now have 29, but we allowed for one omission of a pronoun which makes the total 30 words. Based on this analysis Th shows the influence of OG in 19 out of 30 or 63% of its readings.

The above argument seems convincing, but is there another way to look at the evidence? For example, the above analysis assumes Th borrowed the rendering of the verb in l. 74, but how do we know who knew the meaning of יתנאל? As we have noted, OG was probably corrected toward Th. Second, except for the rendering of the verb in l. 79, Th offers an expected formal correspondence to the MT that could be arrived at by any Greek student at the end of his/her introductory year of Hebrew![48] On this analysis, Th only has a common rendering of the verb in l. 79 and the loan translation for שׂר הסריסים in l. 80. 2 words + 1 omission of a preposition. 3 of 30=10%.

l. 7, 8-The addition of the preposition in l. 7 is not remarkable; and even though the reading of the verb is one of the more obvious choices (1/1) we should view it as a common reading.

l. 13 to 16-The reading of Th in l. 13 looks like Th has rendered ἀπό for the preposition מן and borrowed OG's μέρος for קצת, but it is a correct rendering. The distinct readings for the same Hebrew in l. 57 confirm that Th is not necessarily relying on OG in l. 13. L. 14-15 in Th show formal equivalence to MT (see HR).

---

[47] That is, only if 88-Syh and not 967 is regarded as preserving OG.

[48] The translation of the verb in l. 72 is Th's normal equivalent. See the discussion of l. 65-67, below.

Chapter 1:1-10 57

l. 25, 66, 80, 87, 89-OG and Th share a common loan translation for שר/רב ה/סריסים (also 1:11, 18).

l. 26-Similar to l. 16 it is possible that the compound was inspired by the simple verb in OG, but the hiphil of בוא is translated the same way by Th 2x in 1:18 and it is an obvious choice.[49]

l. 33-Th has the usual OG reading of νεανισκός, though this may have resulted from textual corruption.

l. 44 to 46-See *Lexicology*, l. 44 for οἴκῳ. The remainder are expected equivalents.

l. 50-Th's use of κατά for ב is the only example in the book and the only occurrence of the preposition before 3:28. This might suggest that Th has borrowed from OG. Th's use of κατά also overlaps with OG in 9 other vv. (6:5[4]; 10:15; 11:4, 16, 36; but 4x the MT=0, 3:28; 42[2x]; 43). However, κατὰ ἡμέραν is a good Greek rendering of the Hebrew distributive meaning "every day" (Mayser, II.2. 430ff.), whereas OG has the addition of ἑκάστην as an equivalent for the pronominal suffix. Therefore, there is no reason to conclude that Th was influenced in this rendition by OG.

l. 52, 53-OG and Th have a common reading of τράπεζα, though OG has δεῖπνον in l. 75. It is possible that OG's reading is corrupt because he prefers δεῖπνον in 1:8, 13, 15, 16. However, δεῖπνον is employed by Th in 1:16. So, this might be classified as a distinctive agreement.

l. 58-Th has already established this translation (see l. 43), and it is a SE throughout the LXX.

---

[49] Ziegler's text has the compound verbs for OG also in 1:18 but 967 has the simple forms.

l. 65 to 67-The first three lines read exactly the same in OG and Th, so we could very easily presume that Th has borrowed from OG. However, the only striking features of the reading involve the verb, i.e. it is the same in l. 65 and both omit it in l. 67. There are fifteen possible readings of שׂים in MT.[50] One involves a *Qere* in 11:18 (see *Lexicology*, l. 9), 6x OG=0, and in only 2 places OG employs √τιθέναι (see also 6:18[17]).[51] In contrast, excluding 11:18, Th offers a good translation of שׂים in almost every occurrence and employs √τιθέναι 7x.[52] When we consider the generally close formal correspondence of Th to MT we have to allow for the probability that the verb in l. 67 of MT is a later insertion (see *Text-Critical*). OG and Th would only then agree in their reading of ἐπέθηκεν in l. 65; but it is Th who consistently employs √τιθέναι.

l. 68-The shared reading of βαλτασαρ is distinctive, but there are no means to determine the direction of borrowing. Furthermore, the transcription of a proper name would be more liable to harmonization during the course of textual transmission due to standardization of spelling.

l. 94-97-See *Lexicology* l. 48, 94 concerning the accusative participle in l. 94. It is Th who used this form of √τασσω previously in l. 48 and this is the only place where Th and OG use a form of the verb in the same place. Th employs a more idiomatic rendering of the Hebrew verb in

---

[50] 1:7, 8; 2:5; 3:10, 12; 3:29(96); 4:3(6); 5:12; 6:14(13), 15(14), 18(17), 27(26); 11:17, 18. OG and Th=0 once in 1:7.

[51] OG=0 in 4:3(6); 5:12; 6:14(13), 15(14), 27(26) and 1:7. Except for the use of δώσει in 11:17; 18, OG uses a variety of equivalents or more dynamic renditions for this particular verb. ἐνθυμέομαι in 1:8; προστάσσω in 3:10; φοβέω in 3:12. The remaining two examples are in 2:5 and 3:29(96) where both Th and OG had trouble with MT (see the discussion in 2:1-10).

[52] See 1:7, 8; 3:10; 4:3(6); 5:12; 6:18(17), 27(26). Even in 3:12 where Th has evidently read the verb שׁמע the translation offers a good dynamic equivalent, and in 6:15(14) Th has ἀγωνίζομαι! ὑπετάγη in 6:14(13) and τάξει in 11:17 are then the only places where Th fails to use the expected equivalent.

Chapter 1:1-10   59

l. 97, so it is unlikely that Th is in any way dependent upon OG for the understanding of the syntax. There is also the exact verbal correspondence in l. 95-96, which includes the unusual common reading of πόσιν in l. 96 and the HL βρῶσιν in l. 95. Once again we have to ask, from whom did the reading originate? Is Th merely copying OG, or is the OG that we have a late revision based on Th? There is nothing about the use of βρῶσιν for מאכל (10/30 LXX) that is particularly important, but it is interesting that in the three other occurrences of משתה OG uses a verb twice and leaves it untranslated in 1:16. Th, on the other hand, uses three different equivalents for משתה, two of which are very rare in the LXX. The omission of משתה by OG in 1:16 may indicate that OG actually did not know the meaning of the Hebrew term, although this would be unusual for such a common word. However, in l. 55 OG could have employed the verb quite easily as a contextual guess (and by extension l. 78), but the context did not allow it in 1:16. In any event, it is at least as likely that the rendering in l. 96 is due to revision of OG in the light of Th! The alternative explanation that Th in l. 96 reflects OG, which merely omitted משתה as redundant in 1:16, is less likely for two reasons. First, Th demonstrates considerable independence in the latter half of v. 10, l. 99-107. This is obvious in the choice of terminology (see *Lexicology*, 99, 101, 102, 105) and the syntax (see l. 97 and l. 102). Second, the exact formal correspondence of OG and Th to MT is more characteristic of Th.

In summary, OG and Th have shared readings in l. 8, 13, 26, 33, 46, 52, 58, 65, 67, 68, 79, 94-96 and the five occurrences of ἀρχιευνοῦχος. However, only νεανισκός in l. 33, ἐκτάξαντα in l. 94, πόσις in l. 96, and βαλτασαρ in l. 68 could be called distinctive agreements. There are no means to determine the direction of borrowing for any of the last three, though there is good reason to believe that πόσις is due to Th influence on OG. Given Th's consistent use of παιδάρια for ילדים, it is possible that l. 33 is due to textual corruption. With regard to the remaining common readings, l. 13, 26, 58 are such obvious equivalents that they cannot be considered as evidence of any dependence by Th on OG, and in l. 65, 94-96 OG may also be dependent upon Th. The omission in l. 67 probably reflects a better semitic text; and the other common readings in l. 8, 46, 79 are not particularly important either. There may be significance in the common reading of ἀρχιευνοῦχος, but technical terms and common names are particularly susceptible to harmonization.

The evidence that Th has actually borrowed any readings from OG in 1:1-10 is practically non-existent. On the other hand, there are numerous distinctive disagreements which indicate that Th was translating independently. Overall, Th offers a consistent translation of MT that does not presuppose OG, and employs unique or his own distinctive vocabulary in l. 37, 41, 48, 56, 74, 81, 99, 102, 105. The existence of only four distinctive agreements (in three of which the direction of borrowing is uncertain), so few common readings, and the number of Th readings in this section that are distinctive leads to the conclusion that Th is not a recension of OG in this passage. The agreements may represent Th's occasional borrowing or knowledge of OG, but there is no evidence that Th did a systematic revision of OG. On the other hand, we have only just begun the analysis and perhaps it is better to suspend our judgment. The picture of Th's relationship to OG should become clearer as we proceed.

II.4. *Text-Critical Problems*

l. 18 and 19, 21-The omission in l. 18-19 could be due to the translator's decision to omit the words as redundant. There is also the possibility that the translator omitted בית אלהיו ואת־הכלים by parablepsis. The verb in l. 20 is marked with the ה, but it is followed by כי and l. 21 begins with בית as well. A third possibility is that אלהיו

Chapter 1:1-10

בית was inserted as an explanatory gloss to ארץ־שנער.[53] In this case only ואת־הכלים was deemed redundant, though the phrase is retained in 88-Syh with αὐτά. A decision here is difficult, but the last possibility is probably the one that leads to the original text.[54] L. 21 was omitted as unnecessary by the rendering of אלהיו by εἰδωλείῳ (see *Lexicology*).

l. 28-Charles, 12, is most likely correct when he argues that גולת has been omitted (OG reproduces גדולי in error) from MT. The presence of the addition in Th, which otherwise follows MT so closely, is convincing reason to emend MT rather than view the addition as a gloss from 2:25.[55]

l. 49-See *Syntax*.

l. 67-The verb in MT is a later insertion. See the discussion of Th's relationship to OG, l. 65-67. The verb is also omitted in the Peshitta and Vulgate.

l. 104-We have already noted that this addition is for clarification of who the other youths were (see *Syntax*).

l. 107-OG omits because of the dynamic rendering given to the clause, see *Lexicology*, l. 105.

---

[53] Charles, 8, argues this position, and suggests there is a further addition in MT as well.

[54] Also O. Plöger, *Das Buch Daniel* (*KAT*; Gütersloh: Mohn, 1965) 36; Montgomery, 118. Collins, *Daniel*, 127, suggests all of l. 19-22 may be a later gloss.

[55] Compare the suggestion of Bludau, 51 and Montgomery, 115.

Chapter III

Daniel 2:1-10

The opening 10 verses from chapter 2 are ideal for investigation because OG and Th employ a variety of translation equivalents for MT. This section also offers a number of textual variants between 88-Syh and 967 that provide an indication of how extensive Th's influence on OG actually was. There are some interesting variant readings between OG and MT in 2:1-10 as well.

Table 2

	2:1 Th	2:1 MT	2:1 OG
1	Ἐν τῷ ἔτει τῷ δευτέρῳ	וּבִשְׁנַת שְׁתַּיִם	Καὶ ¹ἐν τῷ ἔτει τῷ δευτέρῳ
2	τῆς βασιλείας	לְמַלְכוּת	τῆς βασιλείας
3	- -	נְבֻכַדְנֶצַּר	Ναβουχοδονοσορ ᴸσυνέβη^S
4	ᴸ(ἠνυπνιάσθη)	חָלַם	εἰς + ὁράματα καὶ +
5	Ναβουχοδον. ᴹᴸἐνύπνιον	נְבֻכַדְנֶצַּר חֲלֹמוֹת	ᴸἐνύπνια ἐμπεσεῖν ²αὐτὸν
6	καὶ ᴸ(ἐξέστη)	וַתִּתְפָּעֶם	καὶ ᴸταραχθῆναι
7	τὸ πνεῦμα αὐτοῦ	רוּחוֹ	- -
8	καὶ ὁ ὕπνος αὐτοῦ	וּשְׁנָתוֹ	ἐν τῷ ³ὕπνῳ^S
9	ἐγένετο ἀπ' αὐτοῦ	נִהְיְתָה עָלָיו	⁴- -
	2:2	2:2	2:2
10	καὶ εἶπεν ὁ βασιλεὺς	וַיֹּאמֶר הַמֶּלֶךְ	[καὶ] ᴸἐπέταξεν ὁ βασιλεὺς
11	ᴸᴹκαλέσαι	לִקְרֹא	ᴸˢεἰσενεχθῆναι^S
12	τοὺς ἐπαοιδοὺς	לַחַרְטֻמִּים	τοὺς ἐπαοιδοὺς
13	καὶ τοὺς μάγους	וְלָאַשָּׁפִים	καὶ τοὺς μάγους

Chapter 2:1-10   65

14	καὶ τοὺς φαρμακούς		לְכַשָּׁפִים	καὶ τοὺς φαρμακούς
15	καὶ τοὺς Χαλδαίους		וְלַכַּשְׂדִּים	^{s}τῶν Χαλδαίων
16	^{M}τοῦ ^{L}ἀναγγεῖλαι		לְהַגִּיד	^{L}[ἀναγγεῖλαι]^{16}
17	τῷ βασιλεῖ		לַמֶּלֶךְ	τῷ βασιλεῖ
18	τὰ ^{L}ἐνύπνια αὐτοῦ		חֲלֹמֹתָיו	τὰ ^{L}ἐνύπνια αὐτοῦ
19	καὶ ἦλθον		וַיָּבֹאוּ	καὶ παραγενόμενοι^s
20	καὶ ἔστησαν		וַיַּעַמְדוּ	ἔστησαν
21	ἐνώπιον τοῦ βασιλέως		לִפְנֵי הַמֶּלֶךְ	παρὰ τῷ βασιλεῖ
	2:3	2:3		2:3
22	καὶ εἶπεν αὐτοῖς		וַיֹּאמֶר לָהֶם	καὶ εἶπεν αὐτοῖς
23	ὁ βασιλεύς		הַמֶּלֶךְ	ὁ βασιλεύς
24	- -^{L}(Ἠνυπνιάσθην)		חֲלוֹם	^{L}Ἐνύπνιον ^{L}ἑώρακα
25	καὶ ^{L}(ἐξέστη)		חָלָמְתִּי	καὶ ^{L}ἐκινήθη
26	τὸ πνεῦμά μου		וַתִּפָּעֶם	^{s}μου τὸ πνεῦμα
27	^{M}τοῦ γνῶναι		רוּחִי	ἐπιγνῶναι +^{s}[οὖν θέλω]+^{6}
28	τὸ ^{L}ἐνύπνιον		לָדַעַת אֶת־הַחֲלוֹם	τὸ ^{L}ἐνύπνιον
	2:4			2:4

The OG and Th Versions of Daniel

29	καὶ ᴸἐλάλησαν	וידברו	καὶ ᴸἐλάλησαν
30	οἱ Χαλδαῖοι	הכשדים	οἱ Χαλδαῖοι
31	τῷ βασιλεῖ	למלך	ˢπρὸς τὸν βασιλέα
32	Συριστί	ארמית	συριστί
33	Βασιλεῦ	מלכא	Κύριε +[βασιλεῦ] +⁷
34	εἰς τοὺς αἰῶνας ζῆθι	לעלמין חיי	τὸν ᴹαἰῶνα ⁸ζῆθι
35	+ˢ(σὺ)ᴸεἰπὸν τὸ ἐνύπνιον	אמר חלמא	ᴸἀνάγγειλον τὸ ᴸἐνύπνιόν⁹
36	τοῖς ᴸπαισί σου	לעבדיך	τοῖς ᴸπαισίν σου
37	καὶ τὴν ᴸσύγκρισινᴹ	ופשרא	καὶ ἡμεῖς σοι ᴸφράσομεν
38	ᴸἀναγγελοῦμεν	נחוא	¹⁰αὐτό
	2:5		2:5
39	ἀπεκρίθη ὁ βασιλεύς	ענה מלכא	ˢἀποκριθεὶς ˢδὲ ὁ βασιλεὺς
40	- -	ואמר	εἶπεν
41	τοῖς Χαλδαίοις	לכשדיא	τοῖς Χαλδαίοις ¹¹διότιˢ
42	Ὁ ᴸλόγος ἀπ' ἐμοῦ	מלתא מני	- -
43	ᴸἀπέστη	אזדא	- -
44	ἐὰν μὴ ᴸγνωρίσητέ ¹⁰μοι	הן לא תהודעונני	Ἐὰν μὴ ᴸ[ἀπαγγείλητέ]¹⁷

Chapter 2:1-10

45	τὸ ἐνύπνιον		μοι +ἐπ' ἀληθείας+
46		קשׁטא	τὸ ᴸἐνύπνιον
47	καὶ τὴν ᴸσύγκρισινᴹ-	תחונני	καὶ τὴν τούτου ᴸ¹⁰κρισιν
48			+ˢδηλώσατέ¹²
49	εἰς ᴸἀπώλειαν ἔσεσθε	לאבדן תתעבדון	ᴸπαραδειγματισθήσεσθε
50	καὶ οἱ οἶκοι ὑμῶν	ובתיכון	καὶ ᴸἀναλημφθήσεται
51	ᴸ(διαρπαγήσονται)	לנולי	ˢὑμῶν τὰ ᴸὑπάρχοντα
52			εἰς τὸ βασιλικόν
	2:6		2:6
53	ἐὰν ˢδὲ τὸ ᴸἐνύπνιον	הן חלמא	ἐὰν ˢδὲ τὸ ᴸἐνύπνιον
54			+ˢδιασαφήσητέ μοι+
55	καὶ τὴν ᴸσύγκρισινᴹ-	ופשׁרה	καὶ τὴν τούτου ᴸ¹⁰κρισιν
56	ᴸγνωρίσητέ +μοι	תהחונני	ᴸ[ἀναγγείλητε]¹⁷
57	δόματα καὶ δορεὰς	מתנן ונבזבה	ᴸλήμψεσθε ˢδόματα
58	Αʹγγοκ λιμη₁ ικι	ויקר שׂגיא	παντοῖα καὶ
59	ᴸλήμψεσθε	תקבלון	ˢδοξασθήσεσθε
60	παρ' ἐμοῦ	מן קדמי	ᴸὑπ' ἐμοῦ

67

The OG and Th Versions of Daniel

68	(ᴸπλὴν)		
61	τὸ ἐνύπνιον	פֵּן	ᴸ112δηλώσατέ ᴸ113 οὖνˢ
62	καὶ τὴνᴸ σύγκρισινᴹ αὐτοῦ	חֶלְמָא	τὸ ἐνύπνιον
63	ᴸἀναγγείλατέ μοι	וּפִשְׁרֵהּ	καὶ κρίνατε
64	2:7	פִּשְׁרֵהּ	2:7
65	ἀπεκρίθησαν	עֲנוֹ	ˢἀπεκρίθησαν ˢδὲ
66	δεύτερον καὶ εἶπαν	תִנְיָנוּת וְאָמְרִין	ἐκ δευτέρου λέγοντες
67	(Ὁ βασιλεὺς ᴸᴹεἰπάτω)	מַלְכָּא יֵאמַר	Βασιλεῦ τὸ ᴸὅραμα
68	τὸ ἐνύπνιον	חֶלְמָא	ᴸεἰπόνˢ
69	τοῖς παισὶν αὐτοῦ	לְעַבְדוֹהִי	14 οἱ ˢδὲ παῖδές σου
70	καὶ τὴν ᴸσύγκρισινᴹ + αὐτοῦ +	וּפִשְׁרָא	ᴸκρινοῦσιν
71	ᴸἀναγγελοῦμεν	נְחַוֵּה	πρὸς ταῦτα
	2:8	2:8	2:8
72	καὶ ἀπεκρίθη	עָנֵה	--καὶ ˢεἶπεν αὐτοῖς
73	ὁ βασιλεὺς	מַלְכָּא	ὁ βασιλεύς
74	καὶ εἶπεν	וְאָמַר	
75	Ἐπ' ἀληθείας	מִן־יַצִּיב	Ἐπ' ᴸἀληθείας

Chapter 2:1-10

76	οἶδα ἐγὼ ὅτι	...	[15]...
77	καιρὸν ὑμεῖς ἐξαγοράζετε	...	καιρὸν ᴸἐξαγοράζετε
78	ᴸκαθότι	...	ᴸκαθόπερ
79	εἴδετε ὅτι		ˢοὖν
80	ᴸἀπέστη ἀπ' ἐμοῦ	...	προστέταχα οὕτως ἔσται
81	τὸ ᴸῥῆμα	...	
	2:9	2:9	2:9
82	ἐὰν οὖν τὸ ἐνύπνιον	...	ἐὰν μὴ [17][ἀπόδωτέ] μοι
83	μὴ ᴸἀναγγείλητέ μοι	...	τὸ ᴸἐνύπνιον[18]
84			+ˢκαὶ τὴν τούτου
85			+[10]κρίσιν + ᴸδηλώσητε
86			+ˢθανάτῳ περιπεσεῖσθε
87	(οἶδα ὅτι)	...	- -
88	- -	...	- -
89	ᴸῥῆμα	...	ᴸσυνείπασθε ˢγάρ
90	ψευδὲς καὶ ᴸδιεφθαρμένον	...	ᴸλόγουˢᴹ
91	ᴸσυνέθεσθε	...	ˢψευδεῖς

70 The OG and Th Versions of Daniel

92	ᴹεἰπεῖν	להחויה
93	ἐνώπιόν μου	קדמי
94	ἕως οὗ	עד די
95	ὁ καιρὸς ᴸἀλλοιωθῇ	עדנא יחלף
96	ᴸ(μεταλλάξαι)ᴸ (--)	להן
97	τὸ ἐνύπνιόν + μου	חלמא
98	ᴸεἴπατέ μοι	אמרו לי
99	+ˢᵍ ²¹εἶδον τὴν νύκτα	
100	καὶ γνώσομαι ὅτι	²²γנדעאנון די
101	τὴν ᴸσύγκρισινᴹ⁻	ופשרה
102	ᴸἀναγγελεῖτέ μοι	תהחון
	2:10	2:10
103	ἀπεκρίθησαν	ענו
104	οἱ Χαλδαῖοι	כשדיא
105	ἐνώπιον τοῦ βασιλέως	קדם מלכא
106	καὶ λέγουσιν	ואמרין
107	Οὐκ ἔστιν ἄνθρωπος	לא איתי אנש

Chapter 2:1-10

108	ἐπὶ τῆς ᴸ(ξηρᾶς)	על־יבשתא	ἐπὶ τῆς γῆς
109	ὅστις τὸ ᴸῥῆμα	מלתא להן	δυνήσεται ᴸεἰπεῖν
110	τοῦ βασιλέως	מלכא	τῷ βασιλεῖ
111	δυνήσεται ᴸᴹγνωρίσαι	להחויה די	ᴸ²³ ἃ ἑώρακεν
112	ᴸκαθότι	כל־קבל די	ᴸκαθάπερ +ˢσὺ ἐρωτᾷς
113	πᾶς βασιλεὺς	מלך רב	καὶ πᾶς βασιλεὺς
114	μέγας	ושליט	--
115	καὶ ᴸἄρχων	מלה כדנה	καὶ²⁴ ᴸδυνάστης
116	ᴸῥῆμα ᴸτοιοῦτο	לא שאל	²⁵τοῦτο τὸ ᴸπρᾶγμα
117	οὐκ ἐπερωτᾷ	לכל־חרטם	οὐκ ²⁶ἐρωτᾷ
118	--ˢἐπαοιδόν-μάγον	ואשף וכשדי	πάντα σοφὸν καὶ μάγον
119	-Χαλδαῖον		καὶ Χαλδαῖον

III.1. *Textual Notes*

1. ἐν τῷ ἔτει τῷ δευτέρῳ (88-Syh)] ἐν τῷ δωδεκάτῳ ἔτει (967) The dating to the 12th year in 967 is probably based on a confusion from Judith 1:1, though it also fixes the chronological difficulties between chapters 1 and 2.[1] Hamm, *I-II*, 141 suggests that the syntax of 967 is correct, but it is more likely that neither 88-Syh or 967 preserves the OG. As noted previously in our discussion of 1:1, OG characteristically employs the genitive for dating and it is Th who employs the dative (1:1; 2:1; 7:1; 8:1; 9:1; 10:1).[2] In this instance 88-Syh reads with Th, while the dative case in 967 may also reflect Th influence even though the number of years was later corrected. A reasonable conjecture would be Ἔτους δευτέρου.

2. τὸν βασιλέα] αὐτόν 88-Syh have replaced the simple pronoun with a more explicit identification of Nebuchadnezzer as "the king". Similar variants occur in 2:4; 3:16, 19.[3]

3. ἐνυπνίῳ] ὕπνῳ If not for this variant it might easily be concluded that the large omission (discussed below) was due to an error in 967. ὕπνῳ "sleep" was changed to ἐνυπνίῳ "vision" either to avoid the repetition of ὕπνος when the correction from Th was added or on the assumption that ὕπνῳ was corrupt (the two words are graphically similar).

4. >αὐτοῦ καὶ ὁ ὕπνος αὐτοῦ ἐγένετο ἀπ' αὐτοῦ This is most likely a later correction toward MT from Th[4] and is a good example of how great the Th influence on OG actually was. If we accept 967's text as original, then OG reads as a dynamic translation that omits redundant

---

[1] McCrystall, 275.

[2] The genitive is found in Th in 3:1, but note that Ziegler has correctly enclosed the words with brackets.

[3] Hamm, *I-II*, 143.

[4] Hamm, *I-II*, 145.

Chapter 2:1-10   73

information in MT. The καί at the beginning of v. 2 might also be omitted as a later correction toward MT.

5. εἰσενεχθῆναι] καλέσαι This is the best example of a corruption in 967 in 2:1-10 due to Th influence or correction toward MT.[5]

6. ἐπιγνῶναι] >οὖν θέλω Hamm, *I-II*, 149 regards 88-Syh as original, but the main reason he gives is because it represents a more dynamic translation. On the other hand, the words could have been added to smooth out the syntax. Perhaps it is best to bracket them to indicate that they are of doubtful authority. See the discussion, p. 111.

7. ζῆθι] ζήσῃ The same variant also occurs in 2:28. יחי appears a total of 5x in MT (see 3:9; OG=0 in 5:10; 6:7[6], 22[21]) and in each case Th reads ζῆθι. The variants in 967 suggest that the imperative of 88-Syh in 2:4 was due to influence from Th. There is no corresponding *Vorlage* for the OG in 2:28, but presumably the correction was due to harmonization to 2:4. 967 agrees with 88-Syh in reading ζῆθι in 3:9, but Hamm, *I-II*, 151 suggests that we read ζήσῃ there also.

8. [βασιλεῦ] See the discussion in *Text-Critical*, 1. 33.

9. ἐνύπνιόν] >σου The additional personal pronoun in 88-Syh may stem from an alternative *Vorlage*, but OG usually does not employ this Hebraism.

10. τὴν σύγκρισιν αὐτοῦ] αὐτό In l. 38 967 reads the personal pronoun αὐτό against τὴν σύγκρισιν αὐτοῦ in 88 (Th=τὴν σύγκρισιν). In this case it is likely that Th's τὴν σύγκρισιν was added to OG as a correction toward MT and the original accusative pronoun was then corrected to a genitive. There are also three other places where 967 reads κρίσιν for σύγκρισιν in 2:1-10 (l. 47, 55, 85), and the variant also occurs in 2:26. Given the fact that σύγκρισις is the stereotyped

---

[5] Charles suggests that the LXX read להביא and that MT should be emended. This is possible, but the OG probably resulted from a simple misreading of the text and/or the translator's expectation of what the text should read, particularly since the context is so similar to 1:3 where להביא does appear. See Charles, *Exegetical Commentary*, 27.

equivalent employed by Th and that κρίσις in 967 accords with OG's usage elsewhere,[6] 967's text should be accepted in all of these cases.

11. ὅτι] διότι 967=88-Syh, but Ziegler accepts Rahlfs' conjecture. Aejmelaeus, notes that "διότι is often corrected to ὅτι in the later transmission of the text."[7] See 3:29(96) for another example of the correction.

12. δηλώσατέ] >μοι In these cases 967 is preferred on the basis that it is the more reliable bearer of the OG. It is possible in the second instance (l. 61) that μοι was mistaken for οὖν (see below).

13. δηλώσατέ] +οὖν The addition of this conjunction does accord with OG's more dynamic approach and it is employed elsewhere in this passage.[8]

14. καὶ οἱ] οἱ δὲ The postpositive conjunction of 967 is the more likely Greek.[9]

15. >οἶδα ὅτι 88-Syh=Th OG shortens MT without losing any vital information.

16. >καθάπερ ἑοράκατε ὅτι ἀπέστη ἀπ' ἐμοῦ τὸ πρᾶγμα We believe that the shorter reading in 967 leads to the best text. In order to attain a better understanding of the issues involved we will begin by printing the texts of MT, Ziegler (=88-Syh), and 967.

MT- כָּל־קֳבֵל דִּי חֶזְוֵיהוֹן דִּי אָזְדָּא מִנִּי מִלְּתָא
Zieg.-καθάπερ ἑοράκατε ὅτι ἀπέστη ἀπ' ἐμοῦ τὸ πρᾶγμα·
καθάπερ οὖν προστέταχα οὕτως ἔσται
967-[   ]
καθάπερ οὖν προστέταχα [   ]

---

[6] κρίσις appears in 2:36, 45; 7:16 and OG generally employs other dynamic equivalents. For a more complete discussion, see p. 98.

[7] Aejmelaeus, "OTI," 123

[8] 2:3?, 6, 8, 9; 3:23, 24, 26(93), 30(97); 5:6; 12:6.

[9] See A. Aejmelaeus, "Clause Connectors," 367-368.

It will be noticed that while the first portion of 88-Syh reads with MT, καθάπερ οὖν προστέταχα οὕτως ἔσται appears to be an addition. However, 967 omits the portion that agrees with MT and has an abbreviated version of the addition. The text that Hamm chooses to read is 88-Syh without οὕτως ἔσται. He argues that the first portion agrees with OG's vocabulary usage elsewhere, and it is lacking in 967 by homoioarchton. Hamm reads the καθάπερ οὖν προστέταχα as a striking translation for the די at the beginning of v. 9 and οὕτως ἔσται as a later addition.[10]

Hamm's reconstruction has much to commend it, but he must assume that the similar reading of Ὁ λόγος ἀπέστη ἀπ' ἐμοῦ in l. 43-44 of v. 5 in Th is OG. This assumption is incorrect. L. 43-44 are asterisked in 88-Syh, omitted in 967, and exhibit the formal correspondence to MT characteristic of Th. Therefore, if we begin with the presupposition that ἀπέστη ἀπ' ἐμοῦ is Th, then our analysis of the addition in 88-Syh changes drastically. Not only does ἀπέστη ἀπ' ἐμοῦ have to be a later addition from Th,[11] but the whole section that agrees with MT (i.e. καθάπερ ἑοράκατε ὅτι ἀπέστη ἀπ' ἐμοῦ τὸ πρᾶγμα) becomes suspect. If we omit the section that agrees with MT as a secondary addition to MT, then Hamm is correct that καθάπερ is the proper equivalent for כל־קבל די, but it is the καθάπερ followed by οὖν προστέταχα and not καθάπερ ἑοράκατε . . . πρᾶγμα.

In other words, 88-Syh preserves the OG, but a more literal translation of MT has been inserted as a correction. Without the secondary addition, καθάπερ οὖν προστέταχα οὕτως ἔσται reads as a dynamic contextual guess for MT. OG's translation of מלה in chapters 2-3 also supports this interpretation. מלה is found 11x in chapters 2-3 and OG employs eight different equivalents:

προστέταχα-2:8? ἕκαστα-2:17

---

[10] Hamm, *I-II*, 163, 165.

[11] Munnich ("Origène," 190) also lists the asterisked addition in 2:5 as a reading that conforms to MT and Th.

λόγος-2:9, 11   πρὸς ταῦτα-2:23
ἃ ἑώρακεν-2:10   πρόσταγμα-2:15?,[12] 3:22
πρᾶγμα-2:10   προσταγή-3:28(95)

The variety of equivalents employed by OG is obvious, and the possibility that προστέταχα was intended as an equivalent for מלה is given credibility by the fact that προστάσσω is etymologically related to two equivalents employed elsewhere by OG: πρόσταγμα in 2:15?; 3:22 and προσταγή in 3:28(95). 967 omits οὕτως ἔσται, but this may have been part of the translation and intended to be an equivalent for היחון.

Ultimately, it is impossible to be sure of the reading of OG in 2:8, but the reconstruction offered above takes the best account for the texts that we have. OG rendered MT with a dynamic equivalent and does not reflect a plus or an alternative *Vorlage*; at least, one cannot be reconstructed with any confidence.

17. ἐὰν μὴ] +ἀπόδωτέ μοι 967 reads ἀπόδωτε μοι where Syh-88 have ἀπαγγείλητέ μοι following τὸ ἐνύπνιον. We believe that there is good reason to suspect that all the readings of ἀπ(ν)αγγέλλω in Ziegler's OG of this passage (l. 16, 44, 56, 85) are later additions and/or corrections to OG.[13] However, on the basis of the manuscript evidence it is impossible to determine whether the dynamic use of ἀπόδωτε is an indication that there were more dynamic renderings employed in l. 16, 44 and 56, or if ἀπόδωτε was a corruption of a secondary addition of ἀπ(ν)αγγέλλω.

18. >ἀπαγγείλητε μοι ἐπ' ἀληθείας The OG of 2:8-9 as it is found in 88-Syh has undergone extensive revision and has several doublets and additions. We have discussed above that ἀπαγγείλητε μοι is a later corruption and it is our view that ἐπ' ἀληθείας is secondary as well. The shorter reading of 967 is to be preferred.

---

[12] A question mark is placed beside 2:15 because there is uncertainty over its reading. 967 has a lacuna, but there is not enough space for πρόσταγμα.

[13] See the discussion of verbs of saying under *Lexicology*, pp. 88 below.

19. τὸ ὅραμα εἴπητε] 3,1,2 88-Syh=MT. Ziegler has correctly conjectured ὅραμα as it is found in 967.
20. >μοι 88-Syh=MT
21. τὴν νύκτα ἑόρακα] εἶδον τὴν νύκτα 967's order and verb τὸ ὅραμα ὃ εἶδον agrees with OG's usage elsewhere in 2:26; 7:1.
22. >τότε 88=967 τότε has been added in Syh to harmonize with MT.[14]
23. ὅ] ἅ OG normally employs a neuter plural relative pronoun when there is no explicit grammatical antecedent (see 1:20; 2:23, 28, 29, 30; 8:19; 9:6; but contrast 3:19).[15]
24. [πᾶς] δυνάστης We have already seen that OG tends to eliminate elements which are redundant in Greek.
25. τοιοῦτο] τοῦτο τό The shared reading of τοιοῦτο in Th and 88-Syh indicates dependence in one direction or the other because it is a HL. If we dismiss any prejudice that Th is borrowing from OG, then it is conceivable that the reading of 88-Syh reflects later corruption toward Th. At the same time, either 967 or 88 could represent an orthographical error. So, the OG witnesses are split and 88-Syh agree with Th. Although there must be a degree of caution evaluating this variant, we cannot assume that Th has borrowed from OG. Furthermore, we have to emphasize that 967 is the more reliable witness to the OG; therefore, the burden of proof is upon those who prefer the reading of 88-Syh.
26. ἐπερωτᾷ] ἐρωτᾷ In l. 117 the simple verb ἐρωτᾷ has been changed to the compound ἐπερωτᾷ due to influence from Th. Note, for example, that the simple form ἐρωτᾷς appears in l. 112.

---

[14] Hamm, *I-II*, 171.

[15] Hamm, *I-II*, 173.

III.2. Analysis of 2:1-10

III.2.i. Morphology

l. 5-Th has a singular for the plural. Since Th usually follows the number of the *Vorlage* and OG has the plural, this difference may stem from an error reading the text.

l. 11, 16, 27, 92, 111-Only in l. 16 and 27 does Th represent the ל of the infinitive construct with an article.

l. 34-OG has the singular for the plural here. עלם occurs 18x, of which 9x there is a plural. The only case in which OG might retain the plural is 7:18(?), while in 4 other places it changes the plural to the favoured singular (2:44[2]; 3:9; 6:27[26]).[16] On two occasions OG employs the adjective αἰώνιος (7:14, 27) for עלם. Given OG's preference for the singular and his omission of מן־עלמא in 2:20, it is probable that Ziegler's reading of the plural in 7:18 is incorrect. Ziegler has OG reading with MT and Th omitting one element.[17]

---

[16] 3x OG=0, 3:33(100); 5:10; 6:7(6) and 3x the *Vorlage* is substantially different in 4:31(34)*bis*; 6:22(21). There are differences in 6:27(26) as well. In order to account for all of the occurrences of עלם, note that it is found 3x in a series in 7:18, 2x in 2:20, and 2x in separate syntagms in 4:31(34). In one instance in 2:44 Ziegler has the plural εἰς τοὺς αἰῶνας according to 88 where 967 has ἕως τοῦ αἰῶνος and Syh also has the singular. The only other time OG retains the plural of MT for עלם is in 7:18 according to Ziegler, but see the note below.
αἰών is used 4x in the Hebrew section of MT, each time in the singular (8:11; 12:3*bis*, 7). In 8:11 and once in 12:3 it is an addition. αἰώνιος is also found for עולם in 9:24; 12:2(2).

[17] See Ziegler, 171. The apparatus reads καὶ ἕως τοῦ αἰῶνος τῶν αἰώνων Syh Iust.] om. τῶν αἰώνων 967; om. καὶ ἕως τοῦ αἰῶνος 88: homiot. I would suggest that either 967 or 88 preserves the original reading. If 967 is original, then OG would have omitted the last of the three occurrences of עלם which is supported by a similar omission in 2:20 and the preference for the singular elsewhere. This reading would explain Syh Iust. as a variant that reflects later harmonization to MT. 88 could have omitted a portion of this text by error as Ziegler indicates, or represent an attempt to fix the singular, or Th influence. On the other hand, we will find more evidence that supports Albertz' position that the OG translator of chapters

Chapter 2:1-10 79

Th follows the number of עלם in MT except in 5:10 and 6:7(6). On two occasions OG and Th both read the adjective αἰώνιος, but once again this does not prove Th dependence on OG. In each instance the use of the adjective is an appropriate rendering for the adverbial עלם; furthermore, עלם is employed as an adverb earlier in 3:33(100) and 4:31(34), and in both cases Th translates with the adjective.

l. 35, 67-Th deals with both of these verbs differently from OG. In l. 35 he adds the personal pronoun for emphasis. Th correctly translates the jussive in l. 67 (see l. 68, *Syntax*).

l. 37, 47, 55, 63, 70, 101-In l. 47, 54 Th omits the pronoun against MT and OG while in l. 71 Th adds it. These differences stem from vocalization, but also demonstrate Th independence from OG. The meaning of the text is not affected either way. Note also the orthographical variation between ה/א in MT.

l. 90-OG employs the plural for the singular, while Th follows MT.

III.2.ii. *Syntax*

l. 3-OG's choice of συνέβη with an accusative and infinitive reflects an idiom in the Greek (see BAG, 777); therefore, there is no reason to suggest an alternative *Vorlage*. For the addition of ὁράματα, see *Text-Critical*.

l. 8-The text is corrupt in the OG, but seems to have undergone revision toward MT under the influence of Th. The clause in l. 9 was omitted as redundant, but the omission of רוחי is harder to explain given its inclusion in l. 26. However, if the καί at the beginning of v. 2 were

---

4-6 is different from the translator of the remainder of the book, so the change to the singular in chapter 7 would only be related to the 3x in chapter 2:4, 44(2).

regarded as a later insertion associated with the hexaplaric addition, then καὶ ταραχθῆναι ἐν τῷ ὕπνῳ ἐπέταξεν would read well; and we can see how the רוּחוֹ would have been regarded as unnecessary. The meaning of OG is basically synonymous with MT.

l. 11-OG uses a different verb (εἰσφέρω) and transforms it into a passive in order to make the meaning of the text explicit (see *Text-Critical*). The choice of the passive may also have been influenced by the one in l. 6.

l. 15-The genitive probably reflects an alternative *Vorlage*, but would make the preceding terms various classes of Chaldeans. See *Text-Critical*.

l. 19-OG employs a hypotactic construction to avoid the parataxis of the Hebrew.

l. 26, 52-Wifstrand notes l. 26 as one of the places where OG does not follow the Hebrew in the position of the personal pronoun.[18] L. 52 should be added to his list.

l. 27-The addition, if original (see *Text-Critical*), serves to make the text read more smoothly by having the king's disturbed spirit being the cause of wanting to know the interpretation of the dream.

l. 27?, 61, 79, 96-The use of postpositive conjunctions like δὲ, οὖν, and γάρ is a sign of a dynamic translator, because employing a postpositive entails a change in the word order of the *Vorlage*.[19] OG employs the conjunction οὖν 9x as a free rendition of MT. Only 2x is it found outside of chapters 2-3.[20]

Th never has this conjunction.

---

[18] A. Wifstrand, "Die Stellung der enklitischen Personalpronomina bei den Septuaginta," *Bulletin de la Société Royale des Lettres de Lund* 1 (1949-50): 49.

[19] See Aejmelaeus, "Clause Connectors," 363-372. δὲ and γάρ are discussed in more detail in later sections.

[20] 2:3?, 6, 8, 9; 3:23, 24, 26(93), 30(97); 5:6; 12:6.

l. 31-OG's choice of the preposition is surprising since the article would do, as in l. 17.

l. 33-See *Text-Critical.*

l. 39, 53, 65, 69-OG employs δè 52x and the distribution is significant: chapter 1-4x; chapter 2-17x; chapter 3-9x; chapter 4-6x; chapter 5-1x; chapter 6-9x; chapter 7-3x; chapter 8-1x; chapter 12-2x.[21] Not only is δè relatively infrequent in chapters 4-6, but it is almost totally absent from chapters 7-12.

Th only has δè 11x, and δè is totally absent from chapters 1, 7-12.[22]

l. 39, 65, 72, 103-All four instances involve the semitic idiom ענה ואמר "answered and said." A literal rendering is the participle/verb (ἀποκρίνω) + finite verb (6x, usually εἶπον). In 3/4 cases Th translates with the formal equivalent, but Th does omit אמר in l. 40 against both MT and OG. OG also has one omission of ענה in l. 72, but exhibits more variety in general. In l. 40 OG has the common literal rendering while in l. 65 the even more formal equivalent participle (λέγοντες) is employed for אמר. Finally, in l. 106 OG has the most idiomatic rendering when אמר is translated with ὅτι as an introduction to direct discourse.[23] Thus, OG displays its characteristic variety, and

---

[21] 1:15, 17, 18; 2:5, 6, 7(2), 13, 16, 24(2), 26, 27, 30, 33(2), 36, 41, 43, 44; 3:12, 15, 16, 23, 25, 46, 49, 51, 28(95); 4:16(19), 19(22), 28(31), 30(33), 34b, 34c; 5:preface; 6:5(4), 6(5), 11(10), 13(12)*bis*, 17(16), 23(22)*bis*; 7:7(2), 16; 8:4; 12:2(2).

[22] 2:6, 15, 24, 30, 41, 42; 3:15, 49; 4:15(18); 5:17; 6:23(22).

[23] Aejmelaeus notes that Daniel's three uses (including 2:5) of ὅτι *recitativum* rank it among the most frequent users, even though we would expect it more often. Similar cases to l. 106 are l. 41 where it is difficult to determine whether the OG is ὅτι or διότι and 2:25 where ὅτι translates כי. See, "*OTI recitativum* in Septuagintal Greek," *Studien zur Septuaginta - Robert Hanhart zu Ehren* (*MSU* 20; ed. D. Fraenkel, U. Quast, and J. Wevers; Göttingen: Vandenhoeck & Ruprecht, 1990) 79-82.

through its variety of renderings demonstrates four main ways that we find the idiom translated in the LXX.[24]

The idiom ענה ואמר is found 30x in the Aramaic section of Daniel. Generally speaking, אמר is most often represented by some form of a finite verb (OG-16x, Th-19x, usually εἶπον). Only 3x does OG use a participle alone (also λέγων in 2:15; 6:21), while Th has one occurrence of the participle alone in 3:16. When OG and Th choose to represent the syntagm with one equivalent it is more often the case that ענה is omitted.

It is when we compare chapters 2-3 with chapters 4-6 that there are significant differences in the TT of both Greek texts, but particularly in Th. For example, the idiom occurs 9x in chapter 2 and Th has the literal rendering of the participle/verb + finite verb 6x.[25] In 2:8, 20 one of the elements is omitted while in 2:15 the whole idiom is left out. In chapter 3:1-20 the idiom occurs 4x: 3:9-Th=omission; 3:14-verb + verb; 3:16-verb + participle; 3:19-omission + verb. In the same section of chapters 2 and 3 OG almost always represents both verbs of the construction and usually has the finite verb as the second element. Besides the differences noted in l. 72 and 106, OG employs the participle alone in 2:15 and in 3:19 OG translates the syntagm dynamically with ἐπιτάσσω.

Significant changes begin to occur where the deutero-canonical additions have been inserted into chapter 3. The idiom occurs 4x in 3:24(91)-3:26(93). In each case Th translates with a single finite verb. OG omits the syntagm once in 3:24(91) and 25(92), translates with a single finite verb once in 3:24(91),[26] and employs καλέω in 3:26(93). This cluster of differences in both OG and Th indicates either that the *Vorlage* is different and/or, possibly, that we are dealing with different

---

[24] See also Aejmelaeus' article, "*Participium Coniunctum* as a Criterion of Translation Technique," *VT* 32 (1982): 387.

[25] Besides 2:5, 7, 10 see 26, 27, 47.

[26] The idiom is attested in 1QDan^b. See *DJD*, 1, 151.

Chapter 2:1-10   83

translators. Similar differences are encountered in chapters 5-6. The syntagm occurs 8x, but Th only represents both elements in 6:14(13); otherwise Th employs a single finite verb.[27] The remaining uses are 3:28(95); 4:16(19)*bis*, 27(30) where Th employs the literal rendering, and 7:2 where both Th and OG omit it. As usual OG has a varied pattern. However, it is significant that even when we exclude the 4x where OG=0 in 3:24-7:2,[28] OG represents both elements 3x (5:13; 6:13[12], 17[16]) where Th only has the finite verb.

Although it is difficult to draw conclusions from the translation of this idiom by itself, it does seem to fit a pattern in the Aramaic section. OG generally represents both elements of the idiom through chapter 3:19 while it does not in 3:24(91)-7:2. The same is true of Th, yet in the majority of cases OG and Th employ different syntactical patterns to translate the idiom. Therefore, Th is not dependent upon OG for his renderings. If we were to examine their lexical choices, we would discover even greater diversity.

l. 41-43-The text in 2:5 offers many difficulties. The reading of the conjunction and the omission of l. 42-43 is somewhat odd given l. 79-81, but should be considered original OG (see *Lexicology* and *Text-Critical*). As a result, the emphasis on the finality of the decree is somewhat less compared to MT, though this is partially compensated for by the addition in l. 45 (if original).

l. 48, 54-It has been argued above (see *Textual Notes*) that these additions probably do not reflect an alternative *Vorlage* at all. If the OG as it stands were original, the creation of distinct clauses would have been motivated by the translator's desire to make explicit the command to tell both the contents of the dream and its meaning.

---

[27] 5:7, 10, 13, 17: 6:13(12), 17(16), 21(20).

[28] 3:24(91), 25(92); 4:16(19)*bis*; 5:7, 10.

l. 57, 58-OG uses alternative means to render these syntagms in MT and offers good idiomatic translations. In l. 57 OG renders one of the co-ordinate nouns with an adjective.[29] OG renders the noun and adjective in l. 58 of MT with the verb in l. 59.

l. 68-Th translates the jussive with its formal equivalent, while OG uses the 2 singular imperative. If Th were following OG closely, it would have been easy to write the vocative βασιλεῦ as in l. 33 before he arrived at the verb and realized that מלכא should be rendered with a nominative. Indeed, it could be argued that OG wrote down the vocative without looking far enough ahead to ensure that the syntax would be correct. It was only after OG came to the verb that he realized his grammatical error, but he was able to change the syntax of the remainder of the verse and still render the basic meaning of the passage.[30]

l. 84-85-We suggest that the addition of OG be preferred (see *Text-Critical*) over MT, but the basic sense of each is the same because the required interpretation of the vision is understood from the context.

l. 86-88-l. 86 is an addition containing the rare word περιπίπτω (1-9), while 87-88 are omitted. The text echoes 2:5 and the overall sense of OG and MT is the same, though OG does emphasize the judgment against the magicians for failing to explain the dream. l. 87-88 exhibit a textual difficulty, because there is no question whether OG and Th could have translated l. 87-88 with a formal equivalent if they had so desired. Both translate רח elsewhere where it occurs in the *Vorlage*.

---

[29] In 2:48 OG renders מתנה with δωρεά, while in 5:17 OG=0. Th renders מתנה 3/3 with δόμα and נבזבה 2/2 with δωρεά (see 5:17).

[30] Soisalon-Soininen ("Beobachtungen," 320-321) notes that the translators were more influenced in their renderings by what they had already translated than by what was to come. They were also limited in their ability to make corrections because of the scarcity of writing material. Therefore, in cases like this, they had to make changes in the grammar.

For example, in 2:13, 15 OG has δογματίζω and in 7:25 νομός. Th has δόγμα in 2:13 as well as in the repeated expression "the law of the Medes and Persians" in 6:9(8), 13(12), 16(15) where OG=0. Th's diversity is also shown by his dynamic rendering in 2:15 ἡ γνώμη ἡ ἀναιδής "the ruthless decree!" and 6:6(5) where he employs νόμιμος. This is further evidence of Th's independence, but in 7:25 Th does have νομός.[31]

l. 89-OG employs the postpositive conjunction γάρ 19x, whereas Th only has it 4x.[32] In chapters 2-6 OG employs the conjunction 5x where MT=0, but in chapters 8-12 it is mainly employed for כי (9/10).[33]

l. 91-OG omits one of the adjectives while Th follows MT.

l. 96-OG transforms the syntax of the clause by the addition of ἐάν, which requires the omission of καί in l. 102.

l. 99-The plus specifies the time when the king had the vision. There is no significant difference in the meaning, though we argue below (*Text-Critical*) that the addition was in the OG *Vorlage*.

---

[31] The common use of νόμος for דת in 7:25 is a distinctive agreement, however there are no means to determine the direction of borrowing. νόμος is only found 4x elsewhere in OG 3:29-MT=0; and in 9:10, 11(2) it is the expected equivalent for תורה. Th does not have νόμος in 3:29, but otherwise has it as the expected LXX equivalent for תורה in 9:10, 11(2). תורה also appears in 9:13 where Th again employs νόμος, but OG has διαθήκη!, which is the SE for ברית.

[32] 2:9; 3:17, 28(95); 4:11(14), 24(27), 34a; 6:6(5), 27(26), 28(27); 8:17, 19, 26; 9:18; 10:11, 14; 11:27, 35, 36; 12:13. Th=OG in 3:17; 8:17, 19; 11:36.

[33] 6x MT=0 in 4:11(14), 24(27), 34a; 6:6(5), 28(27). The only place in chapters 8-12 where γάρ is not employed for כי is 12:13 where MT=0. The other main equivalent for כי in both OG (14/24) and Th (18/24) is ὅτι.

Aejmelaeus ("Clause Connectors," 369) emphasizes that for the proper evaluation of equivalents for כי as a causal conjunction we need to distinguish clearly between this function and the function of כי meaning "that." In 20/24x כי has a causal function. Two exceptions are 12:7, 9 where OG has ὅτι in the sense of "that." In two other cases (9:18; 10:21) OG and Th have ἀλλά for כי where it follows a negative clause and has the sense "but, rather" (see Aejmelaeus, "Clause Connectors," 373). Therefore, OG has γάρ translate the causal sense of כי 9/20 which is almost equal to the use of ὅτι (11/20). The cases where OG has ὅτι are 9:9, 11, 14, 16, 19, 23; 10:12, 19; 11:4, 25, 37.

l. 118-Th does not coordinate with καί against MT and OG.

III.2.iii. *Lexicology*

l. 3-This is the only place where OG uses συνβαίνω (see *Syntax*, l. 3) and it does represent a rather dynamic translation. For the addition of ὁράματα, see the *Text-Critical* discussion.

l. 4, 24-חלם as a verb is only here in Daniel. Th employs words related by etymology to render the verb and cognate accusative, and ἐνυπνιάζομαι is not found in OG. OG uses variety, though συνβαίνω is unusual.

l. 5, 18, 24, 28-OG (5/5) and Th (4/5) both employ the expected ἐνύπνιον as a SE for חלום.[34] Th omits in l. 24, probably in error.

l. 6, 25-Both OG and Th offer good renderings of the Hebrew פעם (2-5, see BDB, 821),[35] though OG once again illustrates variety while Th employs the same rendition. OG uses ταράσσω elsewhere to render different verbs in 11:12 (נפל), 44(בהל). Th also has ταράσσω in 11:44, though in a different person, and uses it 10x in total.[36] OG employs κινέω elsewhere in 3:79; 4:16(19); 11:38,[37] and the verb does not appear in Th. Th uses ἐξίστημι only in these two places, while OG does not employ this compound verb.

l. 10-OG always uses ἐπιτάσσω for אמר in the sense "command" (see 1:18; 2:46; 3:19, 20). Also in 3:24 where MT=0.

---

[34] Also in 1:17.

[35] Also found in Gen 41:8; Judg 13:25; Ps 77:5.

[36] See also 4:2(5), 16(19); 5:6, 9(2x), 10; 7:18, 28.

[37] In 11:38 κινήσει is a contextual guess for יכבד. See p. 53 above.

Chapter 2:1-10   87

l. 11-Both OG and Th use a variety of equivalents for קרא. OG's most frequent equivalent for קרא is (ἐπι)καλέω 3/8 (9:18, 19; 10:1;=Th, 6x OG=0),[38] but OG's variety is seen in the selection of φωνέω (4:11 [14]; 5:7); ἀναβοάω (8:16);[39] κηρύσσω[40] (3:4); εἰσφέρω.

At first glance we might hastily conclude that Th has merely retained OG in 4:11(14); 9:18, 19; 10:1. That this is not necessarily the case can be demonstrated. Overall, Th's TT reveals that he is marching to his own drum. Th employs two main equivalents for קרא: (ἐπι) καλεω 6/14[41] and ἀναγινώσκω 5/14.[42] In all of these instances Th has chosen an appropriate rendering for the context and is not using a mechanical approach. The sensitivity of his choices is exemplified by καλέω in 5:12, because elsewhere he chooses ἀναγινώσκω for the sense of "reading" the writing on the wall. The verbal agreement in 4:11(14) can be explained as coincidence because the rendering is a natural one. Furthermore, Th does not follow OG's choice of φωνέω in 5:7, but employs βοάω instead. Finally, Th employs βοάω in 3:4 where one would expect him to follow the alliteration of OG. The fact that Th has already employed καλέω twice before chapter 9 and that the choices are natural ones in the context also militates against borrowing in chapters 9 and 10. Th also employs perfect forms in 9:18, 19, so Th and OG only share exact verbal agreement in 10:1.

l. 16, 35, 37, 38, 44, 48, 54, 56, 61, 64, 67, 68, 83, 85, 97, 98, 102, 109, 111-This section will examine the translation of verbs of saying.

---

[38] 5:8, 12, 15, 16, 17. OG's presumed *Vorlage* is very different from MT for the second occurrence of קרא in 5:7 as well.

[39] Ziegler has correctly placed καὶ ἐκάλεσε . . . from 8:16 in brackets because it is obviously a doublet from Th. This is an excellent example of the early influence of the Th text on OG, because the doublet is present in 967.

[40] This is a HL in OG. The only place where it occurs in Th is 5:29.

[41] 2:2; 5:12; 8:16; 9:18, 19; 10:1.

[42] 5:7, 8, 15, 16, 17.

We will look at a large number of verbs in this one section, because it will illustrate the complex interplay between the vocabulary of the *Vorlage* and the Greek versions. There are three introductory points to make:
1. In each instance the verb in MT has the meaning "to tell, declare, make known." Other cases where verbs of saying fall outside of this semantic range are not considered. Even this categorization is quite broad.
2. 48 and 54 are underlined because they appear to be pluses in OG.
3. 1. 35, 67, 68 and 99, 100 will not be treated extensively other than to note that אמר/εἶπον is an expected equivalent. However, it should also be noted that OG and Th do use different forms of the verb. To treat all of the occurrences of אמר would require great length and our discussion can proceed without that degree of detail.

In 2:1-10 we are concerned with the translation of 4 semitic verbs: הגיד (hiphil from [נגד]), אמר, √חוה, הודע (haphel or hiphil ידע). These verbs are translated with 6 different verbs in 2:1-10 in OG and Th: ἀναγγέλλω, ἀπαγγέλλω, εἶπον, γνωρίζω, φράζω, δηλόω. διασαφέω[43] also appears in l. 54 of OG (1-11, see LEH, 108), seemingly as an addition.

The first verb we meet is הגיד (infinitive construct) in l. 16, which is translated by the infinitive of ἀναγγέλλω in both OG and Th. The verbal agreement is probably best explained, however, either as coincidence or Th influence on OG. There are two pieces of evidence that lead to the conclusion that Th has not borrowed his rendering from OG. First, apart from the not unexpected uses of אמר/εἶπον mentioned in #3 above, this is the only instance where there is exact verbal agreement in the use of these verbs between OG and Th in this section.

---

[43] 9x in the Maccabean literature and also in Deut 1:5.

Second, in the three other places where הגיד occurs, Th always has ἀναγγέλλω whereas OG renders it consistently with ὑποδεικνύω.⁴⁴
√חוה is found 14x in the pael and haphel, 7 of which are in vv. 2:4-11. The most frequent equivalent in OG is δηλόω, which is used 5/11.⁴⁵ The remaining 6 uses are as follows. In 5:7 it is rendered by ὑποδεικνύω while the appearance of δήλωσις (1/4, not in Th) in 2:27 is a dynamic rendering. The other four renderings are unique and are probably explained as due to stylistic variation since they are clustered within vv. 2:4-11.⁴⁶ Th is far more consistent in his translation of חוה, using ἀναγγέλλω 11/14 and γνωρίζω in the other three.⁴⁷

The reading of ἀναγγέλλω for חוה in l. 56 of OG is interesting, because OG also has an unusual addition of διασαφήσητέ μοι in l. 54. Although l. 54 could be viewed as an addition against MT, it is also very possible that ἀναγγέλλω originated as a gloss to διασαφέω (1-11). This is suggested by the presence of the rare term διασαφέω, the

---

⁴⁴ 9:23, 10:21; 11:2. ὑποδεικνύω occurs 9x elsewhere in OG. In 4:15(18), 34c; 5:9 MT=O. It renders הודע in 2:17, חוה in 5:7, הבין in 10:14; it also occurs in 5:12 where פשר and [חוה] are found and 5:16 where פשר is found once again. In these latter two instances the differences between OG and MT are rather substantial; these are the only occurrences of the verb פשר in MT. One interesting use of ὑποδεικνύω is the difficult construction in 9:22 where it translates השכיל. Except in 7:8 where there was evidently a misreading of the *Vorlage* and 1:17 where the rendering is dynamic, OG uses expected equivalents from the semantic domain of knowing for √שכל elsewhere (1:4; 8:25; 9:13, 22, 25; 11:33, 35; 12:3, 10). Therefore, there is a possibility that OG read להבינך or להודעך for להשכילך in 9:22. The latter would appear more likely because it would involve the omission of ש, and the misreading of ב for כ and נ for ל. It may also have come more easily to the translator because בינה is the following word. Since the Hebrew construction in 9:22 would have caused difficulties for the translator and we can construe a semantic path by which the OG translator rendered the text, it is unlikely that the OG *Vorlage* differed from MT.

⁴⁵ 2:6, 9, 11, 16, 24; 3x OG=0 3:32, 5:12, 15.

⁴⁶ l. 38-φράζω, (1-3, not in Th); l. 56-ἀναγγέλλω or διασαφήσητέ; l. 71-a dynamic translation with κρίνω; l. 112-εἶπον.

⁴⁷ See 2:6, 10; 5:7. Elsewhere in Th γνωρίζω is a SE (17/21) for the haphel and hiphil (only 8:19) of ידע. The exceptions are ἀναγγέλλω in 2:9, 25, 26 and δηλόω in 4:15(18). γνωρίζω does not occur in OG.

frequent use of ἀναγγέλλω by Th, and the fact that we already have questioned the rendering of הגיד by ἀναγγέλλω in l. 16. Though it might be objected that it is characteristic of OG to use variety, the amount of revision on the OG text as we have it can not be underestimated.

There is further corroboration of the possibility that l. 56 is a later revision by the addition in l. 48. In l. 48 δηλόω appears to be an addition, yet δηλόω is consistently employed in the OG to render either √חוה (5/11) or הודע (8/14).[48] Therefore, הודע in l. 44 is the natural equivalent for δηλόω. However, δηλόω looks like an addition because ἀπ-ν-αγγέλλω[49] appears in l. 44 as the formal equivalent for הודע. As in the preceding case, it is possible that ἀπαγγέλλω is the result of later revision of OG, though OG does employ ἀπαγγέλλω to translate הודע in 8:19.

Finally, 967 reads ἀπόδωτε where Syh-88 have ἀπαγγείλητέ following τὸ ἐνύπνιον in l. 82. 967 also omits ἐπ' ἀληθείας from 88-Syh and καὶ τὴν τούτου κρίσιν is an OG plus against MT. The variant reading in 967 justifies our questioning of the earlier readings of ἀναγγέλλω in l. 44 and 56. Does the dynamic use of ἀπόδωτε indicate

---

[48] Otherwise δηλόω appears for גלה in 2:47. The haphel and hiphil of ידע occur 21x in Daniel, but 4x OG=0 (4:3[6], 4[7], 15[18]; 5:15). 2x the text of OG presumes a different *Vorlage* compared with MT (5:16, 17), though ὑποδεικνύω is a possible equivalent in 5:16. Apart from the double translation in 2:5, and the 8x with δηλόω (2:9, 23, 25, 26, 28, 29, 30; 7:16), σημαίνω is found 3x (2:15, 23, 45), ὑποδεικνύω 1x in 2:17 and ἀπαγγέλλω 2x in 5:8; 8:19.

The fact that δηλόω does not occur in chapters 4-6 is one of the proofs of Albertz (p. 163) that chapters 4-6 originate from a different translator. However, as we have seen, δηλόω is used 13(14)/15 to render either הודע or √חוה and there is little evidence for either of these are found in the semitic *Vorlage* of OG in chapters 4-6. The only places where these verbs occur in chapters 4-6 of MT are 4:3, 4, 15; 5:7, 8, 12, 15(2), 16, 17 and the only places where OG might have had them in its *Vorlage* would be 4:15(18); 5:7, 8, 12, 16. The most certain of these are 5:7, 8, 16, but 5:7 certainly appears to have suffered corruption from vs. 8, or possibly from Th, and harmonization toward MT. Therefore, though the absence of δηλόω in chapters 4-6 does support Albertz' thesis, it is not quite as significant as it seems at first.

[49] Note also that 967 reads ἀναγγέλλω.

Chapter 2:1-10   91

that there were more dynamic renderings employed in l. 44 and 56, or was ἀπόδωτε an error? ἀπαγγέλλω or ἀναγγέλλω only occur 9x in Ziegler's OG text. Besides the four occurrences we have so far questioned in l. 16, 44, 56, and 82, ἀναγγέλλω translates אמר in l. 35, and ἀπαγγέλλω translates הודע in 5:8; 8:19. ἀπαγγέλλω also appears in OG pluses in 5:7, 9. A final piece of evidence that indicates that the use of ἀπαγγέλλω in OG is due to later editorial work is the fact that ἀπαγγέλλω also appears in 967 as a variant to παραγγέλλεται in 3:4.[50] We can see then that the use of ἀπαγγέλλω or ἀναγγέλλω is very limited in OG and that there are reasonable grounds to conclude that the appearance of ἀπαγγέλλω or ἀναγγέλλω may be due to later corruption. Furthermore, the 3x that ἀπαγγέλλω appears in chapter 5 have no bearing on OG elsewhere, because chapters 4-6 originate from a different translator. Therefore, the only readings that bear on the four being questioned in chapter 2 are ἀναγγέλλω=אמר in l. 36 and ἀπαγγέλλω=הודע in 8:19.

If we are to accept Ziegler's readings in l. 44, 56, and 82, then either OG was translating a different *Vorlage* or OG changed one clause into two in order to make explicit the command both to **tell** the contents of the dream and to **declare** its meaning. Either of these suggestions is possible, but there are good reasons to doubt the reliability of Ziegler's text. To summarize: 1) Apart from the two attested uses in 2:4 and 8:19 and 3x in chapter 5, OG does not employ ἀν(π)αγγέλλω elsewhere, while Th uses ἀναγγέλλω frequently. 2) In l. 16, 44, and 56 the presence of ἀν(π)αγγέλλω does not reflect OG's translation pattern elsewhere. 3) L. 44 and 56 appear to have additional verbs against MT, but in both cases these verbs seem to be pluses because ἀν(π)αγγέλλω, a verb common in Th, is found in the correct word order position as the equivalent for the semitic verb.

---

[50] The secondary character of the variant is betrayed by the change in person and voice.

l. 27-θέλω appears 4x in OG. MT=0 in 4:17(20); 7:19 for צבא; 8:4 for רזון. Never in Th.

l. 29-λαλέω is a SE for דבר in both OG (17/19) and Th (19/19). The only places where OG departs from this usage are 1:19 and 11:27. The use of the relatively rare ὁμιλέω (1-9) in 1:19 has a more specific sense of conversing than the more general term λαλέω; so it is well-suited to a context that assumes a dialogue. In 11:27 OG employs a compound ψευδολογήσουσιν (HL in LXX!) to translate כזב ידברו. In the 17 other occurrences Th and OG share many exact verbal agreements, but many of these agreements occur in the later chapters.[51] OG and Th also have agreement in the Aramaic section where both employ λαλέω (4/5) as a SE for מלל.[52] We will have to see what a closer inspection of chapters 7-12 reveals, but some of the agreements could easily be coincidental while others may be due to Th influence on OG. For example, in 10:11, 15, 19 OG and Th use the ἐν τῷ + infinitive (λαλῆσαι) to translate the infinitive construct + ב (כ in 10:19). This is an acceptable translation, but very literal and more characteristic of Th.[53] Furthermore, in 8:18 where the exact same construction is found Th has ἐν τῷ λαλεῖν, while OG uses a genitive absolute! Soisalon-Soininen also notes that the frequency of OG's use of the more literal equivalent is disproportionate to OG's treatment of the Hebrew infinitive

---

[51] See 8:13(2x); 9:12, 20, 21, 22; 10:11(2x), 15, 16, 17, 19; 11:36.

[52] See 7:8, 11, 20, 25. In 6:22(21) OG presumably has a different *Vorlage*, and Th has εἶπε. The only other occurrences of the verb are in 3:36=Th; 4:29(32); 4:34(37)*bis* where MT=0.

[53] See Soisalon-Soininen, *Infinitive*, 81, 206. However, there is a slight difficulty with his statistics on p. 188. Soisalon-Soininen's table suggests that ב + infinitive construct is found 7x in Daniel and that in all 7 cases Th employs ἐν τῷ + infinitive. In fact, the Hebrew section of Daniel has 8 cases and there are another 4 in the Aramaic section. Only 6x does Th use ἐν τῷ + infinitive (8:15, 17, 18; 10:11, 15; 11:34). The other instances are 2:25; 3:24(91); 4:24(27); 6:20(19); 8:2; 10:7. 8:2 is omitted by both OG and Th and in 10:7 where they both employ dynamic translations.

Chapter 2:1-10   93

construct as a whole in Daniel.⁵⁴ The fact of these agreements and their Th like character suggests that the OG text has been revised toward Th.

l. 35, 46, 53, 62, 67, 83, 97-Th consistently employs ἐνύπνιον for חלם. There are seven cases where OG employs ὅραμα for חלם including l. 67 and 97. This rendition by OG constituted one of McCrystall's most important proofs of theological *Tendenz* in the OG of Daniel.⁵⁵ In his fourth chapter McCrystall engages in an extensive argument that the OG translator's choice of ὅραμα for ἐνύπνιον in seven out of twenty-five instances reflects the fact that ἐνύπνιον had the connotation of "illusion;" in these instances the translator is updating the terminology in order to make it more acceptable to both Jews and Gentiles.⁵⁶ The argument is based on the fact that Philo, who has adopted the classification of dreams by Stoic philosophers, describes ἐνύπνιον to be "what is illusory." However, the contrast between ἐνύπνιον and ὅραμα is grounded in the classification of dreams in Artemedorus of Daldis (latter half of the second century CE!) who distinguished between ὄνειρος and ἐνύπνιον. McCrystall believes this distinction in dream terminology is also reflected in Josephus who only uses ἔνυπνιον when quoting others. It is found six times in *Antiquities* where Josephus recounts the book of Daniel, five times in *Against Apion* (i. 207, 211, 294, 298, 312), but nowhere in *Jewish War*.

Before we consider some of the details there are two obvious objections that are fatal to McCrystall's argument. First, if the translator really wanted to "update" the terminology, why did he use ἐνύπνιον at all? Second, the argument rests on the attempt to read back the much later dream classification of Artemedorus into OG. Furthermore,

---

⁵⁴ Soisalon-Soininen, *Infinitive*, 189.

⁵⁵ McCrystall's research of the Old Greek translation of Daniel was the first extensive examination of the OG since that of A. Bludau in 1897.

⁵⁶ McCrystall, 152-184.

Artemedorus distinguished between ἐνύπνιον and ὄνειρος, and though ὄραμα was regarded as a type of the latter, the difference in terminology is significant. We also note that the argument from Josephus rests on the five quotations (three different writers) in *Ag. Ap.*, but McCrystall offers no evidence that the people quoted made any distinction between types of dreams and visions. For example, the most negative statement by Agatharchides (i. 211) suggests that the condemnation of ἐνύπνιον has everything to do with incredulity that one should rely on such "hocus-pocus" (i.e. visions), but there is no concern for what term is employed. If his analysis has not already proved troublesome, we can consider McCrystall's presentation of the evidence concerning the use of the terms in the papyri, which are contemporary with the writing of OG. He finds that there is no evidence that ἐνύπνιον and ὄραμα were distinguished in the papyri and even admits that the evidence suggests that the two were used as synonyms![57]

McCrystall's discussion of the dream terminology and how it is employed in the LXX is interesting, however, because it is directly related to our investigation of TT. He notes that ἐνύπνιον is used 10 times in chapters 2 and 4 (for חלם, Hebrew-חלום, 5x) of Daniel and elsewhere only in 1:17 and 8:2. It is found 61 other times in the LXX; and McCrystall divides these uses into three categories. The first are those in which there is no hostility shown towards ἐνύπνιον, and is represented most frequently in Gen 37-42 (24x in the Joseph story), though there are 16 other instances scattered through seven other books. The second category concerns those instances where there is hostility shown towards ἐνύπνιον. This use is found 16 times in six books, most frequently in Jeremiah (6x). The third category exhibits a cautious scepticism towards ἐνύπνιον and is represented by the five occurrences in Sirach.[58] As for ὄραμα, it is found 25 times in the Old Greek of

---

[57] Ibid., 162, 168.

[58] Ibid., 151-152.

Daniel, and in seven[59] of those cases (chapter 2-5 times; chapter 7:1-twice) it translates חלם. Elsewhere in the LXX ὅραμα is found 19 times and in none of these does it translate חלם. Based on these statistics and his analysis of the use of ἐνύπνιον, McCrystall concludes that ἐνύπνια were the focus of prophetic attacks, particularly in Jeremiah, while the "authentic" nature of the ὅραμα is revealed in texts like Jer 39 (32):21; Gen 15:1, 46:2; Num 12:6; Isa 21:2.[60] Therefore, the OG translator incorporated ὅραμα into the translation because of its positive connotations. Can this interpretation be sustained?

In this instance McCrystall confuses the translation with the *Vorlage*, because in all but three of its uses where ἐνύπνιον translates a *Vorlage* in the LXX the semitic term is חלום (חלם),[61] while ὅραμα translates various terms. In other words, ἐνύπνιον was employed as a SE for חלום; therefore, any so-called classification of the uses of ἐνύπνιον cannot be proved from the distribution of the term, because it was universally employed to render חלום (חלם). Whether or not the semitic writers/editors used חלום in a pejorative way is a totally different question and best pursued elsewhere. We might also note that חלם/ὅραμα and [חזו]/ἐνύπνιον occur together in 2:28 (see also 1:17 and 2:1) where there is no discernible difference in meaning (חלמך וחזוי ראשך) so the translator could easily have employed the Greek terms as alternative equivalents.

It is clear that McCrystall has attempted to read a second century dream classification into the OG text of Daniel. However, there may be a possible explanation for the translation technique that resulted in the seven anomalous uses of ὅραμα in Daniel (2:7, 9, 26, 36, 45; 7:1 *bis*). The four cases in chapter 2 could be viewed merely as an attempt to

---

[59] Both ἐνύπνιον and ὅραμα occur in 2:1 to render חלם חלמות. The difference may involve an alternative *Vorlage*, but just as easily could have originated from a touch of hyperbole from the translator.

[60] McCrystall, 164.

[61] The exceptions are Gen 41:1; Mic 3:7; Isa 29:8?.

vary the style due to the frequency of חלם (15 times). For example, חלם (חלום) occurs ten times in the first nine verses and two substitutions of ὅραμα for ἐνύπνιον occur in verses 7 and 9.⁶² However, the rendering of חזו by ὅραμα in v. 19 may provide the key to understanding why the translator used ὅραμα for ἐνύπνιον—because חזו=ὅραμα is a favourite rendering in Daniel OG.⁶³ The third time the translator replaced ἐνύπνιον with ὅραμα is in verse 26. In this verse it is possible that when the translator was confronted with rendering חלמא די־חזית, OG, who preferred to render with ὅραμα, was motivated to substitute the noun for חלמא in place of ἐνύπνιον by the appearance of the verb חזית, which is related etymologically to חזו. This substitution may have been aided by the fact that there was no verb related by etymology to ὅραμα. The result was still a good translation—τὸ ὅραμα ὃ εἶδον. Having established the two terms as alternative equivalents by the previous substitutions and their use as overlapping terms in verse 28, the translator had no hesitation using ὅραμα for ἐνύπνιον in verses 36 and 45 (although חזית also occurs in the latter). There is further support for this suggestion in 2:9 (the second instance of substitution) where the text in 967 contains the plus ὃ εἶδον τὴν νύκτα. The whole phrase—τὸ ὅραμα ὃ εἶδον τὴν νύκτα—can be retroverted as חלמא די־חזית (עמ)ליליא in OG. It is probable that OG had this addition in its *Vorlage*, and (עמ) ליליא די־חזית may have been omitted from MT due to parablepsis.

---

⁶² See also N. Leiter, "Assimilation and Dissimilation Techniques in the LXX of the Book of Balaam," *Textus* 12 (1985): 79-95, who describes the process of using one word and then another to translate the same Hebrew term as dissimilation.

⁶³ In 6/9 occurrences OG translates חזו with ὅραμα: 2:19, 28; 7:1, 7, 13, 15. In 4:2(5), 6(9), 7(10)? OG=0. The places where the rendering does not occur are 4:10(13); 7:2, 20. In 7:20 חזו is used with the meaning of "appearance" so OG employs a different term covering that semantic range. 4:10(13) and 7:2 are rendered differently because of a different concern of the translator. The Aramaic reads חזה הוית בחזוי (also 7:7, 13 where OG has ἐθεώρουν ἐν ὁράματι) and in these two places OG employs ὕπνος for חזו. The use of the same phraseology in 4:10(13) and 7:2 is possible evidence against Albertz' thesis that chapters 4-6 stem from a different translator.

Chapter 2:1-10   97

The text in Dan 7:1-2a is notoriously difficult and there are some indications that this difficulty is due to an editorial splicing together of chapters 6 and 7.[64] The Greek witnesses exhibit difficulties as well, not all of which can be addressed here. However, at this point, we would suggest that the motivation for using ὅραμα 7:1(2x) may be explained similarly to 2:9 and 26. The first occurrence of "dream" is in the phrase חלם חזה. The translator did not have an etymologically related verb for ὅραμα which he preferred for חזה, so he rendered the participle with εἶδεν and חלם with ὅραμα. The remainder of the verse does not follow the Aramaic word order though the elements are represented. The texts run thus:

MT: וְחֶזְוֵי רֵאשֵׁהּ עַל־מִשְׁכְּבֵהּ בֵּאדַיִן חֶלְמָא

OG: παρὰ κεφαλὴν ἐπὶ τῆς κοίτης αὐτοῦ τότε Δανιηλ τὸ ὅραμα ὃ εἶδεν

The main difference is that παρὰ appears in place of וחזוי and OG seems to add ὃ εἶδεν. Some of the difference can be explained, however, if we grant that the translator read וחזוי with חלמא in order to produce τὸ ὅραμα ὃ εἶδεν on the same basis as 2:9, 26 (45?) and earlier in 7:1. What the translator actually read in the *Vorlage* and whether he read the plural noun as the participle cannot be known. However, this proposal does explain both the lexical choice of the translator as well as some of the textual differences.

l. 36-παῖς is an expected equivalent for עבד and appears in OG 11/11. However, Th employs παῖς exclusively for עבד (4/4) in chapters 1-2,

---

[64] See J. E. Miller, "The Redaction of Daniel," *JSOT* 52 (1991): 115-24. However, there is no evidence to support his contention that there was a Hebrew version of chapter 2.

whereas in chapters 3-12 he has the alternative equivalent δοῦλος 6/8.⁶⁵ The exceptions are 3:28(95) and 10:17 where Th again has παῖς, but the basic difference in the pattern in chapters 1-2 is clear.

l. 37, 47, 55, 63, 70, 101-Th employs σύνκρισις as a SE (26/31) for פשר.⁶⁶ OG displays greater variety. In chapters 4-6 the noun is either not in the *Vorlage*⁶⁷ or OG employs σύγκριμα as a SE.⁶⁸ Elsewhere the main equivalent is κρίσις 7/14,⁶⁹ while the remaining cases involve some type of dynamic rendering. In 2:24, 25 OG employs ἕκαστα, which is very similar to the use of πάντα in 2:16, and the neuter pronoun in l. 37. In 2:30 the articular passive infinitive of δηλόω "what has been revealed" is an excellent idiomatic translation. The final two translations involve l. 63 and 70, where פשר is collocated with the verb √חוה (also l. 37, 55, 104). In both of these cases OG transforms the noun into the etymologically related verb κρίνω. L. 70 "they will decide with regard to these things" is another good idiomatic translation. The cluster of uses of the same verb within 2:1-10 means that some of these renderings are probably motivated by the concern for stylistic variation. However, it should be noted that in l. 63 and 70, as in 2:24-25, OG has maintained a similar translation equivalent when one character's words are referred to by another.

---

⁶⁵ The noun עבד is in 1:12, 13; 2:4, 7; 3:26(93), 28(95); 6:21(20); 9:6, 10, 11, 17; 10:17. OG=0 in 6:21(20).

⁶⁶ The exceptions are 2:25; 4:15(18); 5:26=OG, 5:16 (cognate accusative) where σύγκριμα occurs; and 5:15, where it is omitted.

⁶⁷ OG=0 11x. See 4:3(6), 4:4(7), 4:6(9), 4:15(18)*bis*, 4:16(19), 4:21(24); 5:12, 15(2x), 16.

⁶⁸ See 5:7, 8, 16, 26. σύνκριμα is also found in 4:16(19) and 5:17, but the pattern does support Albertz' contention (p. 162) that chapters 4-6 originate from a different translator.

⁶⁹ 2:5, 6, 9, 26, 36, 45; 7:16.

Chapter 2:1-10   99

l. 42, 81, 89, 109, 116-Taken by themselves the 5x that מלה is found in 2:1-10 suggests that Th does not exhibit dependence upon OG. However, there is a translation pattern in both OG and Th that is best understood by looking at chapters 2-3 separately from 4-7.

מלה is found 11x in chapters 2-3 and OG employs at least eight different equivalents:

προστέταχα-2:8?   ἕκαστα-2:17
λόγος-2:9, 11   πρὸς ταῦτα-2:23
ἃ ἑώρακεν-2:10   πρόσταγμα-2:15?,[70] 3:22
πρᾶγμα-2:10   προσταγή-3:28(95)

The variety of equivalents is obvious, and each of the renderings is a good translation. Note, however, that there is uncertainty over what word occurs in 2:15. The translations of 2:8?, 10, 17, 23 are particularly dynamic.[71] Th employs ῥῆμα 9/11, and λόγος in 2:5, 11.

The situation is significantly different in chapters 4-7 where מלה occurs 13x. 5x OG=0, 4:30(33); 5:10, 15, 26; 6:15(14).

λόγος-4:28(31); 6:13(12); 7:1, 11, 16, 28.

ῥῆμα-7:25, 28(27)!

In these chapters not only has the translation been standardized, but ῥῆμα appears twice. The same preference for λόγος is evident in Th who uses it 8/10. ῥῆμα is used only in 5:26 and 7:28. 3x Th=0, 5:10, 15; 7:1.

Both the use of ῥῆμα by OG in chapter 7 and the predominance of λόγος in chapters 4-6 have to be explained. This pattern supports

---

[70] A question mark is placed beside 2:15 because there is uncertainty over its reading. 967 has a lacuna, but there is not enough space for πρόσταγμα as in 88.

[71] We have already argued that λόγος in 2:5 and πρᾶγμα in 2:8 are not original. The suggestion that προστέταχα is the dynamic rendering in 2:8 is based on our reconstruction of the text, but it does reflect OG's other dynamic renderings. προστάσσω is also etymologically related to πρόσταγμα in 3:22 and προσταγή in 3:28(95). Munnich ("Origène," 190) also lists the asterisked addition in 2:5 as a reading that conforms to MT and Th. Note that πρὸς ταῦτα of 2:23 also appears as a dynamic rendering in l. 71.

Albertz' thesis concerning the independence of chapters 4-6, but also raises more questions about chapter 7.

l. 43, 80-Th translates אזדא מני exactly the same in both places. ἀπέστη is a contextual guess for אזדא.[72]

l. 49-52-The reading of the OG has several difficulties and should be considered alongside the similar passage in 3:29(96) where the texts read:

Th-εἰς ἀπώλειαν ἔσονται καὶ οἱ οἶκοι αὐτῶν εἰς διαρπαγήν
MT-הַדָּמִין יִתְעֲבֵד וּבַיְתֵהּ נְוָלִי יִשְׁתַּוֵּה
OG-διαμελισθήσεται καὶ ἡ οὐσία αὐτοῦ δημευθήσεται

McCrystall argues that there is a shift in meaning in the OG in these passages from "physical ruin" to "confiscation."[73] In this instance McCrystall is no doubt correct about the resulting translation, but it is questionable whether this was motivated by any intentional theological *Tendenz*. The first factor we have to consider is the general difficulty presented by the vocabulary of MT. These are the only two passages in MT where the Persian loan-word הדמין "limb" (see BDB, 1089) is found; and נולי[74] occurs elsewhere only in Ezek 6:11. In 3:29 the rare word שוה "be made" (hithpael; also the pael or peil in 5:21) occurs. Given the difficulties of the *Vorlage*, the most logical course of action is to consider whether the OG has misunderstood the text.

With regard to 2:5, Montgomery, 148, has already advanced the explanation that the HL παραδειγματίζω "you shall be made an

---

[72] It is found only here in these two passages in MT. See Montgomery, 148-149, for a discussion of the uncertainty of the meaning.

[73] McCrystall, 80.

[74] The meaning of this word can only be guessed at, as exemplified in the translations. See BDB, 1102 and Montgomery, 148.

Chapter 2:1-10   101

example" for הרמין תתעבדון is based on reading (ה)דְּמִין. The key to the final phrase is the meaning of נולי, at which the translator could only guess from the context. The easiest explanation is that the translator read the hithpeal יתשמון as a peal (which explains the choice of ἀναληφθήσεται), and offered the best guess that he could: "and everything that you own will be expropriated into the treasury."[75] It may be, as McCrystall suggests, that the actual rendering reflects a Hellenistic act of procurement of property; but it would only be natural for the translator's guess to reflect his own cultural circumstances. If we were to refer to this case as theological *Tendenz*, there certainly would not be any great theological consequences; nor could it be deemed as intentional changing of the text.

The translation of וביתה נולי ישתוה by καὶ ἡ οὐσία αὐτοῦ δημευθήσεται in 3:29(96) is very similar to 2:5, except that the translation is probably a guess based on the earlier translation. In this case the OG did not know the meaning of שוה,[76] so the HL δημεύω "confiscate" appears to be a simplification of ἀναληφθήσεται . . . εἰς τὸ βασιλικόν. The major difference between 2:5 and 3:29(96) is that in the latter OG seems to translate הרמין תתעבדון correctly. However, it is possible that διαμελίζω should be emended to read the more common διαμερίζω, which is the reading of 967.[77]

---

[75] See I Esdr 6:31 for a parallel rendering.

[76] OG=0 in 5:21.

[77] Thackeray, 107 notes that the tendency was for ρ to replace λ, but he also states that "instances occur, also, of the reverse change in the κοινή where no consonant follows." The fact that λ was mistakenly written for ρ during the transmission of Daniel is exemplified in 6:22(23) of 967, where ελιψας was later corrected to ερριψας; 11:25 where the addition of παραλογισθήσεται is a corruption from the earlier variant παρογισθήσεται (see Geissen, 259); and the reading of θάλασσης in 10:6. The OG mss. tend to substitute λ for ρ, which suggests that it is a phonetic error. It also means that we should consider the possibility that 967 has the correct reading in 3:96(29).

διαμελ-ρ-ισθήσεται in 3:96(29) is quite interesting because διαμελίζω "dissect" is usually interpreted as a neologism (so LEH, 106), which Montgomery, 148, reconstructed on the basis of an analogy to μέλη ποιήσαντες in 2 Macc 1:16.

There is little doubt that the translation of 3:29(96) was dependent on 2:5, so one has to wonder why παραδειγματίζω was chosen in the first instance. There are four possible options: 1) the translation in 2:5 is based on an alternative reading of the semitic text; 2) the reading in 3:29(96) represents a later correction; 3) there were separate and distinct translators; 4) 3:29(96) should be amended to read διαμερίζω, which is also a contextual guess. The second option always has to remain a consideration, but is unlikely because we would expect the same correction in 2:5. In favour of the first is the possibility that the ה of הדמין was omitted by haplography with the final ה in ומשרה (see *Text-Critical*). This assumes that the translator of both passages was the same. The fourth option accounts for the difficulties in both passages and does not presuppose any theory of multiple translators. Furthermore, if the translator of 3:29(96) did get it right with διαμελίζω, why is there no evidence of correction of 2:5? The third option is also possible, but it would require that the translator of 3:29(96) was later than the translator of 2:5 because he seems to rely on 2:5 for the translation of וביתה נולי ישתוה. Although this solution assumes a rather complex scenario of translation, it has much to commend it. There are a number of differences in TT in 3:20-30(97) that suggest this portion of text was freely edited in order to insert the deutero-canonical material into chapter 3.[78] The evidence does not permit any easy

---

LSJ only has διαμελίζω attested in Plutarch. However, even without 967, we should consider the possibility of reading the far more common διαμερίζω "divide." The problem in reading διαμελίζω is that it would mean OG knew the meaning of the *Vorlage* here, but not in 2:5. On the other hand, the more common διαμερίζω would fit the pattern of orthographic change in OG and would also represent an adequate contextual guess. At some early stage of its transmission the λ could have been substituted for the ρ, and διαμελίζω may have been accepted into the language later.

[78] The evidence for this is discussed in the following chapter on 3:11-20, *A Note on the Additions to Chapter 3*. The third solution also allows for the possibility that διαμελίζω should be emended to read with 967. Regardless of the reading we choose, the translator of 3:29(96) did not depend on 2:5 for the rendering of הדמין תתעבדון.

Chapter 2:1-10   103

resolution of the textual difficulties, but either of the last two solutions are more likely.

Th's translation in 2:5 and 3:29(96) is similar to OG only in that he guessed at the meaning of הדמין תתעבדין. There is, however, a possible explanation for Th's translation of הדמין תתעבדין by εἰς ἀπώλειαν ἔσεσθε (ἔσονται in 3:29[96]). Th might have read תתעבדין as if it were a hithpeal derived from אבד and simply omitted הדמין. The choices of the verb διαρπάζω in 2:5 and the related noun διαρπαγή in 3:29(96), both HL in Daniel, again demonstrate Th independence from OG.

l. 57, 59-Although λαμβάνω is the expected equivalent, the fact that OG and Th both use παραλαμβάνω in the two other occurrences of קבל indicates there may be Th dependence on OG in these later passages.[79]

l. 58-Th employs a SE (see p. 53, above).

l. 60-OG's use of ὑπό makes the personal participation of Nebuchadnezzer in the bestowal of gifts more explicit.

l. 61, 96-OG and Th reflect two different interpretations of להן.[80] OG uses οὖν (+ νυν, l. 96) here for להן, while in 4:24(27) OG=0. Th's rendering with πλὴν in l. 61 (HL in Daniel) understands להן as an adversative and διὰ τοῦτο in 4:24(27) is an excellent rendering as well. The omission by Th in l. 96 is difficult to explain.

l. 75-This is a common rendering for OG and Th. יציב occurs 5x in total in Dan. OG renders with ἀκριβής in 2:45; 6:13(12)[81] where Th

---

[79] See also 6:1(5:31) and 7:18, though the only actual agreement in the former passage is the use of the verb.

[80] See I. Eitan, "Some Philological Observations in Daniel," *HUCA* 14 (1939): 13-14.

[81] OG employs ἀκριβής in 4:24(27) where MT=0. ἀκριβής occurs only 5x elsewhere and not in Th.

uses ἀληθινός, and they share the reading of ἀκρίβεια (1-4!) in 7:16. OG=0 in 3:24(91) where Th has ἀληθῶς. Whether we judge Th to be dependent upon OG in l. 75 and 7:16 depends on our overall assessment of their relationship.

l. 77-This is the only occurrence of זבן in Dan. ἐξαγοράζω is a HL in the LXX, so OG and Th have another distinctive agreement in this verse.

l. 78, 112-OG translates with καθάπερ also in 2:41, 45. Although די כל־קבל occurs 13x altogether, OG only has an equivalent elsewhere in 3:29(96)-διότι and 6:11(10)-καθώς.[82] Th's translations are very interesting. He uses καθότι also in 3:29(96), while in the three remaining cases in chapter 2 he has ὃν τρόπον. The situation changes drastically in chapters 4-6 where ὅτι is employed 5x!, κατενώπιον is used in 5:22, and καθώς in 6:11(10)=OG. As in our investigation of מלה above, there are indications that Th's translation of כל־קבל די in chapters 4-6 is different from chapter 2. The translation of l. 78-81 involves a textual problem, but that does not affect the evaluation of καθάπερ.

l. 89, 91-OG employs the rare term συνεῖπον (1-2) for the hithpael (Qere, HL) of [יזמן]. Th employs another rare word, συντίθημι (1-11). Both are good translations.

l. 90-Th employs διαφθείρω as a SE 6/8 for the Hebrew and Aramaic [שחת].[83] The exceptions both occur in 6:5(4) where OG=0. The latter occurrence in 6:5(4) is within a whole clause that is omitted in Th. In the first instance Th employs παράπτωμα as an idiomatic translation. Th

---

[82] 2:40; 4:15(18); 5:12, 22; 6:4(3), 5(4), 23(22). 2:40 is probably omitted by homoioteleuton.

[83] See also 6:5(4)bis; 8:24(2), 25; 9:26; 11:17.

Chapter 2:1-10   105

also employs παράπτωμα in 4:24(27) for [שלוה]⁸⁴ and in 6:23(22) for חבולא, but παράπτωμα is not found in OG.

l. 92-OG employs a dynamic rendering while Th uses an expected formal rendition of למאמר.

l. 95-The translation of [שנא] offers an interesting example of how difficult it is to determine whether there are separate translators in OG and to describe the relationship between OG and Th.

[שנא] is found 12x in chapters 2-6 and both OG and Th employ ἀλλοιόω as a natural SE. OG translates with ἀλλοιόω 6/7.⁸⁵ The one difference is ἀθετέω (HL in OG)⁸⁶ in 3:28(95), which carries the more appropriate sense of rejecting the command of the king. Th has ἀλλοιόω 10/12 and offers the unique rendering of παρέρχομαι⁸⁷ in l. 95 and παραλλάσσω (1-6) in 6:16(15).

---

⁸⁴ Th's reading is based on a slightly different pointing. In 4:24(27) MT has אַרְכָה לִשְׁלֵוְתָךְ, which could be translated as "length of your prosperity." However, Th has μακρόθυμος τοῖς παραπτώμασί σου "forbearance toward your sin" by reading the pointing of MT as אַרְכָה לִשְׁלִיּוּתָךְ. It is easy to see how ארוכה "healing" and ארכה "lengthening" (the marker of the vowel ו may not have been written), and שלו "neglect, error" and שלוה "ease, prosperity" (with the addition of the pronominal suffix they were written identically in a consonantal text, שלותך) could be confused. The decisive reason why the pointing of MT is accepted as correct by commentators is the fact that the adjective שלה "at ease" appears in 4:1. See Montgomery, 243 and Goldingay, 81. Meadowcroft, 309, incorrectly suggests that "while this translation could owe something to a broadening semantic range of the Aramaic, it also, has a theological point to it." It is true that the resulting text of Th has a different theological slant, but the difference is based in a different reading of the consonantal text and was not due to any interpretive activity.

⁸⁵ 2:9, 21; 3:19, 27(94); 5:6; 6:9(8). OG=0 4:13(16); 5:9, 10; 6:16(15), 18(17). ἀλλοιόω does occur in 4:13(16) but the context is different. Otherwise OG employs ἀλλοιόω in similar types of contexts in 4:16(19), 30a, 34(37), 34a(2) where MT=0 and we can retrovert שנה with confidence. See also J. Barr, "Aramaic-Greek Notes on the Book of Enoch (I)," *JSS* 23 (1978): 187.

⁸⁶ It is also in 9:7 of Th.

⁸⁷ Th employs παρέρχομαι elsewhere in 4:28(31); 6:13(12); 7:14; 11:10, 40. OG overlaps only in 11:10 and has the verb also in 11:26 and 12:1.

In chapter 7 [שנא] occurs 7x, but here the SE for OG is διαφέρω 5/7.[88] The related adverb διαφόρως appears in 7:7 and ἀλλοιόω in 7:25. However, the change in equivalents is not evidence of separate translators, but sensitivity to the differing semantic range of the vocabulary in the *Vorlage*. In 4/5 instances where διαφέρω or the adverb διαφόρως appears the reference has something to do with the "differing" nature of the beasts or the fourth beast in particular. ἀλλοιόω would not have been an appropriate rendering in those contexts, but it is in 7:25 where the reference is to the changing of times and the law. The only possible indication of different translators is in 7:28, where we might expect ἀλλοιόω because it would agree with the OG choices in 3:19, 27(94); 5:6.

Th employs the expected ἀλλοιόω in 7:25, 28; διαφέρω in 7:3, 7, 19; but ὑπερέχω "will rise above" in 7:23 and ὑπερφέρω "will exceed" in 7:24 are excellent translations of the sense. Th, then, is more consistent with his use of ἀλλοιόω in the book and has several marked usages. However, a relationship between Th and OG in chapter seven is indicated not so much by the change in equivalents in chapter 7, but by the fact that they both use διαφέρω, which is only found 11x elsewhere in the LXX.

l. 108-Th's choice of ξηρός (1/1) in contrast to OG's more common γῆ is another mark of independence.

l. 112-The addition of σὺ ἐρωτᾷς may have been motivated by OG's prior changes to the syntax when it brought forward the verb in the ὅτι clause to l. 109 as well as the dynamic rendering ἃ ἑώρακεν in l. 111. The verb in the final כל־קבל די clause is delayed until l. 117, which would have resulted in a more complicated sentence structure in OG if OG had given a formal translation. The insertion of σὺ ἐρωτᾷς makes

---

[88] 7:3, 19, 23, 24, 28.

l. 113-1119 into an independent clause, which explains the insertion of καί in l. 113. The creation of distinct clauses results in some loss in emphasis. MT would be translated "No one can tell the matter of the king; furthermore . . ." while OG has "No one can tell what the king saw as he asks, and no king . . ."

l. 115-Th's rendering with ἄρχων 3/8 reflects independence (also 2:15-OG=0; 5:29). Elsewhere Th demonstrates a dynamic tendency on the four occasions (4:14, 22, 29; 5:21) where שליט occurs within the same nominal clause: די־שליט עליא במלכות אנש(ו)א (OG=0). In each case Th supplies a verb. The latter three are identical: ὅτι κυριεύει ὁ ὕψιστος τῆς βασιλείας τῶν ἀνθρώπων, while in 4:14(17) Th transforms שליט into κύριος and adds ἐστιν. The remaining verse where שליט is found is 4:23(26) where Th employs ἐξουσία as another good translation of the sense of MT.

OG only has one other equivalent for שליט (5:29) where it employs ἐξουσία, though it may also reflect שליט in his *Vorlage* of 4:23(26) where ἐξουσία is found.

III.2.iv. *Summary*

The investigation of 2:1-10 has revealed similar findings to our previous examination of 1:1-10. In the majority of instances OG was translating a *Vorlage* very similar to MT. Although OG is described as a free translation, his faithfulness to his *Vorlage* is manifested, as in 1:1-10, by his overall adherence to the word order of MT. On one occasion OG employed a hypotactic construction (l. 19) to avoid the parataxis of his *Vorlage*. On other occasions he used postpositive conjunctions (δέ in l. 39, 53, 65, 69; οὖν l. 27?, 61, 79, 96; γάρ in l. 89). These characteristics are indicative of OG's style in the early chapters of Daniel, but his freedom is most evident in the diversity of his lexical choices and occasional dynamic renditions. In one instance (1. 67-69) OG changed the syntactic structure unintentionally. There are a number of textual differences between OG's Vorlage and MT, but, for the most part, the differences can be explained as expected corruptions that occur in the transmission of ancient texts (see *Text-Critical*).

In 2:1-10 Th exhibits the expected narrow formal correspondence to MT, though there are several omissions of words (1. 3, 24, 40, 88, 96, 118).[89] However, formal correspondence does not mean that Th was translating mechanically. For example, there are several omissions and additions of minor morphemes (1. 11, 35, 40, 56, 92, 97). The wider investigation of vocabulary also revealed that Th demonstrates a sensitivity to the semantic range of the vocabulary of his *Vorlage*, and turned up occasions where Th employed excellent idiomatic translations.

III.3. *The Relationship Between OG and Th*

It is obvious from the few distinctive agreements and the more numerous disagreements that there is no sense in which we can refer to Th as a recension of OG in 2:1-10. There are only two certain distinctive agreements: ἐξαγοράζω in 1. 77 and Ἐπ' ἀληθείας in 1. 75. However, there are no means to determine the direction of borrowing in the case of the compound verb, nor do these agreements necessarily indicate any borrowing because they both occur within v. 8. In the discussion of 1. 78-81 (see *Textual Notes*) we saw that the agreement between Th and OG in Ziegler's text is due to a secondary addition from Th to 88-Syh, so the distinctive verbal agreement in the preceding lines must be questioned as well. The only other possible shared readings are 1. 16 (coincidence?) and 1. 116 (Th influence?). The distinctive nature of Th's translation is demonstrated by the occasions when Th does not follow OG such as 1. 67-69, 1. 87-89, and the contextual guess in 1. 49-

---

[89] For a full listing of Th omissions against MT, see Schmitt, "Stammt," 19-25.

Chapter 2:1-10   109

52. There are also numerous places where Th employs distinct vocabulary (eg. 1. 4, 6, 24, 25, 51, 61, 95, 108).

In contrast to Th being a recension, we have uncovered more evidence indicating later corruption of the OG due to Th influence. Besides the certain Th influence on 88-Syh in 2:1 and 2:8, it is also possible in 1. 16, 44, 56, and 116. The same relationship between OG and Th is apparent throughout chapter 2: there are occasional verbal agreements and infrequent large agreements (eg. 2:28). This does not exclude the possible acquaintance of Th with OG, which may have occasionally influenced the lexical choice of Th; but it *does* exclude the possibility that Th is a recension of the OG in chapters 1 and 2. As has already been demonstrated, some of these agreements can also be explained as Th readings that have displaced the OG. Therefore, we must seriously consider that *any distinctive agreements in these chapters may reflect secondary corruption of the OG.*

Finally, we have also uncovered evidence that not only corroborates Albertz' thesis that chapters 4-6 originate from a translator different from the other translator(s) of OG, but there is a suggestion that Th's relationship to MT is different in these chapters as well. As to the OG translator of chapters 4-6 we have confirmed that the non-appearance of δηλόω in 4-6 is evidence for a different translator. More importantly, we have also found that the translation of ממלה and the idiom ענה ואמר also support Albertz' view. It is also quite possible that the translation of כל-קבל די corroborates Albertz' thesis. Th's translation pattern of these three elements is also different in chapters 4-6, though only in the case of מלה is there possible influence by OG (or later revision of both?). Th also displays a different pattern of translation for עבד=παῖς/δοῦλος between chapters 1-2 and 3-10.

The employment of postpositive conjunctions also tends to support the picture that is emerging. οὖν only occurs 2/9x in chapters 4-12; and though δέ still appears 16/52x in chapters 4-6, it appears only 6x in chapters 7-12. γάρ is the exception because 10/19x it is used in chapters

8-12 (but 9/10 for כי). OG is definitely more dynamic in the translation of chapters 1-2, but particularly chapter 2.

III.4. Text-Critical Problems

l. 4-The addition of ὁράματα could reflect the ideology of the translator who uses ὅραμα and ἐνύπνιον as overlapping synonyms. In this case the addition would have helped to prepare for the synonymous uses to follow. On the other hand, one of the terms may be a doublet. Given the Greek syntax it is unlikely that there was a differing *Vorlage*.

l. 6-9-OG frequently abbreviates MT and it is unlikely that it represents an alternative *Vorlage*.[90]

l.11-Both Jahn and Charles suggest that the LXX read להביא.[91] This is possible, but the OG probably resulted from misreading the text and/or the translator's expectation of what the text should read,[92] particularly since the context is so similar to 1:3 where להביא does appear.

l. 15-The reading of OG is supported by 1QDan^a: Chaldeans is used as a comprehensive term for the divisions of wise men also in 2:4, 5, 10; 3:8. However, it is only one of a list in 2:10; 4:4(7) OG=0; 5:7, 11 OG=0. It is more likely that OG and 1QDan^a have harmonized to the absolute uses in 2:4, 5 (see also 1:4).

---

[90] Hamm, *I-II*, 145; contrast Collins, *Daniel*, 148.

[91] Charles, 27; G. Jahn, *Das Buch Daniel nach der Septuaginta hergestellt* (Leipzig: Pfeiffer, 1904) 10.

[92] In this case the variant only existed in the translator's mind. See Tov, *Text-Critical Use*, 228-240, where he emphasizes distinguishing between true variants and pseudo-variants.

Chapter 2:1-10

l. 27-We have provisionally accepted this addition as OG. In favour of its retention is the appearance of the postpositive conjunction οὖν, which is found elsewhere in this section. If the plus represents a *Vorlage*, we would most likely reconstruct להן צבית. It is possible that this was omitted from MT through homoioteleuton or homoioarchton with לדעת. However, the order of the Greek looks suspiciously like an addition. Despite the dynamic approach of the OG, for the most part OG does follows the word order of the *Vorlage*.[93] In particular, in OG, as elsewhere in the Biblical corpus, the infinitive invariably follows the verb of wishing, saying etc. to which it is connected. This would be the natural semitic order as well, so we would expect 88-Syh to have the infinitive ἐπιγνῶναι following the addition (see l. 11, 108 for examples). Furthermore, even if the addition is accepted as OG, it appears to be an addition to smooth the syntax.

l. 33-It is highly unlikely that Κύριε originated from an alternative *Vorlage* given the fact that it normally renders the divine name. For the same reason it is difficult to understand why it would have been added. However, Th does use Κύριε to render מרא in 4:16(19), so it is possible that OG read מרא. מלכא in MT would then be explained as a later correction. It is also possible the OG rendered מלכא with Κύριε and this would explain βασιλεῦ as a secondary addition. Either of these scenarios suggests that βασιλεῦ is not OG. In favour of the retention of Κύριε βασιλεῦ as OG is the fact that both are present in 3:9. OG does not witness to an alternative *Vorlage*.

l. 40, 72-The omission by Th in l. 40 and OG in l. 72 of one element of the idiom ענה ואמר does not necessarily indicate a difference in their respective *Vorlagen*. Such omissions are fairly frequent.

---

[93] Wright's (*Difference*, 47) statistics on formal equivalence indicate that OG fails to follow the word order of MT in only 2.16% of the lines.

l. 43-The omission of OG might be explained as error by homoioteleuton from אזרא ... לכשׂריא, but see also l. 43, 80 in *Lexicology*. This omission could have been in the OG *Vorlage*, but the text of MT is preferable in any case. The difference between OG and MT is better explained as an omission in OG, rather than an addition in MT because we can see how the omission occurred and there are numerous places in Daniel where the words of one character are alluded to or repeated verbatim for emphasis.

l. 45-Closely linked to the previous variant is the addition of ἐπ' ἀληθείας in OG. Presumably this addition would reflect מן־יציב as in l. 75. Though it is difficult to see how this variant could have been omitted from MT, it is also difficult to read מן־יציב at this point in the text. Here, the decision will depend upon the disposition of the textual critic, but we are not inclined to view the addition in OG as leading to a better semitic text.

l. 48, 54-We have previously argued that there is reason to believe that these verbs are not additions at all (see *Lexicology*). Even if original, the additions would be attributed to the translator rather than an alternative *Vorlage*.

l. 49-The translation παραδειγματίζω is based on the reading תתעבדון הדמין (see *Lexicology*), but based on the parallel to 3:29(96) MT is to be preferred. It cannot be known whether OG's reading accurately reflects its *Vorlage* and haplography had occurred in MT, or whether his translation stems from a reading error. It could also be that there was a different translator in 3:29(96).

l. 56-The addition of the personal pronoun in Th, which is supported by l. 54 in OG, suggests that the pronominal suffix was read. The Peshitta

Chapter 2:1-10   113

reads the pronominal suffix as well.⁹⁴ The strength of this combination suggests that the pronominal suffix should be added to the verb in MT.

l. 78-81-The text in these lines is very difficult and is obviously corrupt. We have already concluded that OG rendered MT with a dynamic equivalent and does not reflect a plus or an alternative *Vorlage*; at least, one cannot be reconstructed with any confidence.

l. 84-85-The addition καὶ τὴν τούτου κρίσιν would be retroverted as ופשרה as in l. 47 and 54. The use of the demonstrative adjective is a trait of OG (also 2:45) that indicates ופשרה was in his *Vorlage*. OG might also be preferred to MT in this case, because when the king speaks of his dream and interpretation in 2:5-6 they occur together as חלמא ופשרה; whereas when the magicians speak in 2:4 and 7 the terms are employed in separate clauses. OG's reading in l. 86-87 would reflect MT's pattern in 2:5-6.

l. 86-89-It is difficult to judge whether OG reflects an alternative *Vorlage* because of the number of problems in 2:8-9 and how the text echoes 2:5. For example, l. 86 could be a secondary addition based on l. 49, and l. 87-89 might reflect a textual difficulty because the reading of Th also differs from MT. Th borrows from l. 76 for his rendering in l. 87-89, and the similarities between the two are such that Th could accurately reflect a *Vorlage* in l. 87-89 that had been influenced by l. 76. The addition in l. 86 of OG also follows his habit of adding for clarification.⁹⁵ Both OG and Th read more smoothly than MT, and for that reason MT could be original. In the final analysis it is impossible

---

⁹⁴Taylor, 311-313, concludes that P betrays little influence from OG, but was aware of Th; therefore, agreement with Th may be of little text-critical value. In this instance all three witnesses agree against MT.

⁹⁵ So also Collins, *Daniel*, 149.

to determine a retroversion for OG that can account for the differences between the two, so MT should be retained.

l. 99-We have discussed this plus and how it reflects the TT of the OG already (see p. 96). The plus ὃ εἶδον τὴν νύκτα would be retroverted as די־חזית (עמ)לילא and, as in l. 86-87, it reflects the usage3-114 that is found elsewhere in OG Daniel (see 2:26). די־חזית (עמ)לילא may also have been omitted from MT through parablepsis with either the preceding חלמא or the following אמרו. For these reasons, it is probable that the OG addition should be regarded as reflecting a better semitic text.

l. 112-The addition was most likely to simplify the syntax in the Greek and is not based on an alternative *Vorlage*.

l. 114-Whether רב was omitted in OG's *Vorlage* or he chose to leave it untranslated is difficult to decide. It is possible that OG regarded it as redundant. In any case, MT should be retained.

Chapter IV
Daniel 3:11-20

This passage is interesting for our study for several reasons. First, it occurs just prior to the deutero-canonical material found in the versions, and there are clear indications that a later editor reworked the Old Greek text to accomodate these additions. Second, there are definite differences in OG's approach to translation in chapter three, and we will find that OG is much closer to MT and Th here than in 1:1-10 and 2:1-10. Finally, a most interesting aspect of this passage is how the translators dealt with 3:17-18.

The OG and Th Versions of Daniel

Table 3

#	Th	3:11 MT	3:11 OG
	3:11 Th	3:11 MT	3:11 OG
1	ˢκαὶ - - μὴ	וּמַן־דִּי־לָא	καὶ ὃς ἂν μὴ¹ ˢ _ _
2	πεσὼν	יִפֵּל	
3	προσκυνήσῃ	וְיִסְגֻּד	ᴸπροσκυνήσῃ
4	+τῇ εἰκόνι τῇ χρυσῇ+		
5	ἐμβληθήσεται	יִתְרְמֵא	ᴸἐμβληθήσεται
6	εἰς ᴸ _ _ τὴν κάμινον	לְגוֹא־אַתּוּן	εἰς ᴸ _ _ ˢτὴν κάμινον
7	τοῦ πυρός	נוּרָא	τοῦ πυρός
8	τὴν καιομένην	יָקִדְתָּא	τὴν καιομένην
	3:12	3:12	3:12
9	ᴸεἰσὶν ᴸἄνδρες	אִיתַי גֻּבְרִין	ᴸεἰσὶν δέ τινες ᴸἄνδρες
10	Ἰουδαῖοι	יְהוּדָאיִן	Ἰουδαῖοι
11	οὓς ᴸκατέστησας	דִּי־מַנִּיתָ יָתְהוֹן	ˢοὓς ᴸκατέστησας
12	ἐπὶ τὰ ᴸἔργα	עַל־עֲבִידַת	ἐπί _ _
13	τῆς ᴸχώρας	מְדִינַת	τῆς ᴸχώρας

Chapter 3:11-20

14	Βαβυλῶνος	בָּבֶל		τῆς Βαβυλωνίας
15	σεδραχ Μισαχ	שַׁדְרַךְ מֵישַׁךְ		σεδραχ Μισαχ
16	-Αβδεναγω	וַעֲבֵד נְגוֹ		Αβδεναγω
17	ˢοἱ ᴸ(- -)	אֲנָשַׁיָּא אִלֵּךְ		οἱ ᴸἄνθρωποι ἐκεῖνοι
18	οὐχ ˢὑπήκουσαν	לָא שָׂמוּ		οὐκ ˢἐφοβήθησάν σου
19	βασιλεῦ	עֲלָךְ		- -
20	τῷ ᴸ(δόγματι) σου	טְעֵם		τὴν ᴸἐντολὴν
21	τοῖς θεοῖς σου	לֵאלָהָךְ		καὶ τῷ ᴸεἰδώλῳ σου
22	οὐ ᴹλατρεύουσι	לָא פָלְחִין		οὐκ ᴸᴹἐλάτρευσαν
23	καὶ τῇ εἰκόνι	וּלְצֶלֶם		καὶ τῇ εἰκόνι+ˢσου
24	τῇ χρυσῇ	דַּהֲבָא		τῇ χρυσῇ
25	ᾗ ἔστησας	דִּי הֲקֵימְתָּ		ᾗ ᴸἔστησας
26	οὐ ᴹπροσκυνοῦσιν	לָא סָגְדִין		οὐ ᴸᴹπροσεκύνησαν
	3:13		3:13	
27	ᴸτότε Ναβουχοδονοσορ	בֵּאדַיִן נְבוּכַדְנֶצַּר		ᴸτότε Ναβουχοδονοσορ
28	ἐν ᴸθυμῷ καὶ ᴸὀργῇ	בִּרְגַז וַחֲמָה		ᴸᴹθυμωθεὶς ᴸὀργῇ
29	εἶπεν ᴸᴹἀγαγεῖν	אֲמַר לְהַיְתָיָה		προσέταξεν ἀγαγεῖν

118 The OG and Th Versions of Daniel

30	τὸν σεδραχ Μισαχ		שדרך מישך	τὸν σεδραχ Μισαχ
31	-Αβδεναγω		ועבד נגו	Αβδεναγω
32	ᴸ(καὶ)		ענה	ᴸτότε
33	ᴸ- -		נבכדנצר ואמר	
34	ᴸἤχθησαν		להון	ἤχθησαν - -
35	ἐνώπιον τοῦ		הצדא	οἱ ᴸἄνθρωποι
36	βασιλέως		שדרך	πρὸς τὸν
		3:14		βασιλέα
				3:14
37	καὶ ˢἀπεκρίθη		עבד נגו לא	ˢοὺς καὶ ᴸσυνιδὼν
38	Ναβουχοδονοσορ			Ναβουχοδονοσορ
39				+ ὁ βασιλεὺς
40	καὶ εἶπεν αὐτοῖς		ואמר להון	εἶπεν αὐτοῖς
41	Εἰ ᴸἀληθῶς		הצדא	ᴸΔιὰ τί
42	Σεδραχ Μισαχ		שדרך מישך	σεδραχ Μισαχ
43	Αβδεναγω		ועבד נגו	Αβδεναγω
44	τοῖς θεοῖς μου		לאלהי	לאלהי ᴸ- -
45	οὐ - -		לא פלחין	οὐ ᴸ- -

Chapter 3:11-20

46	ᴹλατρεύετε	מפלחין	ᴸᴹλατρεύετε
47	καὶ τῇ εἰκόνι	ולצלם	καὶ τῇ εἰκόνι
48	τῇ χρυσῇ	דדהבא	τῇ χρυσῇ
49	ἣν ἔστησα	די הקימת	ἣν ᴸἔστησα
50	οὐ ᴹπροσκυνεῖτε	לא סגדין	οὐ ᴸᴹπροσκυνεῖτε
	3:15		3:15
51	ᴸνῦν οὖν ˢεἰ	הן איתיכון	ᴸκαὶ νῦν ˢεἰ ˢμὲν
52	ᴸἔχετε ᴸἑτοίμως	עתידין	ᴸἔχετε ᴸἑτοίμως
53	ἵνα	די	ὅπως
54	ᴸὡς ἂν	בעדנא	ᴸἅμα τῷ
55	ἀκούσητε	די תשמעון	ᴹἀκοῦσαι
56	τῆς φωνῆς	קל	- -
57	τῆς ᴸσάλπιγγος	קרנא	τῆς σάλπιγγος
58	σύριγγός τε	משרוקיתא	ˢ- -
59	καὶ κιθάρας	קיתרס	- -
60	σαμβύκης	סבכא	- -
61	καὶ ψαλτηρίου	פסנטרין	- -

62	- -	יתנצבון	- -
63	καὶ παντὸς γένους	כל זני	καὶ παντὸς ἤχου
64	μουσικῶν	זמרא	μουσικῶν
65	πεσόντες	יפלון	πεσόντες
66	προσκυνήσητε	ויסגדון	^{LM}προσκυνῆσαι
67	τῇ εἰκόνι	לצלמא	τῇ εἰκόνι + τῇ χρυσῇ +
68	ᾗ ἐποίησα	די הקימת	ᾗ ^{L}ἔστησα
69	ἐὰν δὲ	והן	
70		לא	^{S}εἰ δὲ μή
71	μὴ προσκυνήσητε	תסגדון	+ γε γινώσκετε ὅτι + μὴ ^{L}προσκυνησάντων
72	^{L}αὐτῇ τῇ ὥρᾳ	בה שעתא	ὑμῶν ^{L}αὐθωρὶ
73	ἐμβληθήσεσθε	תתרמון	^{L}ἐμβληθήσεσθε
74	εἰς ^{L}- - τὴν κάμινον	לגוא אתון	εἰς ^{L}- - ^{S}τὴν κάμινον
75	τοῦ πυρός	נורא	τοῦ πυρὸς
76	τὴν καιομένην	יקדתא	τὴν καιομένην
77	καὶ τίς ἐστιν θεὸς	ומן הוא אלה	καὶ ^{L}ποῖος ^{L}θεὸς
78	ὃς ^{L}ἐξελεῖται ὑμᾶς	די ישיזבנכון	^{L}ἐξελεῖται ὑμᾶς

Chapter 3:11-20

79	ἐκ τῶν ᴹχειρῶν μου		ἐκ τῶν ᴹχειρῶν μου
	3:16	3:16	3:16
80	καὶ ˣἀπεκρίθησαν	יהון	ˢἀποκριθέντες δὲ
81	σεδραχ Μισαχ	אמרין	Σεδραχ Μισαχ
82	-Αβδεναγω	מלכא נבוכדנצר	Αβδεναγω
83	λέγοντες	לה לא	εἶπαν
84	τῷ βασιλεῖ	חשחין	τῷ βασιλεῖ
85	Ναβουχοδονοσορ	אנחנה	Ναβουχοδονοσορ
86		על־דנה	+ Βασιλεῦ
87	Οὐ ᴸχρείαν ἔχομεν	פתגם להתבותך	οὐ ᴸχρείαν ἔχομεν³
88	ἡμεῖς ˢπερὶ		ᴸ⁴ἀποκριθῆναί σοι
89	τοῦ ᴸῥήματος τούτου		
90	ᴸᴹἀποκριθῆναί σοι		ˢἐπὶ τῇ ᴸἐπιταγῇ ταύτῃ
	3:17	3:17	3:17
91	ᴸἔστι ˢᴸγὰρ θεός	אן איתי אלהנא	ᴸἔστιν ᴸγὰρ θεός
92			+ˢἐν οὐρανοῖς
93			+⁵[εἷς] κύριος ἡμῶν

The OG and Th Versions of Daniel

94	ᾧ ἡμεῖς λατρεύομεν		אלהנא די אנחנא פלחין	ὃν ᴸφοβούμεθα
95	ᴸδυνατὸς		יכל	ὅς ἐστιν ᴸδυνατὸς
96	ᴸἐξελέσθαι ἡμᾶς		לשׁיזבותנא	ᴸἐξελέσθαι ἡμᾶς
97	ἐκ τῆς καμίνου		מן אתון	ἐκ τῆς ˢκαμίνου
98	τοῦ πυρός		נורא	τοῦ πυρός
99	τῆς καιομένης		יקדתא	- -
100	καὶ ἐκ τῶν ᴹχειρῶν σου		ומן ידך	καὶ ἐκ τῶν ᴹχειρῶν σου
101	βασιλεῦ		מלכא	βασιλεῦ
102	ᴸρύσεται ἡμᾶς		ישׁיזב	ᴸἐξελεῖται ἡμᾶς
	3:18	3:18		3:18
103	καὶ ˢἐὰν μὴ		והן לא	καὶ ˢτότε
104	γνωστὸν ἔστω σοι		ידיע להוא לך	φανερόν σοι ἔσται
105	βασιλεῦ		מלכא	- -
106	ὅτι τοῖς θεοῖς σου		די לאלהיך	ὅτι οὔτε τῷ ᴸεἰδώλῳ σου
107	οὐ ᴸ- -		לא איתנא פלחין	ᴸ- -
108	λατρεύομεν		פלחין	ᴸλατρεύομεν οὔτε
109	καὶ τῇ εἰκόνι		ולצלם	τῇ εἰκόνι +ˢσου

Chapter 3:11-20   123

110	- -	בְדַהֲבָא	τῇ χρυσῇ
111	ἣ ἔστησας	דִּי הֲקֵים נְבוּכַדְנֶצַּר	ἣν ᴸἔστησας
112	οὗ προσκυνοῦμεν	לָא	ᴸπροσκυνοῦμεν
113	3:19	3:19	3:19
114	ᴸτότε	בֵּאדַיִן	ᴸτότε
115	Ναβουχοδονοσορ	נְבוּכַדְנֶצַּר	Ναβουχοδονοσορ
116	ᴸἐπλήσθη ᴸθυμοῦ	הִתְמְלִי חֱמָא	ᴸἐπλήσθη ᴸθυμοῦ
117	καὶ ἡ ᴸὄψις τοῦ	וּצְלֵם	καὶ ἡ ᴸμορφὴ
118	προσώπου αὐτοῦ	אַנְפּוֹהִי	τοῦ προσώπου αὐτοῦ
119	ἠλλοιώθη	אֶשְׁתַּנִּי	ᴸἠλλοιώθη
120	ἐπὶ σεδραχ Μισαχ	עַל־שַׁדְרַךְ מֵישַׁךְ	ˢ⁶ἐπ' αὐτούς
121	Αβδεναγω	וַעֲבֵד נְגוֹ	
122	καὶ ˢ - - εἶπεν	עָנֵה וְאָמַר	καὶ ˢἐπέταξε
123	ᴸἐκκαῦσαι	לְמֵזֵא	ᴸκαῆναι
124	τὴν κάμινον	לְאַתּוּנָא	τὴν κάμινον
125	ἑπταπλασίως	חַד־שִׁבְעָה	ἑπταπλασίως
126	ἕως οὗ	עַל דִּי	ˢπαρ' ὃ

124   The OG and Th Versions of Daniel

126 (ᴸεἰς τέλος) ᴸἐκκαῇ   מְנוֹ לְמִכְפַּת   ἔδει αὐτὴν ᴸκαῆναι
     3:20   3:20   3:20
127 καὶ ᴸἄνδρας   וּלְגֻבְרִין   καὶ ᴸἄνδρας
128 - - ᴸ(ἰσχυροὺς   גִּבָּרֵי־חַיִל   ᴸἰσχυροτάτους
129 - - ᴸἰσχύϊ)   דִּי בְחֵילֵהּ   ᴸτῶν ἐν τῇ δυνάμει
130 εἶπε   אֲמַר   ἐπέταξεν
131 ᴸᴹ(πεδήσαντας)   לְכַפָּתָה   ᴸσυμποδίσαντας
132 τὸν σεδραχ Μισαχ   לְשַׁדְרַךְ מֵישַׁךְ   ˢ⁷[τὸν σεδραχ Μισαχ
133 Αβδεναγω   וַעֲבֵד נְגוֹ   Αβδεναγω]
134 ᴹἐμβαλεῖν   לְמִרְמֵא   ᴸἐμβαλεῖν
135 εἰς τὴν κάμινον   לְאַתּוּן   εἰς ˢ τὴν ˢ κάμινον
136 τοῦ πυρὸς   נוּרָא   τοῦ πυρὸς
137 τὴν καιομένην   יָקִדְתָּא   τὴν καιομένην

IV.1. Textual Notes

1. >πεσών OG has most likely omitted the participle because it is unnecessary.
2. οἱ ἄνθρωποι ἤχθησαν] 3,1,2 88-Syh has the order of MT.
3. >ἡμεῖς The pronoun has been added in 88-Syh under the influence of MT and Th. Note that it is also omitted in OG in the following verse (l. 94).
4. ἐπὶ τῇ ἐπιταγῇ ταύτῃ ἀποκριθῆναί σοι] 5,6,1,2,3,4 88-Syh=MT.
5. >εἷς 967 omits the numeral here, and it is a difficult task to decide the better text. Hamm *III-IV*, 215 regards 88-Syh as original, because the text would then agree with the monotheistic emphasis that is unique to OG, which is also found in 4:34c(37). However, if chapters 4-6 originate from a different translator, as argued by Albertz, then the numeral would more likely be secondary. We have employed brackets to indicate our doubt as to the authenticity of this reading.
6. ἠλλοιώθη] +ἐπ' αὐτούς 88-Syh have ἐπὶ σεδραχ Μισαχ Αβδεναγω (Syh employs the asterisk), which Ziegler correctly omitted as a hexaplaric addition. The dynamic rendering of 967 is in keeping with OG's style, however, and should be regarded as original.
7. τὸν σεδραχ Μισαχ Αβδεναγω] τοὺς περὶ τὸν 'Αζαρίαν The decision here is difficult. 967 has a more dynamic rendering, which is also found in 3:23. However, there is good reason to believe that 3:20-30(97) have been freely edited in order to accommodate the insertion of the additions to the chapter (see the discussion on p. 145). 967's reading emphasizes 'Αζαρία which ties it to the insertion (v. 23). If the additions to chapter 3 are later, then so are any elements that are linked to them.[1] On the other hand, the reading of 88-Syh agrees with Th.

---

[1] Hamm, *III-IV*, 225 regards 967 as original. If our analysis is correct, the decision about whether to accept 967 would depend upon which stage of the book's literary development we are attempting to reconstruct.

IV.2. Analysis of 3:11-20

IV.2.i. Morphology

l. 22, 26, 46, 50-Either the present or the aorist can be reasonable equivalents for the perfect of HA, and both are abundantly represented in 3:11-20. However, it is interesting to compare l. 22 and 26 to l. 46 and 50. Regardless of the fact that the present probably represents a better choice in l. 22, 26 (as in l. 46, 50), Th's choice of the present in l. 22, 26 where OG reads the aorist is somewhat significant. Barthélemy (*Devanciers*, 63-65), identifies the elimination of the historic present as a characteristic of *kaige*. While these examples are not historical presents, they are more appropriate in the context, and do not exhibit the same formal correspondence to MT as OG.

l. 29-OG avoids the simple coordination of the terms in MT by transforming one noun into the aorist passive participle θυμωθείς.

l. 29, 90, 131, 134-In none of these cases does Th (or OG) represent the ל prefixed to an infinitive.

l. 55, 66-OG employs infinitives for the imperfect forms of MT in l. 55, 66 in an attempt to preserve the sense of the syntax. See *Syntax*, l. 51-66.

l. 71-OG employs the genitive absolute rather than the finite verb because of changes introduced to the syntax. See *Syntax*, l. 69-71.

l. 79, 100-OG prefers to employ the plural for יד,[2] while Th normally follows the number of MT. In fact, only in l. 100 does Th not follow

---

[2] MT only has the plural of יד 3x (2:34, 45; 3:15) and each time OG retains the plural. Otherwise OG prefers the plural even where MT is singular. The plural renders a singular in 1:2; 2:38; 3:17; 7:25; 8:4, 25; 11:11, 16; 12:7. Taylor, 110-111, seems to favour the plural because it is also found in P.

Chapter 3:11-20   127

the number in MT for יד. The change in l. 100 is probably due to harmonization to the earlier use in l. 79.³

IV.2.ii. *Syntax*

l. 1-4-Th's omission of the clause יפל ויסגד לצלם דהבא ומן־די in 3:10 is a rather lengthy minus against both MT and OG, and reflects a tendency of Th, particularly noticeable in chapters 4-6, to omit repeated phrases. Th changes the syntax of MT in 3:10-11 from "Anyone who hears . . . should fall and worship . . . but whoever does not fall and worship . . ." to "Whoever hears . . . and does not fall and worship . . ." The change in syntax explains the addition in l. 4 as necessary to provide the object of worship. The basic meaning of the *Vorlage* is retained, though the elimination of the repeated phrase lessens some of the rhetorical effect.

l. 2-OG's omission of the participle alters the rhetorical effect, but the basic sense is the same.

l. 6, 74, 97, 135-MT has the full expression אתון נורא יקדתא also in 3:6, 21, 23, 26. A formally equivalent translation τὴν κάμινον τοῦ πυρὸς τὴν καιομένην is given by OG and Th in l. 6, 74, 135; 3:6.⁴ OG omits τὴν καιομένην in l. 99 and 3:21;⁵ it has differences in the

---

³ Note that BHS wants us to read the earlier number in the light of the later.

⁴ Indeed, both OG and Th employ the individual Greek words as SE for the corresponding Aramaic. The majority of omissions and/or different readings from the three terms are in 3:21-26(93). For example, יקד only occurs 8x; all in the phrase currently being discussed. אתון is found in 2 additional passages (3:19, 22), and in each case OG and Th translate with κάμινος. נור is also found in 3:22, 24(91), 25(92), 26(93)*bis*, 27(94)*bis*; 7:9(2), 10. Both OG and Th translate with πῦρ, except where it is omitted. OG omits in 3:21, 22, 24(91), 26(93); 7:9. Th omits נור in 3:22, 23, where the context is different due to the inclusion of the deutero-canonical material.

⁵ Asterisked addition in 88-Syh.

readings in 3:23 and 26(93). In 3:23 OG has ἐξελθοῦσα ἡ φλόξ ἐκ τῆς καμίνου and τῆς καμίνου ἔτι καιομένης in 3:26 (93), but both may reflect a different approach to translating compared to the earlier portion of chapter 3.

Th only omits τοῦ πυρὸς in 3:23.

l. 11-This is the only occurrence of the independent object pronoun ית in BA. The relative pronoun οὕς is a literal and idiomatic equivalent for the די + object pronoun.

l. 17-OG=MT while Th omits "these men" and employs a relative clause instead.

l. 18-Both OG and Th translate the semitic idiom שׂים טעם "pay regard to" (+ על person; see BDB, 1113) literally by providing an object for the verb. The idiom also occurs in 6:14(13). There OG=0 and Th employs ὑποτάσσω. It is also possible that Th has read שׁמע in both cases.

l. 23, 109-The addition of σου may be the result of OG making explicit what is implicit in MT, i.e. the image is in the likeness of the king (cf. 2:32, 37),[6] but OG does not add the first person pronoun in l. 47. Regardless of the appearance of the image, to worship it was to acknowledge Nebuchadnezzer's god/idol.

l. 37-40-OG employs a relative phrase to avoid the excessive parataxis in MT. The participle in OG does serve to make the sequence of events explicit ("they were brought . . . when he saw them . . . he said"), but there is no significant difference in meaning. OG's syntax also requires the non-translation of ו in l. 40.

---

[6] See M. Delcor, "Un cas de traduction 'Targumique' de la LXX à propos de la statue en or de Dan. III," *Textus* 7 (1969): 30-35; McCrystall, 81.

Chapter 3:11-20

l. 37, 80, 121-For the variation in the translation of the idiom ענה ואמר, see p. 75.

l. 51-66-Here MT leaves the apodosis unstated.[7] OG employs infinitives in l. 55 and 66, which effectively follow the syntax of MT. ἅμα + dative + infinitive in l. 54-55 = "Together with the hearing . . ." Th has 2 subjunctives in l. 55 and 66, which introduce a slight change, "Now, therefore, if you are prepared: When you hear . . . you should worship."

l. 51-OG employs the idiomatic μέν/δὲ[8] 8x, but the distribution is significant. It occurs in 1:7; 2:24, 33, 41; 3:15, 23, 46; 12:2. The total absence of this construction from chapters 4-11 in the original text of OG is unlikely. Th only has μέν/δὲ in 2:41, 42.

l. 58-62, 119-In l. 119 (see l. 132) OG substitutes a shorter expression for the repeated list of names for stylistic variation. The same motivation accounts for the omission of the instruments in l. 58-62.[9] The list of instruments is also shortened in 3:7, 10; as well as the list of officials in 3:3.

l. 69-71-OG adds l. 70 to emphasize the ominous consequences of not worshipping ("But if not, know for certain/it is a certainty").[10] The introduction of l. 70 also caused 3 changes in the syntax. First, μή was added to l. 69; second, OG's introduction of γινώσκω required an object clause in order to retain the elements in MT; third, OG transforms the finite verb προσκυνέω into a genitive absolute! OG's dynamic

---

[7] *GBA*, §86.

[8] See Smyth, §2895-2916.

[9] In both instances 88-Syh have an asterisked addition.

[10] For γέ, see Smyth, §2821-2829.

translation is faithful to the intention of MT, but slightly more dramatic. At the same time, even though OG added a few elements to create this emphasis, the vocabulary of MT is represented.

l. 86, 105-In the former the vocative מלכא is added, while in the latter the vocative is omitted. Neither makes any significant difference (see *Text-Critical*).

l. 88, 90-Both OG and Th construe על־דנה with פתגם incorrectly.[11] MT = "There is no need for us to make an apology about this."

l. 91, 103-The theological implications of the conditional clauses in 3:17-18 of MT are interesting, but it is not incumbent on us to determine whether it is God's existence or his ability to save that is in question.[12] What is significant for our purposes is that there is an ambiguity in the text, and both OG and Th, in company with the other versions, resolve it.[13] OG and Th affirm the existence of God (OG adds l. 92-93, see

---

[11] Noted by Montgomery, 208; but note that the Peshitta has an addition (מלתא), which makes this connection as well.

[12] The linguistic difficulty in 3:17 is the separation of the particle איתי from the verb יכל. There are two options for translation. The first is offered by Torrey and presupposes that the הן contains the whole protasis. Thus, he translates, "If it be so, (i.e., if the sentence of the king is executed), our God whom we serve, is able to deliver us." See C. C. Torrey, "Notes on the Aramaic Part of Daniel," *Transactions of the Connecticut Academy of Arts and Sciences* 15 (1909): 263. The second option is to translate איתי as a copula (Montgomery, 206). Thus, "If our God whom we serve is able . . ." For an excellent discussion of the issues, see P. W. Coxon, "Daniel III:17: A Linguistic and Theological Problem," *VT* 26 (1976): 400-409. T. R. Ashley notes that medieval rabbinic exegetes debated vigorously over the meaning of this clause and argues that we should seriously consider that the clause questions the existence of God for rhetorical effect. See T. R. Ashley, "A Philological, Literary, Theological Study of Some Problems in Daniel Chapters I-VI; with Special Reference to the Massoretic Text, the Septuagint and Medieval Rabbinic Exegesis of Selected Passages" (Ph.D. Dissertation, University of St. Andrews, 1975).

[13] For a discussion of the translation of 3:17 by the versions, see Coxon, "Daniel III: 17," 402-403.

below) and His ability to save. They confirm God's existence by employing γάρ for הן, but the unified approach is more likely based on an exegetical tradition rather than Th borrowing from OG, because we see it in all the versions.

The translation of the second conditional clause in 3:18 (l. 103) reveals significant differences between OG and Th, which supports the view that there is no dependence of Th on OG in the earlier clause. Th translates l. 103 with formal equivalents "And if not," (i.e., if God does not save us), and the jussive in l. 104 with an imperative "let it be known to you." According to Th, then, the three do not intend to worship the gods whether their God acts or not. Conversely, OG has καὶ τότε φανερόν σοι ἔσται "And then it will be clear to you," which presup-poses that they will be delivered. The explicit belief that they will be delivered is in complete accord with the confession in l. 92-93.[14]

l. 92-93-OG's addition imparts a monotheistic(?) emphasis that strengthens the syntactic change in l. 91.[15] A similar statement on monotheism is found in OG 4:34c.

l. 125-126-OG employs παρα + accusative for a comparative[16] "seven times more than it was (literally: he had seen it) heated." Th reads עד for על and employs εἰς τέλος adverbially.[17] See *Lexicology*, l. 126.

l. 132-967 reads τοὺς περὶ τὸν ’Αζαριαν, which agrees with OG's translation in 3:23. However, it is argued below that a later translator

---

[14] See also Bludau, 45.

[15] The lines are marked with the obelus in 88-Syh.

[16] For the comparative, see Smyth, §1073.

[17] So Montgomery, 211.

has edited 3:20-30(97) in order to insert the additions to chapter 3. It is this reading of 967 in 3:20 that suggests this editing began in 3:20.

IV.2.iii. *Lexicology*

1. 3, 22, 26, 46, 50, 66, 71, 94, 108, 112-The cultic terms סגד and פלח are both rendered by SE in OG and Th. OG employs προσκυνέω 12/12 for סגד,[18] and λατρεύω for פלח 7/9.[19] The choice of equivalents reflects a semantic difference. In the remainder of the LXX λατρεύω is the SE for עבד where it refers to cultic service. προσκυνέω is the SE for שחח in BH and has a more predominant sense of worship. Both OG and Th recognize and maintain that distinction.

OG employs φοβέω in l. 94 as an unusual equivalent for פלח. The motivation for this rendering was to supply a parallel with 3:12 (see *Syntax*). According to OG, the three do not fear the king's decree because they do fear/revere God![20] ὑποτάσσω is a good dynamic translation by OG in 7:27, and only appears elsewhere in OG as a plus to 11:37.

Though Th's choice of δουλεύω in 7:14, 27 is acceptable, there is no semantic difference that would explain why he would not employ the established equivalent λατρεύω. It would support the suggestion that at least chapter 7 originates from a different translator, or that chapter 7 has undergone some revision.

---

[18] 2:46; 3:5, 6, 7, 10, 11, 12, 14, 15, 18, 28. Th omits in 3:10, see *Syntax*.

[19] 3:12, 14, 18, 28(95); 6:17(16), 21(20); 7:14. In 3:17 OG has φοβέω (Th has λατρεύω) and in 7:14 Th has δουλεύω. In 7:27 OG has ὑποτάσσω where Th has δουλεύω again.

[20] It is surprising that Meadowcroft, 159-160, fails to note the obvious literary connection.

l. 5, 73, 134-In chapter 3 OG always employs ἐμβάλλω for רמא 5/5,[21] but in chapter 6 OG has ῥίπτω 4/4.[22] Th employs ἐμβάλλω (9/10), except in 3:24(91) where he has the simple form of the verb. The only other occurrence of רמא is in 7:9 where it has a different sense, and both OG and Th have τίθημι. Once more OG's vocabulary reveals differences within chapters 4-6.[23]

l. 6, 74-OG omits נוא all 10x it appears in Daniel, whereas Th only omits in l. 6, 74 and 3:6.[24] Elsewhere Th has μέσος.

l. 9, 45, 52, 91, 107-Both OG and Th treat איתי as a copula.[25] OG has ἔστιν (εἰσὶν in l. 8) 6/12[26] and omits it in 2:26; 3:14, 18. In three cases OG offers free renditions. OG employs the feminine participle οὖσαν in 2:30 and ἔχω in l. 52. In both these cases Th has the same reading and they would have to be classed as distinctive agreements. In 3:25(92) OG has οὐδεμία ἐγενήθη. Besides the agreements with OG in 2:30 and 3:15, Th also omits איתי in l. 45, 91 and 2:26, but in these cases the particle is made redundant by the presence of a finite verb. Otherwise, Th has 3 person forms of εἰμί 9/14.

---

[21] 3:6, 11, 15, 20, 21. OG=0 3:24(91).

[22] 6:8(7), 13(12), 17(16), 25(24). See 6:18(17) for an equivalent to 17(16).

[23] See also Albertz, 162.

[24] Also in 3:21, 23, 24(91), 25(92), 26(93); 4:7(10); 7:15. 7:15 has the difficult בנוא נדנה, which Th seems to have attempted to render with a contextual guess ἕξει.

[25] GBA, §95. Muraoka states that איתי retains an asseverative force in 2:26 and 3:17, while elsewhere in Daniel it is weakening to a copula. See T. Muraoka, Emphatic Words and Structures in Biblical Hebrew (Jerusalem: Magnes, 1985) 81.

[26] 2:11(2), 28; 3:12, 17, 29(96). OG=0 in 4:32(35); 5:11.

l. 9, 17, 33, 34, 127-OG employs ἄνθρωπος (7x) and ἀνήρ (7x) indiscriminately as equivalents for גבר (19x).[27] In contrast, Th never employs ἄνθρωπος. However, Th also omits translating גבר more often than OG and in one case makes it explicit who the men are (οἱ τακτικοί in 6:6[5]). The omission in 3:12 is due to Th changing the syntax; and Th also omits גבר once in 3:20. Th has a large minus compared to MT in 3:22, while the omissions in 3:13, 23 have no apparent motivation.

l. 11-The same equivalence is shared by OG and Th in 2:24, 49, though Th employs it earlier in 1:11.[28]

l. 12, 13-עבידה is also collocated with מדינה in 2:49 in its only other usage in Daniel, and MT reads exactly the same as l. 11-12. Th has the same equivalent in 2:49, while OG has ἐπι τῶν πραγμάτων τῆς βασιλ. Presumably, OG has omitted עבידה in both cases as unnecessary. Th also employs the collective ἔργα for the Hebrew equivalent מלאכה (HL in Daniel) in 8:27.[29]

Th employs χώρα (9/9) as a SE for מדינה,[30] while OG is more varied in his approach. OG employs χώρα 4x, but also has πόλιν in 11:24 and πρᾶγμα in 2:48, 49 (3:3, 30[97] OG=0). The fact that OG has χώρας in 3:12 suggests that OG employed the dynamic translation πρᾶγμα in 2:49 because of his earlier choice in v. 48.[31]

---

[27] גבר=ἄνθρωπος in 2:25; 3:12, 13, 27(94); 5:11?; 6:25(24); 8:15. גבר=ἀνήρ in 3:8, 12, 20, 21, 22, 23, 25(92). OG (and Th) omits the second גבר as redundant in 3:20 and also omits it in 6:6(5) and 6:12(11). In 3:24(91); 6:16(15) OG=0.

[28] See the discussion of the relationship between Th and OG in 1:1-10, l. 48, 94.

[29] ἔργα is also found in 3:27, 57 in both OG and Th, and in an OG plus in 4:19(22). OG has the singular in 11:17 for מלכות(?).

[30] 2:48, 49; 3:1, 2, 3, 12, 30(97); 8:2; 11:24.

[31] Montgomery, 184, suggests that 2:48 was motivated by 2:49.

Chapter 3:11-20

l. 20–OG employs a variety of equivalents for טעם: γνῶσις 2:14; κρίνω 3:10, 29(96); ἐντολή 3:12.[32] Th favours δόγμα 6/9, but not to the point of misconstruing the meaning of the text. γνώμη renders the sense of "good judgement" in 2:14, while in 5:2 טעם has the sense "taste," which Th translates with γεῦσις. Th employs λόγος in 6:3(2) in a vain attempt to render the meaning of the difficult Aramaic.

Though Th and OG share a much closer relationship in the current passage, the translation of טעם does exhibit significant differences in approach. It should also be noted that OG only employs δόγμα in a plus (6:12a), whereas Th's use of δόγμα mainly for טעם and דתא (see *Syntax*, 2:1-10) represents incomplete lexical levelling.

l. 21, 44, 106–OG's specifies the nature of the gods (εἰδώλῳ) in l. 21 and 106,[33] whereas in l. 44 it has a literal equivalent to MT. Actually, OG's ideology preserves a nice distinction. To the king the statue represents the "gods" θεοῖς (l. 44), but to the three the statue is merely an "idol" εἴδωλον.[34] This distinction explains why OG does not employ εἴδωλον in l. 44.

l. 25, 48, 111–Forms of √ἵστημι were ideal to render קום because of the broad semantic range it afforded, as well as its use as both a transitive or an intransitive verb. Of the 35x קום appears in Daniel the majority are in the Aramaic section and 10 are in chapter 3:1-18.[35] MT has a plus against OG and Th in 3:3, but it is probably a case of

---

[32] OG=0 4:3(6); 5:2; 6:3(2), 6:14(13), 6:27(26).

[33] See also the discussion of 1:2, p. 46.

[34] It is possible that OG's choice of the singular in 3:12, 18 reflects the *Qere* in MT, but given the change in translation equivalents it is difficult to answer this question with any degree of certainty.

[35] 2:21, 31, 39, 44(2); 3:1, 2, 3(3), 5, 7, 12, 14, 18, 24(91); 4:14; 5:11, 21; 6:2(1), 4(3), 8(7), 9(8), 16(15), 20(19); 7:4, 5(2), 10, 16, 17, 24(2); 8:27; 9:12. OG=0 in 3:3(2); 4:14(17); 5:11, 21. 6:20(19)?

dittography in MT.³⁶ The remaining 8 cases in 3:1-18 all have to do with the setting up of the statue (5 in 3 singular haphel perfect; 3 in 2 singular haphel perfect), so it is not surprising to find identical forms in Th and OG.

For the most part, OG and Th employ formal equivalents for the translation of קום. The only dynamic equivalent in OG is 7:17 (ἀπολοῦνται). There are several Th renderings that require comment. Th employs ἐξανίστημι in 3:24(91), which is unique. It is the only occurrence in Th, even though it is a regular equivalent for קום in the LXX.³⁷ In 6:4(3) Th renders עשית להקמותה with a simple finite form of καθίστημι, whereas OG has ἐβουλεύσατο καταστῆσαι. Th has probably omitted translating the HL עשה.

Finally, we must consider the question of Th's relationship to OG. The ratio of agreements between Th and OG for the translation of קום in the remainder of Daniel is not quite as extensive as it is in chapter 3. However, rather than investigating each equivalent we will focus on those instances where OG and Th have the verb καθίστημι. OG and Th share a common reading of the verb in 2:21; 6:2(1), 4(3), so it might be concluded that Th has merely retained OG. On the other hand, Th also employs καθίστημι in 5:11 (OG=0) and in each of these instances Th accurately translates the sense "to appoint." For example, in 5:11 Th has ὁ πατήρ σου ἄρχοντα . . . κατέστ. αὐτόν = אבוך הקימה . . . רב = "your father appointed him head . . ." Th's translations in these instances accord well with his renderings of מנה in 1:11; 2:24, 49; 3:12 that were discussed earlier (see 1:1-10, *Lexicology*). Furthermore, Th employs καθίστημι elsewhere only in 2:38 and 2:48 for the two places where the haphel of שלט appears.³⁸ Therefore, when we consider the faithfulness, consistency and distinctiveness of Th's translation, it is

---

³⁶ OG omits the entire final clause, while Th omits the redundant "which Nebuchadnezzer set up."

³⁷ ἐξανίστημι appears in 5:6 in OG where MT=0.

³⁸ OG has καθίστημι in 2:48, but in 2:38 it employs κυριεύω!

unlikely that Th has borrowed from OG. Most of the common readings are exactly that, common. On the other hand, the shared reading of παρειστήκεισαν in 7:10 is most likely a distinctive agreement.

l. 27, 32, 113-MT employs (ב)אדין 46x in Daniel.[39] There is little point in presenting a comprehensive analysis because τότε is the normal and expected equivalent for (ב)אדין, and καί is a reasonable and frequent choice as well. However, there are several noteworthy points. 1) Except for the omission in 3:3 OG has τότε for (ב)אדין 13/13 in chapter 2-3:21. Th, on the other hand, has δέ in 2:15! and καί in 2:17, 19, 48; 3:3. 2) The frequent use of καί in Th means that the καί in l. 32 may be the equivalent for באדין, rather than for a hypothetical ו (אלך גבריא is omitted in l. 33). 3) OG employs the dynamic equivalents ούτως ούν only in 3:26(93) and 3:30(97). 4) Contrary to the stereotyped usage in chapter 2-3:21, OG only employs τότε about 12/23 in 3:24(91)-7:19 and the alternative equivalents (also καί in 3:26[93]; 5:3, 6, 8; 6:12[11], 14[13], 15[14], 20[19] and δέ in 4:16[19]) only occur in chapters 4-6.[40]

It is not possible to formulate any definite conclusions, but the pattern of translation is similar to what we have found elsewhere. Not only are there unique equivalents in OG around the inclusion of the deutero-canonical additions at the end of chapter 3, but there is also a different approach to translating the term in chapters 4-6.

l. 28, 115-MT has two terms for anger/wrath collocated in l. 28 (רגז is a HL in Daniel). Although OG transforms the first to a participle, Th has the same order of equivalents: θυμός (θυμόω OG) then ὀργή. The

---

[39] 2:14, 15, 17, 19(2), 25, 35, 46, 48; 3:3, 13(2), 19, 21, 24(91), 26(93)bis, 30(97); 4:4(7), 16(19); 5:3, 6, 8, 9, 13, 17, 24, 29; 6:4(3), 5(4), 6(5), 7(6), 12(11), 13(12), 14(13), 15(14), 16(15), 17(16), 19(18), 20(19), 22(21), 24(23), 26(25); 7:1, 11, 19.

[40] 3:24(91)?; 5:9, 13, 17?, 29; 6:7(6), 13(12), 19(18), 26(25); 7:1, 11, 19. OG=0 5:24; 6:4(3), 5(4), 6(5), 16(15), 17(16), 22(21), 24(23). Th's ratio of 15/31 in 3:24(91)-7:19 (Th=0 in 5:24?) is about the same as 2-3:21.

nature of this agreement is underscored in l. 115 where both OG and Th employ θυμός for חמא instead of ὀργή as in l. 28. The same type of agreement occurs with the cognate Hebrew term חמה. In 11:44 OG and Th both render חמה with θυμός, but in 9:16 they both have ὁ θυμός σου καὶ ἡ ὀργή σου where MT reads אפך וחמתך. The order θυμός, then ὀργή is not a fixed collocation in the LXX either, so 9:16 may be a distinctive agreement.[41] However, the formal equiv-alence to MT suggests that OG has suffered corruption.

There are further reasons that suggest that any distinctive agreement in these terms is due to textual corruption. For example, in the only other occurrence of חמה in 8:6, OG has the expected θυμός; but Th has ὁρμή (1-11 in LXX!, though it could be a corruption from ὀργῇ). If we broaden the investigation, we find that OG and Th employ ὀργή to render the substantive זעם in 8:19 and 11:36. However, when זעם occurs as a verb in 11:30 OG employs ὀργίζω and Th has θυμόω. Nor does Th share OG's reading of ὀργή in the addition (doublet?) to 9:26, or OG's error in 11:18. In the other occurrence of אף in the sense of anger in 11:20 (see also 9:16) OG employs ὀργή, whereas Th renders literally with πρόσωπον. Finally, we should note that OG employs both θυμόω (8:7) and ὀργίζω (11:11) to translate מרר in the hithpalpal (יתמרמר) "to be embittered," but Th has 2 HL in the LXX: ἐξαγριαίνω and ἀγριάνω!!

l. 29, 34-OG and Th have common readings for אתה throughout Daniel (12x), but the significance is minimal because the Greek renderings are expected.[42] In 3:26(93) OG simplifies פקו ואתו to ἐξέλθατε while Th

---

[41] In fact, ὀργή more often precedes θυμός (50x) in the LXX than the other way around (38x). See also T. Muraoka, *A Greek-English Lexicon of the Septuagint* (Louvain: Peeters, 1993) 111, 173 where Muraoka notes that θυμός and ὀργή are employed as overlapping synonyms in the LXX.

[42] אתה is 12x in Daniel. 3:2, 13(2), 26(93); 5:2, 3, 13, 23; 6:17(16), 18(17); 7:13, 22. OG=0 5:13; 6:17(16).

Chapter 3:11-20   139

has a good dynamic translation ἐξέλθετε καὶ δεῦτε "Come out and come here!"[43]

l. 37-This is the only occurrence of συνοράω for the translated books of the Hebrew Bible, though it does occur 9x in the Maccabean literature.

l. 41-OG renders the sense of MT, but it is uncertain whether he actually knew the meaning of the infinitive צרא.[44] Th offers a literal equivalent.

l. 51-The adverb כען appears 7x in MT, though OG only seems to have it in his *Vorlage* in 3:15 and 2:23. Th reflects a difference in his approach. In the 5x that the adverb stands alone, including 3:15, Th translates with νῦν οὖν.[45] However, in 5:15 where the conjunction ו is attached, Th translates with καὶ νῦν. According to Ziegler, the νῦν is not part of Th's text in 2:23, but there is some support for its inclusion.

l. 52-The equivalent ἑτοίμως (1-4) for עתיד (HL in Daniel) in OG and Th is a common reading in l. 52.

l. 54-בעדנא די also occurs in 3:5 where OG has ὅταν and Th employs ᾗ ἂν ὥρᾳ. Th's rendering is more dynamic in 3:15. See *Syntax*, l. 49-64.

l. 57-There are five or six musical instruments listed in 3:5, 7, 10, 15. 3 of the names of the instruments are certainly Greek loan words

---

[43] For δεῦρο and δεῦτε, see E. Eynikel and J. Lust, "The Use of ΔΕΥΡΟ and ΔΕΥΤΕ in the LXX," *ETL* 67 (1991): 57-68.

[44] See Torrey, "Notes," 261-62.

[45] 3:15; 4:34(37); 5:12, 16; 6:9(8).

(κίθαρις, ψαλτήριον, συμφωνία), and two (קרן, שרק) are semitic.[46] OG only gives a complete list in the first instance and prefers to abbreviate in vv. 7, 10, 15. The main point of interest in the list is the word συμφωνία. It was believed that συμφωνία is specifically mentioned as a favourite individual instrument in connection with Antiochus Epiphanes, but Coxon has argued that it should be understood in the sense of a group of musicians.[47] The sense of the term is uncertain, but Th and OG seem to understand it as orchestral music. Th omits συμφωνία all 4x in which it appears. This suggests that he understood it in terms of a band or orchestra; therefore, he omitted it as redundant because of the following "and all kinds of music." The reading of OG depends on the text we choose as original. 88-Syh and 967 translate all six terms in 3:5, but 88-Syh lists them in a way that suggests συμφονία refers to an individual instrument. 967 reads "and a symphony of all kinds of music," which should probably be accepted as OG.[48] In the later vv. (7, 10, 15) OG omits συμφωνία as redundant.

l. 68-OG may employ ἵστημι for עבד because he expected to read קום due to the previous collocation of (רהבא) לצלם (די הקימ(ת)) in 3:2, 3, 5, 7, 12, 14, though he also has συνίστημι in 7:21. The expected equivalent for the verb עבד in both OG (3/7) and Th (10/12) is ποιέω.[49]

---

[46] For a discussion of the instruments, see Coxon, "Greek Loan-Words," 24-40; P. Grelot, "L'Orchestre de Daniel III 5, 7 10, 15," *VT* 29 (1979): 23-38; K. A. Kitchen, "The Aramaic of Daniel," *Notes on Some Problems in the Book of Daniel* (ed. D. J. Wiseman et al.; London: Tyndale, 1965) 48-50.

[47] Bevan, 41, includes the quote from Polybius; see Coxon, "Greek Loan-Words," 32.

[48] συμφωνία in OG could be the result of later harmonization to MT.

[49] 2:5; 3:1, 15, 29(96), 32(99); 4:32(35)*bis*; 5:1; 6:11(10), 23(22), 28(27); 7:21. OG=0 in 3:32(99); 4:32(35)*bis*; 6:23(22)?, 28(27). Neither OG or Th understand MT in 2:5 and 3:29(96).

Chapter 3:11-20   141

l. 72-שעה only appears 5x in Daniel: 4x in the temporal expression בה־שעתא (3:6, 15; 4:30[33]; 5:5) and once prefixed with כ (4:16). OG has various equivalents. αὐθωρὶ (1-2) in 3:15 appears to be a neologism (LEH, 70), while in 3:6 OG omits translating it. ἕως δε πρωὶ may be an equivalent in 4:30(33), though like 4:16(19) the *Vorlage* is uncertain. Other than the neologism in 3:15, ἐν αὐτῇ τῇ ὥρᾳ in 5:5 is the most significant equivalent for בה־שעתא because it almost certainly stems from Th! In the other three cases where בה־שעתא appears, Th always has αὐτῇ τῇ ὥρᾳ. The only difference in 5:5 is the addition of ἐν, but the literalness of the reading and the consistency with which it is found in Th leads to the conclusion that the reading ἐν αὐτῇ τῇ ὥρᾳ of OG in 5:5 is Theodotionic.

l. 78, 96, 102-The main equivalent for שיזב (shaphel, see BDB, 1115) in both OG (5/8) and Th (7/9) is ἐξαιρέω.[50] The other equivalent for OG is σῴζω in 3:28(95); 6:21(20), 28(27).[51] Th has ῥύομαι in 3:17 and ἀντιλαμβάνω! (HL in Daniel) in 6:28(27). It is possible that Th has followed OG's use of ἐξαιρέω for שיזב, but it is also possible that Th made the same equivalence. The 2x that Th changes equivalents can be explained as stylistic variation, and it is noteworthy that Th changes equivalents in 3:17 while OG does not.[52] Analysis of related vocabulary sharing the sense of deliverance reveals similar findings. For example, other than 3:88, Th only has σῴζω in 11:41 and 12:1 where the Hebrew equivalent is מלט (niphal). These are the only appearances of מלט in Daniel and the reading is shared with OG in 12:1. However, in 11:41 OG=0, so we cannot assume Th dependence on OG in 12:1.

Another semitic term for deliverance, נצל (haphel in BA), occurs 5x in Daniel. OG has ἐξαιρέω in 3:29(96); 6:16(15)=15(14) and

---

[50] שיזב is in 3:15, 17(2), 28(95); 6:15(14), 17(16), 21(20), 28(27)*bis*. OG=0 once in 6:28(27) where שיזב appears twice and OG reads quite differently.

[51] OG has σῴζω also in 3:88; 11:42; 12:1.

[52] See the discussion of OG and Th's relationship.

ῥύομαι in 8:4, 7. Th overlaps in 6:15(14), whereas in 3:29(96); 6:28(OG=0) he has ῥύομαι and in 8:4, 7 ἐξαιρέω.

l. 87-OG and Th employ the common reading χρείαν ἔχομεν for חשׁה (HL in MT; BDB, 1093). This reading also shares the same feature as the common reading in l. 52, i.e. both employ ἔχω.

l. 88, 90-OG and Th have ἀποκρίνω for תוב. Th has the same equivalence where תוב has the sense of "answer" in 2:14. There OG has εἶπεν.[53]

l. 88, 90-MT also has פתגם in 4:14(17) where OG=0 and Th has λόγος.

l. 95-OG and Th only have δύνατος elsewhere in 11:3 for גבור (HL in Daniel).[54] The reading in l. 95 might be a distinctive agreement (though the equivalence is also found in (Gen 32:28[29]; Num 13:31[30], 22:38), but there is no way to prove the direction of borrowing. However, it is noteworthy that OG and Th have extensive agreement with one another and formal agreement with MT in l. 95-101.

l. 115-OG and Th have a common reading, which more likely stems from OG. πίμπλημι is nowhere else in Th while OG has it again in 12:4.[55]

---

[53] Elsewhere תוב has the sense of return in 4:31(34), 33(36)bis, and in each case Th renders with ἐπιστρέφω (OG=0).

[54] גבור=δύνατος is a common equivalent in the LXX.

[55] מלא appears 4x in MT: 2:35 OG=πατάσσω, Th=πληρόω; 9:2 OG= ἀναπλήρωσις, Th=συμπλήρωσις; 10:3 OG=συντελέω, Th=πλήρωσις. OG's rendering in 2:35 is probably based on his reading מחת for מלת. מחת is found earlier in the verse as well as in 2:34.

Chapter 3:11-20   143

l. 116-εἰκών is the SE for צלם for both OG (14/17) and Th (16/17),[56] but would not have been appropriate to describe the "appearance" of the king's face. The choice of equivalents in 3:19 is interesting because μορφή is a HL in OG, whereas Th has it 5x for זיו.[57] ὄψις is an equivalent for מראה in 1:4 of Th, whereas OG has it for מראה in 1:13, 15 (Th=ἰδέα).

l. 118-The translation of שנא was discussed in the previous section on 2:1-10. 4x elsewhere MT has זיו collocated with שנא "his appearance was changed" and in each case Th employs ἀλλοιόω.[58]

l. 122, 126-OG employs the simple καίω for אזא while Th has the compound ἐκκαίω. The only other occurrence of אזא is in 3:22 (peal perfect) where both read ἐξεκαύθη. OG exhibits lexical levelling by employing καίω for both אזא and יקד (3:6, 11, 15, 20, 23), whereas Th makes a distinction through employing the compound. Therefore, it is very possible that the compound in 3:22 of OG reflects Th influence.

l. 126-Th has the dynamic rendering of εἰς τέλος for חזה. Th translated it adverbially (i.e. "utterly"), but it is unlikely that his text differed from MT.[59] This is a good example of Th's independence from OG.

l. 128-129-MT piles up the superlatives in depicting the "men, mighty men of strength who were in his service" who were to throw the three

---

[56] צלם is found elsewhere in 2:31(2), 32, 34, 35; 3:1, 2, 3(2), 5, 7, 10, 12, 14, 15, 18. OG omits in 2:32 and once in 3:3. Th omits in 3:10, but has it as a plus in 3:11 (see *Syntax*, 1. 1-4).

[57] 4:33(36); 5:6, 9, 10; 7:28. OG=0 in all cases except in 5:6 where it has ὅρασις.

[58] 5:6, 9, 10; 7:28. OG has ἀλλοιόω in 5:6; OG=0 in 5:9, 10; διαφέρω in 7:28.

[59] Montgomery, 211, suggests that Th read חזה as if it were from the root of אזא.

into the fire. OG renders גברי־חיל with a superlative, and a formally equivalent rendition of די בחילה. Th simplifies to ἰσχυροὺς ἰσχύι "strong in strength." Th's more dynamic rendering should be regarded as another clearly independent translation.

l. 131-OG has συνποδίζω (3/3) for כפת, whereas Th has πεδάω 4/4.[60] Both words are employed in the LXX (see HR), but Th's choice suggests independence.

IV.2.iv. *Summary*

As in 1:1-10 and 2:1-10, OG was no doubt translating a *Vorlage* virtually identical with MT. However, OG's relationship to MT has a different character in 3:11-20 when compared to the previous sections we have examined. As in the previous sections OG adheres quite closely to MT, but here OG does not exhibit the same variety in his choice of lexical equivalents and the close formal correspondence to MT (note the number of articles!) is unusual. This may be partly explained by the high degree of repetition in the vocabulary. However, it is also striking that in 3:11-20 OG always has qualifying adjectives and participles with articles in the attributive position (eg. τῇ εἰκόνι τῇ χρυσῇ) rather than employing a shorter form. There are omissions against MT, but these primarily involve words that occur frequently in chapter 3. Though OG demonstrates a closer formal correspondence to MT in this passage, there are still some interesting free translations. For example, OG changes the conditional clauses in 3:17-18 in order to remove any ambiguity about the existence of God or His ability to save. The addition emphasizing monotheism in l. 92-93 of 3:17 ensures that we are in no doubt about OG's theological views. The addition in l. 70 is different from l. 92-93 because it does not introduce any fundamental

---

[60] 3:20, 21, 23, 24(91). OG=0 in 3:24(91) but has an extra appearance of συνποδίζω in 3:22. OG has πεδάω in 4:30a.

differences in meaning, though it did require OG to make changes in the syntax. OG has a few dynamic equivalents (l. 37-συνιδὼν; l. 72-αὔθωρὶ; l. 94-φοβούμεθα) and displays some freedom in word order by employing postpositive conjunctions (δὲ in l. 9, 69, 80; γὰρ in l. 91). In 3:11-20 Th demonstrates an expected formal correspondence to MT, but not to the point of mechanical literalness. Once again, Th has occasional omissions against MT and even changes the syntax at the beginning of v. 11. Th also employs some variety in equivalents (l. 102, 116, 126, 131) that distinguish him from OG. Th's expression of the superlative in l. 128-129 is also dynamic.

The investigation of 3:11-20 has also found further evidence to confirm Albertz' thesis. First, we have confirmed that OG's use of ῥίπτω for רמא in chapters 4-6 is distinct from the choice ἐμβάλλω elsewhere. Second, OG employs τότε as a SE for (ב)אדין in chapter 2-3:21, which is distinct from 3:24(91)-7:19. Third, the idiomatic μέν/δὲ only occurs once outside of chapters 1-3, but this finding has been anticipated by the results of our investigation of 2:1-10.

There is also the possibility that a significant piece of evidence links chapters 4-6 with the rest of OG, or, at least chapter 3. It depends upon whether we read "one" εἷς in 88-Syh as OG, but the emphasis on monotheism in 3:17 would then parallel 4:34c. Albertz argues that one of the reasons why the later translator of chapters 1-3, 7-12 adopted the earlier "popular" edition of chapters 4-6 into his edition was because the earlier translator of chapters 4-6 shared the same theological concerns. Albertz offers the parallel between 3:17 and 4:34c as a prime example of this shared theology.[61] However, if that were the case, we might expect to find additional emphasis on monotheism elsewhere in chapters 1-3 or 7-12 and the numeral is not found in 967. So, although it can be maintained that OG chapters 4-6 stem from a different translator when

---

[61] Albertz, 164.

compared with chapters 1-3; 7-12, the correspondence between 3:17 and 4:34c exemplifies the problem of reconstructing OG and its compositional history.

IV.3. A Note on the Additions to Chapter Three

A further complication in reconstructing the compositional history of OG is the inclusion of the Prayer of Azariah and the Song of the Three Young Men in chapter 3. Whether the additions stem from a semitic *Vorlage* is beyond the limits of this investigation, nor is it strictly within our purview to decide whether the additions were part of the OG text. However, what we have found suggests that the additions have been inserted into the OG. There are differences in content between MT, Th and OG in the verses immediately prior to and following the insertion in 3:21-30(97), but the primary difference is in 3:24(91). MT does not provide a reason why the king was alarmed and rose to his feet, but presumably he can see the four from where he sits. In OG and Th the king rises to his feet in amazement because he hears them singing, and then he declares to his friends (nobles in Th) that there are four beings in the fire. Despite the differences in content, the narrative sequence, apart from the inclusion of the deutero-canonical material in the Greek texts, is basically the same in MT and the Greek versions. Therefore, we can be reasonably certain that the *Vorlage* for OG and Th was very similar to that preserved in MT. Even though the *Vorlagen* for MT and OG were very similar, there are several translation equivalents that OG employs that are unique to 3:20-30(97). These are summarized below:

1. OG has ἐξελθοῦσα ἡ φλόξ ἐκ τῆς καμίνου in 3:23 where MT has לנוא־אתון־נורא יקדתא and τῆς καμίνου ἔτι καιομένης in 3:26(93) where MT has אתון־נורא יקדתא (compare 3:6, 11, etc.).

2. OG has οὐδεμία ἐγενήθη in 3:25(92) for לא־איתי.

Chapter 3:11-20   147

3. OG employs οὕτως οὖν only in 3:26(93) and 3:30(97) for באדין.

4. OG renders שׁנא with ἀθετέω (HL in OG) in 3:28(95) instead of the SE ἀλλοιόω (6/7).

5. A strong piece of evidence that the deutero-canonical material has been inserted into the text is the translation of הדמין יתעבד and וביתה נולי ישׁתוה in 3:29(96)=2:5. For the latter OG has καὶ ἡ οὐσία αὐτοῦ δημευθήσεται "his belongings will be confiscated" in 3:29(96), which seems to be a simplification of καὶ ἀναληφθήσεται ὑμῶν τὰ ὑπάρχοντα εἰς τὸ βασιλικόν in 2:5. Yet, the same translator. who depends on 2:5 for the translation of one difficult text, ignores 2:5 for the translation of הדמין תתעבדון. Instead of an equivalent similar to παραδειγματισθήσεσθε in 2:5, the translator has διαμελ(ρ)ίζω. The best way to explain the differences between how the same *Vorlage* is rendered in 2:5 and 3:29(96) is to posit a later translator (redactor) of 3:29(96). The later redactor simplified the translation given by the translator of 2:5 for וביתה נולי ישׁתוה because he did not know the meaning either. On the other hand, the redactor employed his own equivalent for הדמין תתעבדון rather than follow the earlier translator's lead because in that case he knew the meaning of MT.[62]

6. The translation in 3:23 of τοὺς περὶ τὸν 'Αζαριαν for שׁדרך מישׁך ועבד נגו (see 3:20 of 967) prepares for the insertion of the Prayer of Azariah.

7. It was also noted that the translation of ענה ואמר (see 2:1-10) changes after 3:19, but, in this case, it is not possible to distinguish 3:20-30(97) from chapters 4-6.

The differences in TT by OG in 3:20-30(97) are consistent with the position that a later translator/ redactor has freely edited this section

---

[62] See the discussion of *Lexicology*, l. 49-52, in 2:1-10.

in order to accommodate the insertion of the Prayer of Azariah and the Song of the Three Young Men.[63]

IV.4. *The Relationship Between OG and Th*

It would seem that the lexical equivalent in l. 115 is a distinctive agreement in which Th is dependent upon OG. The readings in l. 52, 87 and 95 are also distinctive, but there are no means to determine the direction of dependence. The conjunction γάρ is a common reading in l. 91, but it is not necessarily distinctive because it may stem from an exegetical tradition. Likewise, the omissions of גוא in l. 6 and 74 (also 3:6) are common readings, but it is difficult to judge their value because Th does translate גוא 7x elsewhere while OG always omits it.

The evidence for Th's independence from OG in this passage is also more limited than in the two previous sections. We noted above the lexical equivalents (l. 20, 102, 116, 126, 131) and syntactical features (l. 1-4, 128-129) that distinguish Th from OG, and they do indicate independence in approach. However, the extent of the verbal agreement accompanied by several distinctive agreements indicates that there is a closer textual relationship between OG and Th.

Once again, on the basis of a close analysis of this passage, it is not possible to conclude that Th has revised the OG text. There are two reasons for this position. First, many of the shared lexical equivalents are expected renderings employed throughout the LXX (קום=ἵστημι; נור=πῦρ; יקד=καίω; צלם=εἰκών; דהב=χρυσός) and, therefore, cannot be harnessed as evidence that Th has revised OG. Second, the consistent use of the attributive adjective (τῇ εἰκόνι τῇ χρυσῇ) and

---

[63] OG's choice of κρίνω in 3:10, 29(96) where MT has שים טעם are unique equivalents that link the translator of 3:21-30(97) to the previous chapters. Presumably when the redactor spliced the deutero-canonical additions into 3:21-30(97), he had a translation of 3:21-30 from the same translator as chapter 3. On the other hand, the rendering of σώζω for שיזב in 3:28(95)=6:21(20), 28(27) is one link between the editor of the insertion and chapters 4-6.

phrases like εἰς τὴν κάμινον τοῦ πυρὸς τὴν καιομένην is decidedly unlike the OG that we have witnessed previously. Where are the prepositive genitives? Why is the participle in the attributive position? And why is OG so monotonous? Unfortunately, the paucity of textual witnesses for OG suggests that Th and OG are closer in this passage than they may have been originally. Given the decidedly formal, Theodotion like, correspondence between OG and MT and the accumulating evidence that Th readings have infiltrated OG,[64] it is a reasonable hypothesis that some of these verbal agreements are the result of secondary influence of Th on OG. For example, the formal correspondence to MT in l. 95-101, which includes the distinctive agreement of δύνατος in l. 95, is likely the result of textual corruption.

A closer examination of the statistics also reveals that OG influence on Th is minimal. Although there are numerous ways by which we could attempt to "count" the frequency with which Th retains OG in 3:11-20, if we total the number of individual lexemes in OG, including some of the omissions (which Th followed), then we get 264. If we count each lexeme in Th that reads with OG, no matter how insignificant it is, we get 174 or 66%. However, articles, personal pronouns, prepositions, conjunctions, and negatives account for 75 agreements and proper names number 27. That only leaves 72 (37%) agreements. As we have already noted, most of these agreements are themselves questionable indicators of Th dependence on OG. The insignificance of two translators employing translation equivalents that are common to all books of the LXX for the determination of whether one is a revision of the other will be demonstrated in the following section on 8:1-10.

IV.5. *Text-Critical Problems*

---

[64] In our discussion of 3:11-20 we have uncovered only two places where Th influence on OG is possible and neither is in 3:11-20. We can be reasonably certain that ἐν αὐτῇ τῇ ὥρᾳ in 5:5 stems from Th. It is also possible that the compound verb ἐξεκαύθη in 3:22 stems from Th.

The omissions and additions against MT have been commented on already during the course of the analysis of TT. In summary, it may be that one or another minus or plus is based on a minus or plus in the respective *Vorlagen* of OG or Th, but there is only one instance where there are good grounds to emend MT. A few cases are noted below.

l. 6, 74-The omission of גוא by Th (also 3:6) in these places is difficult to explain (see *Lexicology*).

l. 33-OG and Th both omit אלך, and this may be grounds to emend MT, but Th also omits אלך in l. 17 where OG has it and Th does have occasional omissions.

l. 67-The addition of τῇ χρυσῇ[65] in OG could be based on an alternative *Vorlage* reading דהבא, but it also looks like harmonization with previous uses (omitted in Th, Peshitta and Vulgate). There are no grounds to emend MT.

l. 70, 92-93-These additions almost certainly reflect the ideology of the translator. The former only involves a slight emphasis on the consequences of not worshipping the image. The latter is a definite example of *theological Tendenz* because the translator adds a confession (of monotheism?) where the meaning of MT is ambiguous.

l. 86, 105-It is possible that OG's βασιλεῦ in l. 86 is based on מלכא in his *Vorlage*, which was omitted in MT (or added in OG's *Vorlage*) due to the preceding למלכא. On the other hand, OG may have inserted βασιλεῦ as a means to introduce this important section of direct address. In a similar fashion, OG omitted מלכא in l. 105 because he had retained

---

[65] It is marked with the obelus in 88-Syh.

Chapter 3:11-20   151

it in l. 101 and it would have been redundant to translate it again in l. 105. There are no convincing grounds to emend Mt in either case.

l. 99-OG has a definite tendency to shorten and omit elements, especially those that are frequently repeated. The omission of יקדתא in OG (compare l. 8, 76) falls into this category.[66]

l. 119-The substitution of ἐπ' αὐτούς for the list of names is more likely another example of OG abbreviating the monotonous repetition of MT in chapter 3 and is not based on a *Vorlage* with עליהן.[67]

---

[66] Collins, *Daniel*, 177, emends based on OG (967).

[67] For the dramatic irony conveyed by the repetition of the lists in MT, see Meadowcroft, 141-145. Collins, *Daniel*, 177, emends MT.

Chapter V
Daniel 8:1-10

Sharon Pace Jeansonne made extensive notes on this portion of text in her investigation of the OG of Daniel.[1] For that reason, in this section our sole concern will be to evaluate her conclusion that Th is a recension of the OG. As in the previous sections, we will begin with an alignment of the texts and then follow that with a discussion of Th's relationship to the OG. In order to facilitate the discussion the readings will be divided exactly as Jeansonne did. The readings in Th that Jeansonne judged to retain OG will be underlined while those she judged to be dependent upon OG will be double-underlined.

It should be noted that there are only a couple of textual notes because the majority of 967 for this passage was available to Ziegler among the Chester Beatty papyri. A small section of vv. 5-7 has since become available in the fragment published by Roca-Puig.

---

[1] Jeansonne, 32-57.

Table 4

	8:1 Th	8:1 MT	8:1 OG
1	Ἐν ἔτει τρίτῳ	בִּשְׁנַת שָׁלוֹשׁ	Ἔτους τρίτου
2	τῆς βασιλείας	לְמַלְכוּת	βασιλεύοντος
3	Βαλτασαρ	בֵּלְאשַׁצַּר	Βαλτασαρ
	τοῦ βασιλέως	הַמֶּלֶךְ	- -
4	ὅρασις	חָזוֹן	ὅρασιν
5	ὤφθη πρός με	נִרְאָה אֵלַי	ἣν εἶδον
6	ἐγώ	אֲנִי	ἐγώ
7	Δανιηλ	דָּנִיֵּאל	Δανιηλ
8	μετά	אַחֲרֵי	μετά
9	τὴν (ὀφθεῖσάν)	הַנִּרְאָה	τὸ ἰδεῖν
10	μοι	אֵלַי	με
11	τὴν (ἀρχήν)	בַּתְּחִלָּה	τὴν πρώτην
	8:2	8:2	8:2
12	(	וָאֶרְאֶה	καὶ εἶδον
13		בֶּחָזוֹן	ἐν τῷ ὁράματι
14		וַיְהִי	
15	)	בִּרְאֹתִי	τοῦ ἐνυπνίου μου
16	καὶ ἤμην	וַאֲנִי	ἐμοῦ ὄντος
17	ἐν σούσοις	בְּשׁוּשַׁן	ἐν Σούσοις
18	τῇ βάρει	הַבִּירָה	τῇ πόλει
19	ἥ	אֲשֶׁר	ἥτις
20	ἐστιν ἐν χώρᾳ	בְּעֵילָם	ἐστὶν ἐν χώρᾳ
21	Αιλαμ	הַמְּדִינָה	Ἐλυμαΐδι
22	- -	וָאֶרְאֶה בֶחָזוֹן	- -
23	καὶ	וָ	ἔτι
24	ἤμην	אֲנִי הָיִיתִי	ὄντος μου
25	ἐπί	עַל־	πρός
26	τοῦ Ουβαλ	אוּבָל	τῇ πύλῃ
27	- -	אוּלָי	Ωλαμ

Chapter 8:1-10   155

	8:3	8:3	8:3
28	καὶ ἦρα	וָאֶשָּׂא	ἀναβλέψας
29	τοὺς ὀφθαλμούς μου	עֵינַי	
30	καὶ εἶδον	וָאֶרְאֶה	εἶδον
31	καὶ ἰδοὺ	וְהִנֵּה	- -
32	κριὸς	אַיִל	κριὸν
33	εἷς	אֶחָד	ἕνα μέγαν
34	ἑστηκὼς	עֹמֵד	ἑστῶτα
35	πρὸ	לִפְנֵי	ἀπέναντι
36	τοῦ Ουβαλ	הָאֻבָל	πύλης
37	καὶ αὐτῷ	וְלוֹ	καὶ εἶχε
38	κέρατα	קְרָנָיִם	κέρατα
39	- -	וְהַקְּרָנַיִם	- -
40	ὑψηλά	גְּבֹהוֹת	ὑψηλά
41	καὶ τὸ ἓν	וְהָאַחַת	καὶ τὸ ἓν
42	ὑψηλότερον	גְּבֹהָה	ὑψηλότερον
43	τοῦ ἑτέρου	מִן־הַשֵּׁנִית	
44	καὶ τὸ ὑψηλὸν	וְהַגְּבֹהָה	καὶ τὸ ὑψηλὸν
45	ἀνέβαινεν	עֹלָה	ἀνέβαινε
46	ἐπ' ἐσχάτων	בָּאַחֲרֹנָה	8:4 μετὰ δὲ ταῦτα
	8:4	8:4	
47	εἶδον	רָאִיתִי	εἶδον
48	τὸν κριὸν	אֶת־הָאַיִל	τὸν κριὸν
49	κερατίζοντα	מְנַגֵּחַ	κερατίζοντα
50	κατὰ θάλασσαν	יָמָּה	πρὸς ἀνατολὰς
51	καὶ βορρᾶν	וְצָפוֹנָה	καὶ πρὸς βορρᾶν
52			καὶ πρὸς δυσμὰς
53	καὶ νότον	וָנֶגְבָּה	καὶ μεσημβρίαν
54	καὶ πάντα	וְכָל־	καὶ πάντα
55	τὰ θηρία	חַיּוֹת	τὰ θηρία
56	οὐ	לֹא־	οὐκ
57	στήσονται	יַעַמְדוּ	ἔστησαν

58	ἐνώπιον αὐτοῦ	לְפָנָיו	ἐνώπιον αὐτοῦ
59	καὶ οὐκ ἦν	וְאֵין	καὶ οὐκ ἦν
60	ὁ (ἐξαιρούμενος)	מַצִּיל	ὁ ῥυόμενος
61	ἐκ χειρὸς αὐτοῦ	מִיָּדוֹ	ἐκ τῶν χειρῶν αὐτοῦ
62	καὶ ἐποίησε	וְעָשָׂה	καὶ ἐποίει
63	κατὰ	כְּ	ὡς
64	τὸ θέλημα αὐτοῦ	רְצֹנוֹ	ἤθελεν
65	καὶ ἐμεγαλύνθη	וְהִגְדִּיל	καὶ ὑψώθη
	8:5	8:5	8:5
66	καὶ ἐγὼ	וַאֲנִי	καὶ ἐγὼ
67	ἤμην	הָיִיתִי	
68	(συνίων)	מֵבִין	διενοούμην
69	καὶ ἰδοὺ	וְהִנֵּה	καὶ ἰδοὺ
70	τράγος	צְפִיר־	τράγος
71	αἰγῶν	הָעִזִּים	αἰγῶν
72	ἤρχετο	בָּא	ἤρχετο
73	ἀπὸ	מִן־	ἀπὸ
74	(λιβὸς)	הַמַּעֲרָב	δυσμῶν
75	ἐπὶ	עַל־	ἐπὶ
76	πρόσωπον	פְּנֵי	προσώπου
77	πάσης	כָל־	- -
78	τῆς γῆς	הָאָרֶץ	τῆς γῆς
79	καὶ οὐκ ἦν	וְאֵין	καὶ οὐχ
80	ἁπτόμενος	נוֹגֵעַ	ἥπτετο
81	τῆς γῆς	בָּאָרֶץ	τῆς γῆς
82	καὶ τῷ τράγῳ	וְהַצָּפִיר	καὶ ἦν τοῦ τράγου
83	κέρας	קֶרֶן	κέρας
84	- -	חָזוּת	ἓν
85	ἀνὰ μέσον	בֵּין	ἀνὰ μέσον
86	τῶν ὀφθαλμῶν	עֵינָיו	τῶν ὀφθαλμῶν[1]
	8:6	8:6	8:6
87	καὶ ἦλθεν	וַיָּבֹא	καὶ ἦλθεν

Chapter 8:1-10

88	ἕως	עַד־		ἐπὶ
89	τοῦ κριοῦ	הָאַיִל		τὸν κριὸν
90	τοῦ τὰ κέρατα ἔχοντος	בַּעַל הַקְּרָנַיִם		τὸν τὰ κέρατα ἔχοντα
91	οὗ	אֲשֶׁר		ὃν
92	εἶδον	רָאִיתִי		εἶδον
93	ἑστῶτος	עֹמֵד		ἑστῶτα
94	ἐνώπιον	לִפְנֵי		πρὸς
95	τοῦ (Ουβαλ)	הָאֻבָל		τῇ πύλῃ
96	καὶ ἔδραμε	וַיָּרָץ		καὶ ἔδραμεν
97	πρὸς αὐτὸν	אֵלָיו		πρὸς αὐτὸν
98	ἐν (ὁρμῇ)	בַּחֲמַת		ἐν θυμῷ
99	τῆς ἰσχύος αὐτοῦ	כֹּחוֹ		ὀργῆς
	8:7		8:7	8:7
100	καὶ εἶδον αὐτὸν	וּרְאִיתִיו		καὶ εἶδον αὐτὸν
101	(φθάνοντα)	מַגִּיעַ		προσάγοντα
102	ἕως	אֵצֶל		πρὸς
103	τοῦ κριοῦ	הָאַיִל		τὸν κριόν
104	καὶ (ἐξηγριάνθη)	וַיִּתְמַרְמַר		καὶ ἐθυμώθη
105	πρὸς αὐτὸν	אֵלָיו		ἐπ' αὐτὸν
106	καὶ (ἔπαισε)	וַיַּךְ		καὶ ἐπάταξεν
107	τὸν κριὸν	אֶת־הָאַיִל		- -
108	καὶ συνέτριψεν	וַיְשַׁבֵּר		καὶ συνέτριψεν
109	—	אֶת־		τὰ
110	(ἀμφότερα)	שְׁתֵּי		δύο
111	τὰ κέρατα αὐτοῦ	קְרָנָיו		κέρατα αὐτοῦ
112	καὶ οὐκ	וְלֹא־		καὶ οὐκέτι
113	ἦν	הָיָה		ἦν
114	ἰσχὺς	כֹחַ		²ἐν τῷ κριῷ
115	ἐν τῷ κριῷ	בָּאַיִל		ἰσχὺς
116	τοῦ στῆναι	לַעֲמֹד		στῆναι
117	ἐνώπιον αὐτοῦ	לְפָנָיו		κατέναντι τοῦ

				τράγου
118	καὶ ἔρριψεν αὐτὸν		וַיַּשְׁלִיכֵהוּ	καὶ ἐσπάραξεν αὐτὸν
119	ἐπὶ τὴν γῆν		אָרְצָה	ἐπὶ τὴν γῆν
120	καὶ (συνεπάτησεν) αὐτόν		וַיִּרְמְסֵהוּ	καὶ συνέτριψεν αὐτόν
121	καὶ οὐκ		וְלֹא־	καὶ οὐκ
122	ἦν		הָיָה	ἦν
123	ὁ ἐξαιρούμενος		מַצִּיל	ὁ ῥυόμενος
124	τὸν κριὸν		לָאַיִל	τὸν κριὸν
125	ἐκ		מִ	ἀπὸ
126	χειρὸς αὐτοῦ		יָדוֹ	τοῦ τράγου
	8:8	8:8		8:8
127	καὶ ὁ τράγος		וּצְפִיר	καὶ ὁ τράγος
128	τῶν αἰγῶν		הָעִזִּים	τῶν αἰγῶν
129	(ἐμεγαλύνθη)		הִגְדִּיל	κατίσχυσε
130	ἕως		עַד־	
131	σφόδρα		מְאֹד	σφόδρα
132	καὶ ἐν		וּכְ	καὶ ὅτε
133	(τῷ ἰσχῦσαι αὐτὸν)		עָצְמוֹ	κατίσχυσε
134	συνετρίβη		נִשְׁבְּרָה	συνετρίβη
135	τὸ κέρας		הַקֶּרֶן	αὐτοῦ τὸ κέρας
136	τὸ μέγα		הַגְּדוֹלָה	τὸ μέγα
137	καὶ ἀνέβη		וַתַּעֲלֶנָה	καὶ ἀνέβη
138	- -		חָזוּת	ἕτερα
139	κέρατα τέσσαρα		אַרְבַּע	τέσσαρα κέρατα
140	ὑποκάτω αὐτοῦ		תַּחְתֶּיהָ	κατόπισθεν αὐτοῦ
141	εἰς τοὺς τέσσαρας		לְאַרְבַּע	εἰς τοὺς τέσσαρας
142	ἀνέμους		רוּחוֹת	ἀνέμους
143	τοῦ οὐρανοῦ		הַשָּׁמָיִם	τοῦ οὐρανοῦ
	8:9	8:9		8:9
144	καὶ ἐκ		וּמִן־	καὶ ἐξ

Chapter 8:1-10

145	τοῦ	הָ	
146	ἑνὸς	אַחַת	ἑνὸς
147	αὐτῶν	מֵהֶם	αὐτῶν
148	ἐξῆλθε	יָצָא	ἀνεφύη
149	κέρας	קֶרֶן	κέρας
150	ἓν	אַחַת	ἰσχυρὸν
151	ἰσχυρὸν	מִצְּעִירָה	ἓν
152	καὶ (ἐμεγαλύνθη)	וַ‏תִּגְדַּל־	καὶ κατίσχυσε
153	(περισσῶς)	יֶתֶר	καὶ ἐπάταξεν
154	πρὸς	אֶל־	ἐπὶ
155	τὸν νότον	הַנֶּגֶב	μεσημβρίαν
156	- -	וְאֶל־	καὶ ἐπ'
157	- -	הַמִּזְרָח	ἀνατολὰς
158	καὶ	וְ	καὶ
159	πρὸς	אֶל־	ἐπὶ
160	(τὴν δύναμιν)	הַצֶּבִי	βορρᾶν
	8:10	8:10	8:10
161	(ἐμεγαλύνθη)	וַ‏תִּגְדַּל	καὶ ὑψώθη
162	ἕως	עַד־	ἕως
163	τῆς (δυνάμεως)	צְבָא	τῶν ἀστέρων
164	τοῦ οὐρανοῦ	הַשָּׁמָיִם	τοῦ οὐρανοῦ
165	καὶ ἔπεσεν	וַ‏תַּפֵּל	καὶ ἐρράχθη
166	ἐπὶ τὴν γῆν	אַרְצָה	ἐπὶ τὴν γῆν
167	ἀπὸ	מִן־	ἀπὸ
168	τῆς (δυνάμεως) τοῦ οὐρανοῦ	הַצָּבָא	τῶν ἄστρων
169	καὶ ἀπὸ	וּמִן־	καὶ ἀπὸ
170	τῶν ἄστρων	הַכּוֹכָבִים	αὐτῶν
171	καὶ συνεπάτησεν αὐτά	וַ‏יִּרְמְסֵם	κατεπατήθη

V.1. Textual Notes

1. ὀφθαλμῶν] > αὐτοῦ 88-Syh=MT
2. ἰσχὺς ἐν τῷ κριῷ] 2,3,4,1 88-Syh=MT

V.2. The Relationship Between OG and Th

Jeansonne has divided the text into 171 readings ("judgeable units"). According to her findings, in 69 readings (40%) Th has retained OG, and in an additional 30 (18%), Th is dependent upon OG. On this basis she concludes,

> This sampling of readings confirms that θ' [Th] is indeed a recension of the OG since a total of 58% of the readings show the OG influence on θ'. In 72, or 42%, the θ' readings are distinct, revised in the interest of already well-known principles, that is, grammatical fidelity to M and standardization of word equivalencies.[2]

There are two discrepancies between Jeansonne's statistics and the text above. First, it is not always clear from her notes and discussion what Th readings she considers to be dependent upon OG. Thus, there are only 28 readings that have been double underlined, and many of these are my guesses of what Jeansonne intends to represent as Th dependence on OG. Second, Jeansonne has omitted τοῦ οὐρανοῦ from l. 168 of Th.[3]

---

[2] Jeansonne, 57.

[3] Another misprint is ראראה for ואראה in l. 30 (8:3).

As to Jeansonne's analysis of the relationship between Th and OG, many points can be disputed. In the following we will look at each verse individually and consider the following aspects of relationship: 1) Cases where Jeansonne asserts Th retains OG; 2) Cases where Jeansonne suggests that Th is dependent upon the reading of OG; 3) Evidence of Th independence. We will find that in many cases OG and Th exhibit verbal agreement, but the Greek translation equivalent is the SE for the whole LXX. We assume that the reader is knowledgeable of the really obvious agreements (eg. ὁράω=ראה, εἰς=אחד) in order to avoid producing endless (and rather pointless) statistics.

V. 1

Th retains OG (4x)-The equivalents in l. 6, 7, 8 are common LXX equivalents and are of no significance in determining whether Th is a revision. Jeansonne, 49, suggests that Th's retention of the spelling βαλτασαρ in l. 3 is good evidence that Th is a recension, because we would expect a more precise transliteration for בלאשצר. Although Jeansonne's argument has some merit, one cannot build a case on the translation of proper names, especially when they would be so prone to harmonization during the course of transmission.[4] This cannot be classified as a distinctive agreement.

Th dependent upon OG (5x)-In all 5 cases (l. 1, 2, 4, 5, 10) Jeansonne marks these lines with a "b" to indicate that Th "alters the grammatical forms and style of the OG to mirror more closely its *Vorlage*."[5] If Jeansonne does intend to suggest that Th is dependent upon OG in these 5 cases, it is a surprising claim indeed. Th does exhibit a formal equivalence to MT, but that hardly requires that Th revised OG. Why

---

[4] The same spelling is found in 1:7, see 1:1-10.

[5] Jeansonne, 33.

should Th be dependent upon OG for such obvious equivalents as ב/ἐν, שנת/ἔτει, שלוש/τρίτῳ, למלכות/τῆς βασιλείας, חזון/ὅρασις, etc.?

Independent Th readings (2x)-None of Th's translation in v. 1, apart from the possible exception of Βαλτασαρ, requires that Th had any knowledge of OG. Th's independence is suggested by the reading in 1. 9 where he renders the difficult Hebrew with a participle[6] and by the choice of ἀρχήν in 1. 11, but neither of these is particularly distinctive.[7]

V. 2

Th retains OG (2x)-Th shares the OG reading in 1. 17 and 20. The first is for the city, Susa, and is therefore expected and insignificant. The second is more important because OG and Th not only have a verbal agreement (ἐστιν ἐν χώρᾳ), but also follow the same word order against MT "which is in the province of Elumaidi/Ailam."[8] However, as we saw in the last section, Th employs χώρα as a SE for מדינה (9/9).[9] It is possible that Th is dependent upon OG's word order, but, with the exception of 8:2, מדינה always appears as a construct when designating an area (2:48, 49; 3:1, 12, 30[97]). In those cases Th has χώρα-X and this is the natural order of the Greek, so it would have been quite natural for Th to employ the reading that we have. The immediate differences between OG and Th in 1. 18, 19, 21 also militate against Th dependence.

---

[6] For the use of the article to introduce a relative clause, see *GKC* §138k.

[7] תחלה occurs elsewhere in 9:21, 23 where both OG and Th employ ἀρχή. Jeansonne, 49, states that Th "standardizes ἀρχή 'first' for תחלה," but she does not note that OG has the same reading in the other two places.

[8] The double underline under Αιλαμ is intended, albeit inadequately, to indicate that Jeansonne suggests that Th is dependent on the OG word order.

[9] 2:48, 49; 3:1, 2, 3, 12, 30(97); 11:24.

Chapter 8:1-10   163

Th dependent upon OG (3x)-The fact that Th has the same word order as OG in l. 20-21 was discussed above. It is difficult to be certain, but Jeansonne appears to suggest that Th is dependent upon OG for l. 16 and 24.[10] Once again, the conclusion is hardly warranted. Th, like OG, translates the *Vorlage*, and in the first instance Th had to provide a tense appropriate to the context.

Independent Th readings (1x)-The transliterations in l. 21 and 26, and the correct translations in l. 18, 19, 23, and 25 only demonstrate that Th was more than capable of translating independently. However, any minus in Th against OG, especially one as large as l. 12-15, has to be regarded as a distinctive disagreement. If Th were merely revising OG, then virtually every translation equivalent in OG that can be positively linked to MT should be represented in some way in Th.

V. 3

Th retains OG (8x)-There is definitely no significance for the SE ὁράω=ראה in l. 30, κριός=איל (8/8) in l. 32,[11] and κέρας=קרן in l. 38.[12] The verbal agreement of ὑψηλός=גבה in l. 40, 42, 44 is more significant not only because these are the only places where גבה appears in Daniel, but also because of the forms in l. 42 and 44. ὑψηλός does not appear elsewhere in Th, but OG has it in 4:7(10) (misreading of כנוא?) and 9:15. This might suggest that since OG employs ὑψηλός elsewhere, then Th has borrowed from OG in 8:3. However, as a survey of HR reveals, although the adjective גבה is translated

---

[10] Jeansonne, 50, #14.

[11] 7/8 occurrences of איל are in 8:1-10. 8:3, 4, 6, 7(4), 20.

[12] קרן 23x, but 4x it refers to a musical instrument (3:5, 7, 10, 15). Otherwise κέρας is a SE in OG (18/19) and Th (17/19). OG and Th share an omission in l. 39 which is probably secondary in MT and Th also omits once in 7:20. The remaining passages are 7:7, 8(4), 11, 20, 21, 24; 8:3, 5, 6, 7, 8, 9, 20, 21.

sporadically by various equivalents in the LXX, the main equivalent is ὑψηλός.[13] Therefore, we should not be surprised that Th employs ὑψηλός in 8:3.

Likewise, if we consider the specific forms employed by OG and Th in 1. 42 and 44, there is nothing we would not expect to find if Th were translating independently. The comparative form in 1. 42 is expected for the comparative מן. The substantive in 1. 44 is linked to the verbal agreement in the verbs in 1. 45 as well as to the agreement of the substantives in 1. 41. The verb עלה in 1. 45 only occurs outside of 8:3 in 8:8 and 11:23. In all cases Th reads ἀναβαίνω because it is the SE throughout the LXX.[14] The expression in 1. 41 (καὶ τὸ ἓν for והאחת), like that in 1. 44, is a formal equivalent for MT. All of the vocabulary agreements shared by OG and Th are the SE that are found throughout the LXX, and in every case the texts exhibit formal equivalence to MT. It is unlikely that OG and Th could have such extensive agreement in 1. 40-45 independently, but Th dependence on OG cannot be assumed either.

Th dependent upon OG (3x)-If Jeansonne intended to identify 1. 33, 34, 37 as dependent upon OG, we must question the basis for such a judgment.[15] There is nothing about OG's reading that is presupposed by Th, unless one has already prejudged that Th is revising.

Independent Th readings (0x)-Throughout the verse Th merely exhibits formal equivalence to MT, and there is no Th reading that is a

---

[13] For example, the adjective נבה is rendered by the singular equivalents ἕξις in 1 Kgdms 16:7; μετέωρος in Isa 5:15; ὑπερήφανος in Ps 101(100):5; ὑπεροχή in 1 Kgdms 2:3. Otherwise the adjective נבה is rendered 27x by ὑψηλός outside of Daniel from Genesis (eg. 7:17) to Ezekiel (eg. 40:2).

[14] In 11:23 OG has evidently read the preposition על because it translates with ἐπί.

[15] We should note that 4QDanᵃ and 4QDanᵇ read גדול with 967, but that is not evidence that Th is revising OG. It only demonstrates that their *Vorlagen* were different.

distinctive disagreement against OG. For example, Th employs various but appropriate equivalents for נשא.[16]

V. 4

Th retains OG (9x)-7 of the 9 agreements are well established formal SE and do not require comment. The participle in l. 49 from κερατίζω (1-11) is a common reading, but κερατίζω is the SE (9/11) for נגח in the LXX;[17] therefore, the lexical equivalence is of no consequence. It may be significant that both OG and Th employ a participle, but it does correspond to MT. The other reading of possible significance is in l. 59. However, as in l. 80 below, Th always renders the particle of negation with οὐκ + a third person form of εἰμί.[18]

Th is dependent upon OG (4x)-In all 4 cases Th provides the expected formal equivalence to MT. For example, רצון occurs 4x in MT and Th employs θέλημα 4/4.[19] Th even has a future for the imperfect verb in MT in l. 57 where the aorist (see OG) would have been appropriate.

Independent Th readings (1x)-Once again Th's translation exhibits formal correspondence to MT in this verse. The equivalence μεγαλύνω= גדל (hiphil, also l. 129, 152, 161) might be regarded as a distinctive disagreement because Th employs it as a SE (7/8), whereas OG never

---

[16] Also 1:16; 2:35; 10:5; 11:12, 14. Only in 1:16 (ἀναιρέω) and 11:12 (λαμβάνω) do OG and Th have verbal agreement.

[17] נגח also appears in Exod 21:28, 31(2), 32; Deut 33:17; 3 Kgdms 22:11; Ps 44(43):5; Ezek 34:21; Dan 11:40; 2 Chr 18:10. נגח is not translated once in Exod 21:31 where it is redundant, but OG and Th both have συγκερατίζω in 11:40 which is a distinctive agreement (HL in LXX!).

[18] See 1:4; 8:27; 9:26; 10:21; 11:15, 16, 45. Th usually has οὐκ ἔστιν. OG often renders similarly to Th, but omits in 1:4, has οὐκ in 8:5, οὐδεὶς ἦν in 8:27 and οὐθεὶς ἦν in 10:21.

[19] OG renders with a verb again in 11:3, while it has θέλημα in 11:16, 36.

makes this equivalence. In fact, OG only employs μεγαλύνω once in 2:48 for רבה.[20]

V. 5

Th retains OG (13x)-Each of these verbal agreements is the expected SE that is employed throughout the LXX.[21] However, בין=ἀνὰ μέσον requires some comment, because O'Connell and Bodine suggest it is a *kaige* characteristic. בין appears 4x in MT and in each case OG and Th employ ἀνὰ μέσον.[22] This "characteristic" is nothing more than an expected Greek equivalent.[23]

Th is dependent upon OG (3x)-The equivalents in l. 79 and 82 were discussed previously under vv. 3 and 4 respectively. The participle of ἅπτω is both a formal equivalent for MT and the SE for נגע throughout the LXX. See the discussion of l. 101 under *Independent Th readings* in v. 7.

Independent Th readings (2x)-In the discussion of wisdom vocabulary in 1:1-10 we have seen that Th employed his own pattern of equivalents for MT. That conclusion is supported by the OG and Th renderings for the

---

[20] OG's main equivalent is ὑψόω (8:4, 10, 25; 11:36, 37). In 8:8, 9 OG employs κατισχύω as a dynamic equivalent. OG and Th share a distinctive agreement in 8:11 where both have ῥύομαι. 8:11-14 is similar to 9:24-27 in that the OG text is significantly different from MT. The difference is that in 8:11-14 Th follows OG very closely. For a detailed discussion and attempt to resolve the problem see, David, 357-380. Bogaert ("Relecture," 207-210), also argues for an alternative *Vorlage* and, based on the TT elsewhere in OG and Th, that conclusion is justified.

[21] The only exception to this statement is τράγος=צפיר "he-goat," because τράγος is not employed for the only other occurrences of צפיר in 2 Chr 29:21; Ezra 8:5. However, τράγος is the exact equivalent, and the choice is also determined by the fact that צפיר is collocated with עז whose SE is αἴξ.

[22] 8:5, 6, 21; 11:45.

[23] See also Greenspoon, *Joshua*, 301-302; Gentry, 407.

Chapter 8:1-10   167

verb בין (usually hiphil) in l. 68. Th employs συνίημι as a SE (16/22), while OG prefers διανοέομαι (11/22).[24] In l. 74 Th employs λίψ (HL in Daniel) for מערב (HL in Daniel), while OG exhibits lexical levelling by choosing the same equivalent (δυσμή) that he did in v. 4 for ימה.[25]

V. 6

Th retains OG (4x)-The readings in l. 87, 92, 96, 97 are expected equivalents. For example, רוץ in l. 96 is a HL in Daniel, but the SE (57/64) throughout the LXX is τρέχω (the common aorist forms are from √δράμω).

Th dependent upon OG (3x)-The equivalence in l. 89 is obvious and has been discussed above. Similarly, the lexical equivalence in l. 93 and the perfect participle is expected.[26]

In l. 90 Th appears to be dependent upon OG because of the use of the participle from ἔχω. Th employs ἔχω 8x and in 5 cases he shares a reading with OG.[27] There are also two similar readings to l. 90 in 8:17, 20. In 8:17a there is exact verbal agreement between OG and Th,

---

[24] 1:4, 17; 8:5, 16, 17, 23, 27; 9:2, 22, 23(2); 10:1, 11, 12, 14; 11:30, 33, 37(2); 12:8, 10(2). Th has συνετίζω in 8:16; 9:22; 10:14, ἐννοέω once in 9:23 (see OG in 11:33) as a stylistic variant and his use of διανοέομαι is in 1:4. In 10:1 Th omits by homoioarchton. OG has σύνεσις in 1:17, προνοέω 11:37(2), ὑποδείκνω in 10:14, συνίημι in 11:33 (with Th!), προσέχω in 12:10, and σοφός in 1:4. In three cases OG has textual differences: omission in 8:16 and 9:23; προσῆλθεν (reading ויבא) in 9:22.

[25] OG also has δυσμή in 6:15(14) where MT=0.

[26] Th employs the perfect participle of ἵστημι 7x in Daniel and only on one occasion do OG and Th have a common form, 12:1. The other passages are 2:31; 7:16; 8:3; 10:16; 11:16.

[27] Th has ἔχω in 3:15, 16; 4:8; 8:6, 17, 20; 10:4, 16. Recall from the previous discussion of 3:11-20 that there is no way to determine the direction of dependence in 3:15, 16.

but the use of ἔχω for אצל is a fairly common practice in the LXX.²⁸ However, MT also has בעל הקרנין in 8:20, which OG renders with the same equivalent as l. 90; whereas Th has ὁ ἔχων τὰ κέρατα. Montgomery, 332, notes that the syntagm בעל הכנפים appears in Eccl 10:20 and Rahlfs' text reads ὁ ἔχων τὰς πτέρυγας as the translation. The fact that Th follows Eccl 10:20 (see also the apparatus for 7:13[12]) in 8:20 is evidence that he has independent knowledge of how to translate בעל הקרנין. Therefore, Th's agreement with OG in l. 90 is surprising. It may be that Th has borrowed from OG in l. 90, but the independent translation in 8:20 suggests that the agreement is due to textual corruption.

Independent Th readings (2x)-It was noted in the discussion of 3:11-20 that ὁρμῇ (1-11) for חמה in Th l. 98 is distinctive, though it could be an error for ὀργῇ.²⁹ Another example of Th's independence is the fact that he chooses to transliterate in l. 95 rather than employ OG's translation.

V. 7

Th retains OG (11x)-The equivalents in l. 100, 109, 111, 113-115, 119, 121, 122, and 124 exhibit formal correspondence to MT using the standard equivalents employed in the LXX. συντρίβω=שבר is also the SE for the LXX. Th has it 8/8 whereas OG employs it 5/8.³⁰

---

²⁸ See, for example, Neh 2:6, 3:23; Mic 1:11; Ezek 1:15, 19.

²⁹ See also Ezek 3:14 for the same equivalence, though Montgomery, 332, regards it as an error.

³⁰ 8:7, 8, 22, 25; 11:4, 20, 22, 26. OG has the dynamic rendering ἀποδίδωμι in 8:25; a textual problem in 11:22; and ἀποστρέφω (reading ישיבהו 3 singular imperfect + 3 masculine singular suffix from שיב) in 11:26.

Chapter 8:1-10

Th dependent upon OG (2x)-Both 1. 103 and 116 are expected equivalents.

Independent Th readings (5x)-The normal SE for נגע is ἅπτω, but Th has φθάνω in l. 101. Th makes the same equivalence in 12:12, and these must be regarded as distinctive because OG does not employ φθάνω at all.[31] In the discussion of vocabulary for wrath/anger in 3:11-20 we noted that ἐξαγριαίνω in l. 104 is a HL in the LXX, and this also must be regarded as a distinctive disagreement. The reading in l. 106 should also be considered a distinctive disagreement. This is the only occurrence of נכה in MT and the equivalents chosen by OG (πατάσσω) and Th (παίω, HL) are both employed as SE in the LXX. However, παίω is found only 26x compared with πατάσσω, which appears about 400x. If Th were revising OG we would expect him to have retained πατάσσω. The fourth distinctive Th reading is in l. 110 where Th renders שתי more dynamically with ἀμφότερα, as opposed to OG, which has the formal equivalent δύο. The same difference in equivalents is found in 11:27 (OG never has ἀμφότερος). Finally, Th's choice of συμπατέω (6-11, never in OG) for רמס "trample" 2/2 in l. 120 and l. 171 should also be considered distinctive because Th has obviously employed his own vocabulary.[32]

V. 8

---

[31] נגע appears in 8:5, 7, 18; 9:21; 10:10, 16, 18; 12:12. OG has προσάγω in 8:7; 9:21 and συνάπτω (συνάγω?) in 12:12. Other than the mentioned differences, both OG and Th have ἅπτω.
  Th also employs φθάνω as a SE (8/8) for מתא. See 4:8(11), 17(20), 19(22), 21(24), 25(28); 6:25(24); 7:13, 22.

[32] The equivalence συμπατέω=רמס is made earlier in 3 Kgdms 7:17, 20; 9:33; 14:9; Nah 3:14. Th also has συμπατέω in 7:7, 19 (רפס); 7:23 (רוש); 8:13 (מרמס).

Th retains OG (9x)-All 9 equivalents correspond to MT and usual usage in the LXX, and most have already been discussed previously. Two of the equivalents that have not been mentioned are in l. 131 and 136. מאד appears only in l. 131 and 11:25, and in both cases OG and Th read σφόδρα (see HR). גדול appears 15x and Th renders with μέγας (13/15).[33] In two instances he employs πολύς (11:28, 44), which is reserved primarily for שׂגיא in chapters 2-7 (11/12)[34] and רב in the Hebrew sections.

Th dependent upon OG (2x)-The reading in l. 135 is expected. Both OG and Th read a plus, κέρατα in l. 139. It is most likely that OG and Th had קרנים in their *Vorlage*.[35]

Independent Th readings (2x)-It is possible that we should consider the reading in l. 133 as distinctive. This is suggested not so much by this particular reading, as Th merely gives a formal equivalent, but by Th's translation of עצם in Daniel. In 8:24 Th has κραταιός where OG employs a dynamic equivalent, and in 11:23 Th employs ὑπερισχύω where OG has ἰσχυρός. The reading in l. 129 is also a possible distinctive disagreement (see the discussion in 8:4). καὶ ἐν in l. 132 is not mentioned as a distinctive reading because Th has probably read וב for כו. Therefore, Th was just producing a formal equivalent for what he read in the *Vorlage*.

V. 9

---

[33] 8:8, 21; 9:4, 12; 10:1, 4, 7, 8; 11:2, 13, 25(2), 28, 44; 12:1. OG has ἰσχυρός in 10:1, 7; 11:25, 44; πολύς in 11:13, 25, 28; μέγας elsewhere.

[34] 2:6, 12, 48; 4:7(10), 9(12), 18(21); 5:9; 6:15(14), 24(23); 7:5, 28. Both OG and Th omit in 2:31.

[35] Contrast Jeansonne, 54, who states that either "horn" was in the *Vorlage* or it "could represent an expansion in the OG retained inadvertently by θ'." This statement is typical of Jeansonne's analysis in that she has assumed that Th is a recension without subjecting the agreements to careful examination.

Chapter 8:1-10   171

Th retains OG (5x)-Th exhibits the expected formal correspondence to MT in all 5 cases (l. 144, 146, 147, 149, 158).

Th dependent upon OG (2x)-The reading ἕν for אחת is expected. However, the reading in l. 151 is probably a distinctive agreement, though it is possible that OG and Th reflect a textual variant. As Jeansonne, 55, points out, OG and Th appear to be translating a form of עצום "mighty" in l. 151 for צמירה "strong." The reading of the Greek versions does make sense in the context. If it is a distinctive agreement, there is no way to determine the direction of dependence.

Independent Th readings (3x)-OG provides a dynamic equivalent for יתר in l. 153. Th's use of the adverb correctly interprets the adverbial construction in MT. περισσῶς in Th should also be considered distinctive. Th has περισσῶς 4-7[36] in the LXX, and it is not found in OG. The meaning of MT in l. 160 appears to be "beautiful land."[37] The text (צבי) presented problems for both OG and Th. OG reads βορρᾶν as if MT had צפונה (see l. 51). The reading may have been unintentional, but OG was probably puzzled by MT and assumed a scribal error had been committed. For this reason, OG seems to have guessed that another direction was intended. Th reads הצבא (see l. 163), but it should be considered a distinctive reading because he has also omitted l. 156-157.[38] If Th were following OG, there would not have been so great a divergence. The reading in l. 152 is possibly distinctive (see 8:4).

V. 10

---

[36] Also 7:7(2), 19.

[37] See Montgomery, 339 for discussion.

[38] That Th is translating independently is supported by the other three occurrences of צבי in MT. Th transliterates in 11:16, 41, 45 whereas OG omits in 11:41 and has θέλησις in 11:16, 45.

Th dependent upon OG (5x)-All five readings are expected equivalents for MT (l. 162, 164, 166, 167, 169).

Independent Th readings (3x)-Th's choice of συμπατέω in l. 171 has already been discussed in v. 7. OG identifies צבא with the "heavenly host" in l. 163, 168, whereas Th renders with δύναμις 3/4. OG and Th do have a shared reading in 8:11 (ἀρχιστράτηγος=הצבא שר), but the rendering is the SE for שר צבא in other books of the LXX.[39] The reading of ἐμεγαλύνθη in l. 161 is possibly distinctive as well (see 8:4). The addition of τοῦ οὐρανοῦ in l. 168 is probably based on an alternative *Vorlage*, so it would not count as a distinctive disagreement.

V.3. *Summary*

An analysis of the texts of OG and Th in 8:1-10 reveals how important it is to be precise in the choice of terminology. Jeansonne asserts that there are 69 readings where Th retains OG and 30 readings where Th is dependent upon OG. Neither of these statistics can be considered accurate. The fact that OG and Th have 69 common readings does not oblige us to conclude that Th has "retained" OG. Such an assessment requires that a significant number of distinctive agreements exist between the two texts and that there is evidence to prove the direction of borrowing. Such evidence is wanting in 8:1-10. There are only three probable distinctive agreements (ἰσχυρός=צעיר l. 151; l. 39-44; τοῦ τὰ κέρατα ἔχοντος l. 90) in the reconstructed texts of 8:1-10. As to the 30 dependent readings, it is hard to know what 30 Jeansonne believes are dependent upon OG, because dependence assumes that Th somehow had to rely upon OG for his choice of equivalents. In order to hold such a view we would have to assume that Th was incompetent

---

[39] OG and Th omit in 8:12. OG seems to offer guesses for צבע in 8:13 and 10:1 (ἐρημόω, πλῆθος confusion from Aramaic צבא).

Chapter 8:1-10   173

to translate without reference to OG. As we have seen throughout this passage, indeed in all the passages we have examined, Th was more than competent as a translator. Th adopted a method of formal equivalence in his translation and was quite consistent in his choice of equivalents. Where available, Th normally chose those equivalents that were employed as SE in the other books of the LXX. Therefore, without strong distinctive agreements and proof of the direction of borrowing, there is no statistical significance when OG and Th agree in the translation of common vocabulary. Besides the three agreements mentioned above, there are only three other possible distinctive agreements in 8:1-10 (βαλτασαρ l. 3; ἐστιν ἐν χωρᾳ l. 20; καὶ οὐκ ἦν l. 59). We have already seen that these three are all exceedingly weak as evidence that Th has borrowed from OG.

Let us examine the first three agreements again. The best evidence for Th dependence on OG is ἰσχυρός=צעיר in l. 151. As Jeansonne states, it is possible that OG and Th had עצום in their *Vorlage*, but her other suggestion that "it is possible that the concern of θ' with word order in this case caused the translator not to notice the sense" is gratuitous.[40] Th does not follow OG when OG does not know MT. This has been evident throughout our investigation and is demonstrated by the omission of חזות in l. 84, 138; the transliterations in l. 21, 95; and the attempt to translate צבי in l. 160. If עצום was not in their *Vorlagen*, then it is more probable that one text is corrupt. There also seems to be a relationship between OG and Th in l. 40-45 and l. 90, but in neither case is it certain. Regarding l. 90 we have seen that Th follows the form of Eccl 10:20 in 8:20. Therefore, the fact that Th agrees with OG in l. 90 could indicate that Th has been corrected toward OG. Finally, there is extensive agreement in l. 40-45, but it is agreement that exhibits formal correspondence to MT. In conclusion,

---

[40] Jeansonne, 55.

there are three distinctive agreements between OG and Th, but in no case is it certain that Th actually borrows from OG.

On the other hand, the evidence that Th is translating independently is strong. Not only does Th offer a formal translation of MT, but we have found 11 cases of distinctive disagreements in Th (l. 12-15, 68, 74, 98, 101, 104, 106, 110, 120/171, 153, 160, 163/168) along with another 4 possible distinctive readings (l. 9, 11, 65/129/152/161, 133). These distinctive readings are not merely cases where Th does not agree with OG. They underscore instances where Th employs translations that have no connection with OG. At the same time, these distinctive readings are part of Th's well-established pattern of formal correspondence to MT.

In conclusion, there is only one possible conclusion. There is no sense in which we can refer to Th as a revision of OG in this passage. In fact, there is virtually no evidence in 8:1-10 that Th had knowledge of OG at the time of translation. Given the paucity of textual witnesses to OG it is possible (probable?) that in some of the cases where OG and Th have verbal agreement Th readings have actually displaced the OG. However, we do not have enough textual witnesses to prove this last suggestion.

Chapter VI
Daniel 12:1-13

The OG text of chapter 12 is unlike the sections that we have considered previously because it has more textual differences, particularly additions, when compared to MT. For our purposes, however, a comparison of the texts of OG and Th provides important indicators of the secondary revision and corruption of OG. The textual differences between OG and Th will be discussed initially under the rubric of *Syntax*.

Table 5

The OG and Th Versions of Daniel

	12:1 Th	12:1 MT	12:1 OG
1	καὶ ἐν τῷ ᴸκαιρῷ	ובעת	καὶ κατὰ τὴν ᴸὥραν
2	ἐκείνῳ	ההיא	ἐκείνην
3	ἀναστήσεται Μιχαηλ	יעמד מיכאל	ᴸπαρελεύσεται Μιχαηλ
4	ὁ ᴸ(ἄρχων) ὁ μέγας	השר הגדול	ὁ ἄγγελος ὁ μέγας
5	ὁ ἑστηκὼς	העמד	ὁ ἑστηκὼς
6	ἐπὶ τοὺς υἱοὺς	על־בני	ἐπὶ τοὺς υἱοὺς
7	τοῦ λαοῦ σου	עמך	τοῦ λαοῦ σου
8	καὶ ἔσται	והיתה	ˢᴸἐκείνῃ
9	ᴸκαιρὸς θλίψεως	עת צרה	ἡ ᴸἡμέρα θλίψεως
10	ˢοἵα οὐ γέγονεν	אשר לא־נהיתה	ˢοἵα οὐκ ἐγενήθη
11	ἀφ' οὗ γεγένηται	מהיות	ἀφ' οὗ ἐγενήθησαν^M
12	ἔθνος	גוי	– –
13	ἕως	עד	ἕως
14	τοῦ ᴸκαιροῦ ἐκείνου	העת ההיא	τῆς ᴸἡμέρας ἐκείνης

Chapter 12:1-13

15	καὶ ἐν τῷ	בָּעֵת	καὶ ἐν ἐκείνῃ
16	ᴸκαιρῷ ἐκείνῳ	הַהִיא	τῇ ᴸἡμέρᾳ
17	ᴸσωθήσεται	יִמָּלֵט	ᴸὑψωθήσεται[1]
18	ὁ λαός σου	עַמְּךָ	ˢπᾶς ὁ λαός[M]
19	πᾶς ὁ ᴸ(- -)	כָּל־הַנִּמְצָא	ὃς ἂν εὑρεθῇ
20	γεγραμμένος	כָּתוּב	ἐγγεγραμμένος
21	ἐν τῷ βιβλίῳ	בַּסֵּפֶר	ἐν τῷ βιβλίῳ
	12:2		12:2
22	καὶ πολλοὶ	וְרַבִּים	καὶ πολλοὶ
23	-τῶν ᴸκαθευδόντων	מִיְּשֵׁנֵי	τῶν ᴸκαθευδόντων
24	ἐν γῆς ᴸ(χώματι)	אַדְמַת־עָפָר	ἐν τῷ ᴸπλάτει τῆς γῆς
25	ᴸἐξεγερθήσονται	יָקִיצוּ	ᴸἀναστήσονται
26	οὗτοι εἰς ζωὴν	אֵלֶּה לְחַיֵּי	ˢοἱ μὲν εἰς ζωὴν
27	αἰώνιον	עוֹלָם	αἰώνιον
28	καὶ οὗτοι	וְאֵלֶּה	οἱ δὲ
29	εἰς ὀνειδισμὸν	לַחֲרָפוֹת	εἰς ᴸὀνειδισμὸν
30	καὶ εἰς αἰσχύνην	לְדִרְאוֹן	οἱ δὲ εἰς ᴸδιασποράν

178   The OG and Th Versions of Daniel

31	αἰώνιον	עולם	[καὶ ᴸ²αἰσχύνην] αἰώνιον	
	12:3		12:3	
32	καὶ οἱ ᴸσυνιέντες	והמשכלים	καὶ οἱ ᴸσυνιέντες	
33	ᴸ(ἐκλάμψουσιν)	יזהרו	ᴸφανοῦσιν	
34	ὡς ἡ λαμπρότης	כזהר	ὡς ³οἱ ᴸφωστῆρες	
35	τοῦ ᴸστερεώματος	הרקיע	τοῦ ᴸοὐρανοῦ	
36	καὶ ᴹἀπὸ τῶν δικαίων	ומצדיקי	ˢκαὶ οἱ κατίσχοντες	
37	τῶν πολλῶν	הרבים	τοὺς λόγους μου ᴹ	
38	ὡς οἱ ἀστέρες	ככוכבים	ὡσεὶ τὰ ἄστρα	
39			+ˢτοῦ οὐρανοῦ	
40	εἰς τοὺς αἰῶνας	לעולם	εἰς τὸν αἰῶνα	
41	καὶ ᴸ(ἔτι)	ועד	τοῦ αἰῶνος	
	12:4		12:4	
42	καὶ σὺ Δανιηλ	ואתה דניאל	καὶ σὺ Δανιηλ	
43	ᴸἔμφραξον	סתם	ᴸκάλυψον	
44	τοὺς ᴸλόγους	הדברים	τὰ ᴸπροστάγματα	
45	καὶ ᴸσφράγισον	וחתם	καὶ ᴸσφράγισον	

Chapter 12:1-13

46	τὸ βιβλίον	הספר	τὸ βιβλίον
47	ἕως ᴸκαιροῦ	עד עת	ἕως ᴸκαιροῦ
48	ᴸσυντελείας	קץ	ᴸσυντελείας
49	ἕως ᴸ(διδαχθῶσιν)	ישטטו	ἕως ἂν ᴸἀπομανῶσιν⁴
50	πολλοί	ותרבה	πολλοί
51	καὶ ᴸπληθυνθῇ	הדעת	καὶ ᴸπληθῇ
52	ἡ ᴸγνῶσις		+ἡ γῆ+ ᴸἀδικίας
	12:5	12:5	12:5
53	καὶ εἶδον ἐγὼ Δανιηλ	וראיתי אני דניאל	καὶ εἶδον ἐγὼ Δανιηλ
54	καὶ ἰδού	והנה	καὶ ἰδού
55	δύο ἕτεροι	שנים אחרים	δύο ἕτεροι
56	ᴸεἱστήκεισαν	עמדים	ᴸἑστήκεισαν
57	εἷς (ˢἐντεῦθεν)	אחד הנה	εἷς ˢἔνθεν
58	τοῦ χείλους	לשפת	- -
59	τοῦ ποταμοῦ	היאר	τοῦ ποταμοῦ
60	καὶ εἰς (ἐντεῦθεν)	ואחד הנה	καὶ εἰς ἔνθεν
61	τοῦ χείλους	לשפת	- -

180   The OG and Th Versions of Daniel

62	τοῦ ποταμοῦ	הַיְאֹר		
	12:6		12:6	
63	καὶ εἶπεν τῷ ἀνδρὶ	וַיֹּאמֶר לָאִישׁ		καὶ ᴹεἶπα ˢτῷ ἑνὶ
64	τῷ ᴸἐνδεδυμένῳ	לְבוּשׁ		τῷ ᴸπεριβεβλημένῳ
65	τὰ ᴸ(βαδδίν)	הַבַּדִּים		τὰ ᴸβύσσινα
66	ˢὃς ἦν ἐπάνω	אֲשֶׁר מִמַּעַל		ˢτῷ ᴸἐπάνω
67	τοῦ ὕδατος	לְמֵימֵי		ˢ_ _
68	τοῦ ποταμοῦ	הַיְאֹר		
69	Ἕως πότε τὸ ᴸπέρας	עַד־מָתַי קֵץ		ˢΠότε οὖν ᴸσυντέλεια
70	+ˢὧν εἴρηκας			+ˢὧν εἴρηκάς μοι
71	τῶν ᴸ(θαυμασίων)	הַפְּלָאוֹת		τῶν ᴸθαυμαστῶν
72				+ˢκαὶ ὁ καθαρισμὸς
73				+τούτων
	12:7		12:7	
74	καὶ ἤκουσα	וָאֶשְׁמַע		καὶ ἤκουσα
75	τοῦ ἀνδρὸς	אֶת־הָאִישׁ		ˢτοῦ ᴸπεριβεβλημένου
76	τοῦ ᴸἐνδεδυμένου	לְבוּשׁ		

Chapter 12:1-13

77	τὰ ᴸ(βαδδιν)		τὰ ᴸβύσσινα
78	ˢὃς ἦν ἐπάνω	ⁿ܀ܢ ܕܘܝܐ ܠܥܠ	ˢὃς ἦν ἐπάνω
79	τοῦ ὕδατος	ܕܡܝܐ	τοῦ ὕδατος
80	τοῦ ποταμοῦ	ܕܢܗܪܐ	τοῦ ποταμοῦ
81			+ˢᵛἕως καιροῦ συντελείας
82	καὶ ᴸὕψωσε	ܘܐܪܝܡ	καὶ ᴸὕψωσε
83	τὴν δεξιὰν αὐτοῦ	ܝܡܝܢܗ	τὴν δεξιὰνᴹ
84	καὶ τὴν ἀριστερὰν	ܘܣܡܠܗ	καὶ τὴν ἀριστεράνᴹ
85	αὐτοῦ		
86	εἰς τὸν οὐρανὸν	ܠܫܡܝܐ	εἰς τὸν οὐρανὸν
87	καὶ ὤμοσεν	ܘܝܡܐ	καὶ ᴸὤμοσε
88	ἐν τῷ ζῶντι	ܒܚܝ	τὸν ζῶντα
89	τὸν αἰῶνα	ܠܥܠܡ	εἰς τὸν αἰῶνα +ˢθεὸν
90	ὅτι	ܕ ܥܠܡܝܢ	ὅτι
91	Εἰς καιρὸν καιρῶν	ܠܙܒܢܝܢ	εἰς καιρὸν καὶ καιροὺς
92	καὶ ἥμισυ +ˢκαιροῦ	ܘܦܠܓܗ	καὶ ἥμισυ +ˢκαιροῦ
93	ˢἐν τῷ συντελεσθῆναι		ˢἡ συντέλεια χειρῶν

182   The OG and Th Versions of Daniel

94	διασκορπισμὸν	רצץ	ἀφέσεως
95	(γνώσονται	עם־קדש	λαοῦ ἁγίου
96	- -)	תכלינה	καὶ συντελεσθήσεται
97	πάντα ταῦτα	כל־אלה	πάντα ταῦτα
	12:8		12:8
98	καὶ ἐγὼ ἤκουσα	ואני שמעתי	καὶ ἐγὼ ἤκουσα
99	καὶ οὐ ᴸδιενοήθην	ולא אבין	καὶ οὐ ᴸδιενοήθην
100			+ˢπαρ' αὐτὸν τὸν καιρὸν
101	καὶ εἶπα Κύριε	ואמרה אדני	καὶ εἶπα Κύριε
102	τί τὰ ἔσχατα	מה אחרית	τίς ἡ ᴸλύσις
103	τούτων	אלה	τοῦ ᴸλόγου τούτου
104			+[ˢκαὶ ⁵τί
105			+αἱ παραβολαὶ αὗται]
	12:9		12:9
106	καὶ εἶπεν	ויאמר	καὶ εἶπέν +ᴹμοι
107	ᴸ(Δεῦρο) Δανιηλ	לך דניאל	ᴸΑπότρεχε Δανιηλ
108	ˢὅτι ᴸἐμπεφραγμένοι	סתמים	ˢὅτι ᴸκατακεκαλυμμένα

Chapter 12:1-13

109	καὶ ᴸἐσφραγισμένοι		מחתמים	καὶ ᴸἐσφραγισμένα	
110	οἱ ᴸλόγοι		הדברים	τὰ ᴸπροστάγματα	
111	ἕως ᴸκαιροῦ		עד עת	ἕως ἄν ˢ - -	
112	πέρας		קץ	- -	
		12:10			
113	ἐκλεγῶσιᴹ		יתבררו	ᴸ - -	
114	καὶ ᴸ(ἐκλευκανθῶσιν)		ויתלבנו	ᴸπειρασθῶσιν καὶ	
115	καὶ ᴸπυρωθῶσιν		ויצרפו	ᴸἁγιασθῶσιν	
116	πολλοί		רבים	πολλοί	
117	καὶ ᴸ(ἀνομήσωσιν)		והרשיעו	12:10 καὶ ᴸἁμάρτωσιν	
118	ᴸἄνομοι		רשעים	οἱ ᴸἁμαρτωλοί	
119	καὶ οὐ ᴸσυνήσουσιν		ולא יבינו	καὶ οὐ μὴ ᴸδιανοηθῶσι	
120	ᴸ - - (ἄνομοι)		כל רשעים	πάντες οἱ ἁμαρτωλοί	
121	καὶ οἱ ᴸ(νοήμονες)		והמשכילים	καὶ οἱ ᴸδιανοούμενοι	
122	ᴸσυνήσουσιν		יבינו	ᴸπροσέξουσιν	
		12:11		12:11	
123	καὶ ἀπὸ ᴸκαιροῦ		ומעת	ˢἀφ' ᴸοὗ ἄν	

The OG and Th Versions of Daniel

	OG	Hebrew	Th
124	ᴸ(παραλλάξεωςᴹ)	הוסר	ᴸἀποσταθῇ
125	τοῦ (ἐνδελεχισμοῦ)	התמיד	ἡ θυσία [ᴸδιὰ παντὸς]
126		ולתת	+ˢκαὶ ἑτοιμασθῇ
127	καὶ ᴹδοθήσεται		ᴹδοθῆναι
128	βδέλυγμα	שקוץ	τὸ ˢβδέλυγμα
129	ἐρημώσεως	שמם	τῆς ἐρημώσεως
130	ἡμέραι χίλιαι	ימים אלף	ἡμέρας χιλίας
131	διακόσιαι ἐνενήκοντα	מאתים ותשעים	διακοσίας ἐνενήκοντα
	12:12	12:12	12:12
132	μακάριος ὁ ᴸὑπομένων	אשרי המחכה	μακάριος ὁ ᴸἐμμένων
133	καὶ ᴸ(φθάσας)	ויגיע	⁶ὅτι ᴸσυνάψει⁷
134	εἰς ἡμέρας χιλίας	לימים אלף	ἡμέρας χιλίας
135	τριακοσίας	שלש מאות	τριακοσίας
136	τριάκοντα πέντε	שלשים וחמשה	τριάκοντα πέντε
	12:13	12:13	12:13
137	καὶ σὺ ᴸ(δεῦρο)--	ואתה לך לקץ	καὶ σὺ ᴸβάδισον--
138			+ˢὀπόθου⁸

Chapter 12:1-13

139		+ἔτι γάρ εἰσιν
140		+ἡμέραι καὶ ὧραι
141		+εἰς ᴸἀναπλήρωσιν
142		+συντελείας
143	καὶ ᴸἀναπαύου	וְתָנוּחַ [καὶ ᴸἀναπαύσῃ
144	καὶ ᴸἀναστήσῃ	וְתַעֲמֹד καὶ ἀναστήσῃ
145	εἰς τὸν ᴸκλῆρόν σου	לְגֹרָלְךָ ἐπὶ τὴν ᴸδόξαν σου
146	εἰς ᴸσυντέλειαν	לְקֵץ εἰς ᴸσυντέλειαν
147	ἡμερῶν	הַיָּמִין ἡμερῶν]

VI.1. *Textual Notes*

1. Ziegler's text reads σωθήσεται for OG (with Th) against the reading of 88-Syh, which is accepted here.[1] מלט only appears elsewhere in 11:41 where OG=0 and Th has the expected σώζω. Th's reading is an obvious equivalent in 1. 17, but there is no reason to expect that Th is witnessing to the OG. There are also no obvious inner Greek grounds to explain 88-Syh as a corruption. The emphasis on resurrection in this passage is unparalleled in the Hebrew Bible,[2] and given the context ὑψωθήσεται "will be raised/exalted" renders the sense rather well. ὑψωθήσεται should be accepted as OG.

2. αἰσχύνη is in all probability a later gloss from Th.[3]

3. ὡς] +οἱ 88-Syh=MT, but the article might have been added because it is better Greek.

4. ἀπομανῶσιν] >οἱ OG never adds the article elsewhere to πολλοί (see 8:25, 11:10, 18, 26, 34, 44; 12:9[10]).

5. τίνες] τί Syh-88(τίνος by error) exhibits correction for grammatical agreement.

6. καί] ὅτι 88-Syh=MT.

7. συνάψει] >εἰς 88-Syh=MT.

8. ἀναπαύου] ἀπώθου 88-Syh harmonizes to the later use and/or it the result of Th influence. This variant is affected by the larger discussion concerning the authenticity of 1. 143-147, which we believe are a doublet from Th (see p. 192).

VI.2. *Analysis of 12:1-13*

VI.2.i. *Morphology*

---

[1] 967 has a lacuna for this portion of text. Montgomery, 473 simply refers to 88-Syh's reading as an error.

[2] See Collins, *Daniel*, 394-398.

[3] So also Ziegler, 17.

l. 11-OG has a 3 plural verb, which could mean that he understood nation as a reference to gentile nations, not Israel. Thus we would translate, "that time of affliction unlike any other (literally: such has not been) since they (i.e. the nations) came into existence." Alternatively, OG may have intended the plural subject as an implicit comparison with previous periods of affliction in Israel's past. In this case we would translate "that time of affliction unlike any other since they (i.e. our times of affliction) began." The latter option is the plainest reading of the OG. It is also possible that the translator was working along on the text and assumed that the comparison was intended in MT; therefore, OG may have employed the plural form before he realized that the grammatical subject was גוי.[4] In any case, OG's change of subject required the omission of גוי.

l. 18, 83, 84-OG omits translating the pronominal suffix as unnecessary (contrast l. 37, 106 where personal pronouns are added).
l. 36-Th reads the מ as a preposition (מִצַּדִּיקֵי) rather than a hiphil participle.
l. 37, 106-OG occasionally adds personal pronouns against MT and Th.
l. 63-OG employs the first person "I said" from v. 5 for "one said" in MT. Th has a formal equivalent to MT.

l. 113, 114, 115, 117-Montgomery, 478, states that Th has retained the subjunctive mood in these verbs from OG. If this is the case, it would be the only sign of dependence in this verse. Furthermore, the imperative in l. 107 followed by the causal ὅτι in l. 108 (see *Syntax*) makes a purpose clause, hence the subjunctive mood, perfectly explicable.

---

[4] We encountered a similar situation in 2:7.

l. 124-Th transforms the verb into a noun. He may have read תמיד הסרת (genitive construct from סרה).

l. 127-Th employs a finite verb rather than an infinitive. OG employs the passive infinitive in order to accommodate the change he has made in the syntax (see *Syntax*, l. 126).

VI.2.ii. *Syntax*

l. 8-It seems OG has read העת ההיא for והיתה עת. The demonstrative adjective creates an asyndetic clause where MT has parataxis.

l. 10-11-OG and Th follow MT quite closely and translate the sense of the syntax, but the common reading of the adjective οἵα "such as" makes it appear that one is dependent on the other. However, OG and Th also employ οἷος for אשר in 9:12 to give a good idiomatic rendering, and there is little reason to suspect dependence in that verse.

l. 18-19-OG transposes πᾶς before λαός "the whole people." In order to ensure that the statement "the whole people will be raised" is not mistaken for universalism, OG clarifies with the rendering ὃς ἂν εὑρεθῇ "whomever is found" for הנמצא.

l. 26-30-OG renders the repetition of אלה in l. 26, 28 idiomatically with the article + μὲν/δὲ/δὲ while Th corresponds to MT. OG's addition of the second δὲ makes three groups to be raised whereas MT has two. It is possible that לחרפות was an early explanatory gloss on לדראון,[5] but the versions support its inclusion. Th adds καὶ in l. 30 to smooth the syntax.

---

[5] Jeansonne, 101-102.

Chapter 12:1-13   189

l. 36-37-According to Montgomery, 473, OG has translated ומצריקי הרבים as if it were וחזיקי דברי. This judgment is based on accepting the reading of 88-Syh and 967 (κατισχύοντες) as OG. Ziegler reads the participle from κατίσχω instead, and the conjecture does make sense. To read "those who keep my words" is more in keeping with the context than "those who overpower my words." The problem with the conjecture is that there is no semitic equivalent that can be retroverted from κατίσχοντες that is similar to ומצריקי. OG has to represent some type of dynamic equivalent or a contextual guess for a text that gave OG problems. For example, OG could be a dynamic equivalent for a text that he read as וצריקי מרבים "the righteous of the many."

l. 39-OG adds l. 39 in harmonization with l. 35, though it could be a scribal addition.

l. 57-OG and Th employ equivalent expressions for the idiom "one on this side of the river and one on that side of the river." These are the only occurrences of ἔνθεν/ἐντεῦθεν in Daniel. The fact that Th employs a different adverb from OG suggests Th is an independent translation because there would be no reason for Th to switch equivalents deliberately. OG abbreviates the translation of l. 57-62, but the same sense is transmitted (see *Text-Critical*).

l. 63, 75-In both cases OG has a more idiomatic rendering than Th who employs a formal equivalent ἀνδρι + participle. OG omits האיש as redundant in l. 75.

l. 66, 78-Th employs the same formal rendering for the relative clause אשר ממעל. The agreement between OG and Th in l. 78 is either insignificant or the OG has been corrupted by Th (see *Text-Critical*, l. 67-68).

l. 67-68-OG may have omitted למימי היאר by parablepsis (עד־מתי ממעל . . .), or omitted the information as unnecessary, because it was sufficient to designate which of the two figures was being referred to in 12:5 by simply stating that it was the one "on the upper side."

l. 69-OG renders more to the sense of the compound interrogative "When, therefore, is the end," and οὖν alters the word order. Th employs a formal rendering. עד־מתי also appears in 8:13 where Th employs the same equivalent and OG has Ἕως τίνος.

l. 70-OG and Th have a common addition ὧν εἴρηκας (OG + μοι), and this addition makes it explicit that the "end" referred to is the one spoken of by Michael, the great angel, in v. 4 (see *Text-Critical*). MT does not explicitly identify either of the two figures in v. 5, and this identification is clearly wrong when compared to 10:5, 13 (Gabriel?, see 9:21). The addition is a distinctive agreement.

l. 72-73-OG's addition[6] is based on 11:35 where OG twice reads the verb καθαρίζω (for צרף, qal infinitive construct; לבן, hiphil infinitive construct).[7] The purification of the wise ones in 11:35 is connected with the time of the end, and, in the following verse, there is a reference to the boastings of Antiochus. OG interpreted the פלא "wondrous events" in l. 70 as an allusion to the נפלאות "boasting of wonderful things" by Antiochus in 11:36 (see *Lexicology*, l. 71). Therefore, OG added l. 72-73 in order to clarify that there will not only be an end to the boastings of Antiochus, but also "the purification of these ones" (i.e. "the wise ones" in l. 32; 11:35).

---

[6] καὶ ὁ καθαρισμός is marked with the obelus in 88-Syh.

[7] Both of the translations in 11:35 are unique in the LXX, and though there is some change in meaning the OG equivalents do impart the basic sense of the *Vorlage*. OG only has καθαρίζω elsewhere in 8:14 where it is once more a singular equivalent for צדק (niphal perfect; a distinctive agreement with Th!).

Chapter 12:1-13

l. 81-The addition in OG has the one clothed in linen on the upper side of the river "until the time of the end."

l. 89-OG makes explicit who it is that lives forever by the addition of θεόν in apposition to the preceding substantive, though θεόν could have originated as a marginal note that was later incorporated into the text.

l. 92-OG and Th share a common addition of καιροῦ, which is implicit in MT, though the agreement might be because מועד was in their *Vorlage* (see *Text-Critical*).

l. 93-96-Both OG and Th had difficulties with this text. Evidently OG transposed יד after וככלות, which would explain l. 93 (see *Text-Critical*). However, the translation of ἀφέσεως for נפץ is unique. McCrystall argues that OG engaged in deliberate theological *Tendenz* by reading מצה (which can express "deliverance") for נפץ.[8] However, is this an example of intentional theological *Tendenz*, or was it motivated by a misunderstanding of the *Vorlage*? This is not to say that OG's theology did not play any role in this rendering, but the type of programmatic theological manipulation of MT by OG envisaged by McCrystall is extreme.[9] In the first place, the translator may have been uncertain about the exact meaning of the phrase, and McCrystall has shown a possible semantic path by which OG arrived at the rendering.

---

[8] McCrystall, 84.

[9] McCrystall argues that the rendering in 12:7 is theologically motivated based on the OG interest in following the chronological system of the MT, which is based on the Jubilees' calendar (McCrystall, 234). To a great extent McCrystall's view of 12:7 depends on his ability to prove that MT used the Jubilees calendrical system and that OG knew this and inserted slight modifications. This view rests on his interpretation of three texts: 7:25, 9:24-27, and 12:7. Although it has not been our concern to establish whether MT does in fact reveal that it used the Jubilees' calendrical system, in the course of this work we have given considerable reason to doubt McCrystall's view that the OG translator actually intentionally introduced significant changes to MT for theological purposes.

Second, the translation bears similar characteristics to the addition in l. 72-73. It has been suggested that the addition in l. 72-73 was motivated by the translator drawing a parallel in 12:6 with the connection between the boastings of Antiochus and the purification of the wise ones at the time of the end in 11:35-36. OG may have understood that the text implied the same referents in 12:7. The context is the time of the end, which brings the end of the powers (i.e. those who are boasting), and the release of the holy people (i.e. the wise ones). Finally, the resulting translation by OG is in keeping with the context, because there is an emphasis on the time of the end bringing purification, blessing, and reward in vv. 10(9)-12.

Ultimately, the explanation offered here for 12:7 has much in common with McCrystall's. The difference is that McCrystall presumes that OG correctly understood MT and then deliberately introduced changes, whereas the suggestion here is that the process is probably more subliminal. It would be more appropriate to say that OG, in company with every reader, interpreted a difficult text according to his own understanding. If anything, there was more intentional *Tendenz* in the addition of l. 72-73 than in the translation of l. 94.

Th had his own problems with l. 94-96. He translates נפץ correctly with διασκορπισμός, but the appearance of γνώσονται in l. 93 suggests that he read (ו)ידעתם (3 plural perfect consecutive[?] from ידע) for יד־עם and he or his *Vorlage* omitted קדש תכלינה. The significant point for our purposes is that OG is obviously closer to MT than Th, and Th's translation is clearly distinct from OG.

l. 100-OG adds this line to make explicit what is implicit in MT.

l. 104-105-Ziegler encloses these lines in square brackets to indicate that their originality is doubtful. The preceding lines exhibit traits of dynamic equivalence and correspondence to MT, which would indicate that they are original and not later correction toward MT (see

Chapter 12:1-13   193

Lexicology). However, παράβολος could be based on אחידות "riddles" (see 5:12), which would grant these lines a strong claim to originality. So, we have a double reading in which there are no easy means to determine which lines were originally intended to translate the *Vorlage* (see *Text-Critical*). Although l. 104-105 could have been added later, they also could be an additional comment of the original translator, similar to other pluses in OG. In that case, OG makes explicit the uncertainty regarding the time of the coming of the end. Such a comment would be appropriate given the fact that Antiochus had come and gone between the period of the final redaction of MT and the translation by OG.

l. 108-OG and Th both use ὅτι when γάρ would have been a more appropriate rendering of כי.[10] Other shared examples of this Hebraism are 9:16, 19, 23; 11:4, 37, while OG employs γάρ properly against Th's ὅτι in 9:18; 10:11, 14; 11:27, 35.[11]

l. 111-112-The omission by OG results in a redivision of the sentence and cuts across the verse division.

l. 123-OG renders עת in l. 123 with the relative οὗ and omits the coordinate conjunction, which makes l. 123-125 subordinate to the predicate in l. 122. The OG of l. 121-125 might be translated, "But the wise will pay attention from [the time] when the perpetual sacrifice is taken away."
l. 126-The addition in OG retains the connection between the removal of the daily sacrifice and the "abomination of desolation," but also makes

---

[10] See Aejmelaeus, "OTI," 118-126. Aejmelaeus notes that the usage of ὅτι for γάρ in such instances is particularly Septuagintal and "frequently occur[s] in connection with commands or prohibitions," (Aejmelaeus, 118, see l. 107).

[11] The complete listing for the occurrences of כי (24x) in Daniel is 8:17, 19, 26; 9:9, 11, 14, 16, 18(2), 19, 23; 10:11, 12, 14, 19, 21; 11:4, 25, 27, 35, 36, 37; 12:7, 9.

it explicit that there is a sequence involved: the sacrifice is taken away, "and the abomination of desolation is prepared to be given."

l. 128-129-The same Hebrew terms are collocated in 9:27 and 11:31. In 9:27 the expression is plural, and OG and Th have the common reading βδέλυγμα τῶν ἐρημώσεων. In 11:31 OG has βδέλυγμα ἐρημώσεως, while Th has βδέλυγμα ἠφανισμένον.[12] Th has the cognate noun ἀφανισμός in 9:18, 26 (not in OG), so the agreement of ἐρήμωσις in 9:27 and 12:11 might be distinctive. However, the verbal agreement is not surprising when we consider the popular currency of the phrase (see 1 Macc 1:54), particularly in the later Christian tradition (Matt 15:14! Mark 13:14). So the agreement in 9:27 and 12:11 could be because Th employed a known phrase. At the same time, the fact that they read differently in 11:31 suggests that the agreements in 9:27 and 12:11 are probably due to later scribal corruption. Either way, the agreements cannot be considered as evidence that Th is a revision of OG.

l. 138-142-The lines in OG are generally regarded as a large addition to MT and this might be the case.[13] On the other hand, we have to consider the possibility that these lines are actually OG and l. 143-147 are a later correction toward MT. In favour of this possibility is that the conclusion of the verse has a high degree of verbal agreement with Th and it corresponds to MT. The main difference is in l. 145 where OG

---

[12] Contrast Jeansonne, 18, who states in error, "When θ' revised ο' the expression [βδέλυγμα ἐρημώσεως] was retained in all three occurrences (Dan 9:27, 11:31, 12:11)."

√שקץ occurs also in 4:16(19) OG=0; 8:13, 27; 9:17, 18, 26, 27. βδέλυγμα=שקוץ is a SE in the LXX, so it is only ἐρημώσεως that could be used as evidence that Th has borrowed from OG.

[13] Montgomery, 478; Collins, *Daniel*, 370; Lacoque, 247. Plöger, 170, argues that l. 138-142 are an equivalent for לקץ. The addition is marked with the obelus in 88-Syh.

has δόξαν for κλῆρόν, but this could based on a corrector reading לגרלך for לנרלך.[14]

The suggestion that l. 138-142 is OG faces two objections. The first is based on the preconception that Th is a revision of OG; therefore, the reason why l. 143-147 are so close in Th and OG is that Th has retained OG's reading. By now it should be obvious that we have every reason to dispense with that presupposition. On the one hand, Th's translation of l. 143-147 provides the expected formal equivalence to MT and does not require knowledge of OG. On the other hand, the OG looks a great deal like a doublet and we have proved Th influence on OG elsewhere.

The more significant objection against reading l. 138-142 as OG and 143-147 as a later doublet is that l. 138-140 are not equivalent in meaning to MT. In l. 143-147 MT has "and rest and you will rise to your lot at the end of the days." L. 138-142 in OG have, "Go away,[15] for there are yet days and hours until the fulfilment of the end." Some of the discrepancy in OG's reading might be accounted for by textual differences. For example, OG may have read ונרח for ותנוח and possibly וכ עוד for ותעמר, but it is unlikely that we could (or should even attempt to) reconstruct a whole catalogue of textual corruptions to account for OG's reading in l. 138-142. One of the main reasons for the creation of doublets in the LXX—and Th is in one sense a rather large doublet—was that there was a perceived inadequacy in the original translation. Therefore, it could be argued that there would not have been a need to add the correction from Th, if the OG had been closer to MT in the first place.

There is one final consideration that may support the position that l. 143-147 is a later addition to OG. It is generally agreed that the

---

[14] See Montgomery, 478.

[15] 967's reading of ἀπώθου is accepted as OG against ἀναπαύου in 88-Syh, which has been influenced by Th and/or the reading in l. 143.

epilogue in 12:5-13 consists of a later addition to MT.[16] Therefore, it is possible that OG was translating a slightly different *Vorlage*, which did not contain the specific promise of personal resurrection for Daniel in l. 138-140. However, this suggestion is less plausible because the OG is generally close to MT in the previous verses.

Although we can do no more than raise the possibility that l. 143-147 are a later addition to OG, it is necessary to do so because it brings into focus two questions: 1) How faithfully has the OG text been preserved? 2) How great was Th influence on the OG witnesses that have survived? We will consider these questions in more detail in the summary of our conclusions. Suffice it for now to say that the answer to these two questions makes it plausible that l. 143-147 are a later addition to OG.

VI.2.iii. *Lexicology*

l. 1, 9, 14, 16, 47, 111, 123-Th employs καιρός as a SE for עת (15/16), while OG displays more variety using ὥρα 5x, καιρός 4x, and ἡμέρα 3x.[17] The dynamic equivalent is ἡμέρα, which appears 3x in 12:1. In keeping with the eschatological outlook of the context OG equates עת צרה in l. 9 with יום צרה, which is found 20x in the Hebrew Bible. יום צרה is usually translated ἡμέρα θλίψεως (eg. Gen 35:3; 2 Kgdms 19:3; Isa 37:3; Obad 1:12, 14; Nah 1:7; Hab 3:16). OG retains

---

[16] Collins, *Daniel*, 371, and Montgomery, 474 regard the epilogue as later but integrated with the remainder of the book, while Hartman and Di Lella, 277, regard it as a gloss. Charles, 392 and Lacoque, 249 regard vv. 11-13 as later glosses.

[17] See 8:17; 9:21, 25; 11:6, 13, 14, 24, 35, 40; 12:1(4), 4, 9, 11. Th follows OG with ὥραν θυσίας ἑσπερινῆς in 9:21 which is evidence for borrowing or a corrupt text. OG=0 in 9:25; 12:9; and there are textual difficulties in 11:24; 12:11 (see *Syntax*, l. 123). The fact that Th employs καιρός reveals that it is a perfectly legitimate rendering, but it is possible that OG's reading in 11:14 (also in 11:13; 35; 12:4) is actually Th because καὶ ἐν τοῖς καιροῖς ἐκείνοις is a formal equivalent to MT and we might have expected OG to employ his more favoured ὥρα.

Chapter 12:1-13   197

ἡμέρα to render עת in l. 14, 16, because the antecedent is still that day of affliction.

l. 3-OG employs a dynamic equivalent, but given the problems OG had in reading the text and the textual differences, he very well could have read the 3 singular imperfect of עלל.

l. 4-The translation of שר might be regarded as a distinctive reading in Th. Apart from its uses in compounds (6x) Th renders שר with ἄρχων 9/11.[18] OG demonstrates variety by employing στρατηγὸς (10:13, 20[2], 21), δυνάστης (9:6, 8; 11:5), and ἄγγελος (l. 4). OG shares a reading with Th in 10:13 εἷς τῶν ἀρχόντων τῶν πρώτων, and we have to suspect Th influence on OG. OG employs ἄρχων only 4x elsewhere, and only in 2:48 is there an equivalent in MT (רב, but even there it may be a doublet translation with ἡγούμενον).[19]

l. 17-See *Textual Notes* for ὑψωθήσεται.

l. 19-Th omits מצא against OG as redundant.

l. 23-OG and Th share a HL καθεύδω for the HL ישן. It is possible that this is a distinctive agreement, but the euphemism of sleep for death may have been arrived at independently.[20]

---

[18] 8:25(2); 9:6, 8; 10:13(2), 20(2), 21; 11:5; 12:1. OG and Th share a common difference in the reading of שר שרים in 8:25. OG has ἀπωλείας ἀνδρῶν, Th ἀπωλείας πολλῶν. Montgomery, 354, is surely correct when he states that they read שר נברים / רבים. The difference in the OG and Th readings suggests that there is no dependence, but the similarities reflect an alternative *Vorlage*.

[19] MT=0 in 3:38; 97(30)?; 4:15(18).

[20] The euphemism was well known and used. See T. H. McAlpine, *Sleep, Divine and Human in the Old Testament* (*JSOTS* 38; Sheffield: JSOT, 1987).

l. 24-OG employs πλάτος (also in 9:27, not in Th) "breadth" as a dynamic equivalent for the construct אדמת, while Th's rendering with χῶμα (1-15) might be considered distinctive.[21]

l. 25-Th employs the compound ἐξεγείρω elsewhere in 7:4 and 11:25. Although either OG or Th's rendering is appropriate for the HL קיץ (hiphil) and Th's choice is not particularly distinctive, it does demonstrate his independence from OG.

l. 29-ὀνειδισμός is the expected SE for חרפה (4/4) in OG and Th,[22] though it may have originated as a gloss to דראון (see *Syntax, Text-Critical*).

l. 30-31-OG renders דראון (1-2, Isa 66:24) "abhorrence" with a contextual guess διασπορά.

l. 32, 99, 119, 121, 122-OG and Th's vocabulary for בין was discussed previously in 8:1-10 (though it should be noted that OG's προσέχω "give attention to" in l. 122 is a good dynamic rendering). משכילים and Th's translation of √שכל was treated in 1:1-10 (see pp. 47). Neither OG or Th's translation indicates that they discerned any special significance in the משכילים and the investigations of vocabulary for the domain of knowing have demonstrated that Th was working to his own agenda. Recall, for example, that Th employed συνετός in 11:33 and νοήμονες (1-10) in 12:10, because in both cases משכילים is collocated with יבינו.[23] The fact that Th clearly favoured συνίημι for משכילים and that his two exceptions in 11:33 and 12:10 can be explained does raise

---

[21] Talmon suggests that ארמת עפר is a double reading of synonyms, but there is good evidence to retain both. See "Double Readings in the Massoretic Text," *Textus* 1 (1960): 167-68.

[22] 9:16; 11:18(2); 12:2.

[23] The particular choice of νοήμων in 12:10 may also be explained by phonological motivation. In the preceding lines, Th employs √ἄνομος 3x (l. 117, 118, 120) to render √רשע.

questions, however, about the verbal agreement with OG in l. 32. OG has ἐπιστήμων in 1:4; ἐννοέω in 11:33; διανοέομαι in 12:10; but συνίημι in 11:35 (genitive plural masculine participle=Th) and 12:3 (nominative plural masculine participle=Th)!²⁴ Given OG's other choices for משכילים and the fact that συνίημι is clearly a favoured Th equivalent, we are more than justified to question the authenticity of OG's participles in 11:35 and 12:3. συνίημι is not collocated with any other term for knowing in 12:3, so it is particularly doubtful that we have OG in l. 32.

l. 33-34, 117-118-Phonological motivation is evident in the choices of OG and Th for the translation of יזהרו כזהר in l. 33-34. OG employs the rare φωστήρ (1-6) with φαίνω, which retains at least some of the consonance in MT. Th's choices ἐκλάμπω and λαμπρότης are even closer in sound (λαμπ). ἐκλάμπω (1-8) and λαμπρότης (1-6) are also rare in the LXX; therefore, they are excellent examples of Th's distinctive vocabulary.

The same phonological processes were at work in l. 117-118 where OG and Th again employ different equivalents. In this instance, OG's choices were guided by the fact that ἁμαρτωλός is the main SE for רשע in the LXX. Although Th's ἄνομος is also employed for רשע, it is not used as frequently or as consistently as ἁμαρτωλός.

l. 34-OG exhibits lexical levelling by employing οὐρανός for רקיע (unique in LXX) and שמים (l. 84). στερέωμα is the expected equivalent.

l. 41-Th has read עור for עד. Such an error can also be regarded as a distinctive disagreement, because, if Th were following OG, he would not have made such an obvious mistake.

---

²⁴ συνίημι only appears one other time in OG (11:33) where OG again agrees with Th (συνήσουσιν).

l. 44, 110-The translation of דבר offers further evidence of the distinctive nature of Th's translation. If we discount the 3 occurrences in chapter 1, OG employs πρόσταγμα as a SE 14/18.²⁵ The only exceptions are 10:6, 9 where λαλιά "speaking" is a better idiomatic rendering,²⁶ and 10:12(2) where OG has ῥῆμα. Th's SE for chapters 9-12 is λόγος (17/18; Th=0 in 10:1 by homoioteleuton).

l. 43, 45 and 108, 109-MT has the same verbs collocated (סתם וחתם, passive participle) in 12:9. The SE for חתם in the LXX is σφραγίζω so it is not surprising to find agreement in OG and Th.²⁷ However, there are differences in the rendering of סתם. There are only two points worthy of note. First, κατακαλύπτω by OG in l. 107 is a HL in Daniel. Second, סתם also occurs in 8:26. In 8:26 Th uses σφραγίζω as the common term meaning "to seal," while OG has φράσσω (1-8). The differing vocabulary indicates independent translations.

l. 48, 69, 112, 142, 146-As in the previous two paragraphs, עד־עת קץ is found in both 12:4 and 12:9. The Th reading in 12:4 is most likely OG. עת קץ appears with a preceding preposition 5x, and in every case except 12:4 Th renders קץ with πέρας (see 8:17; 11:35, 40). Th also employs πέρας to render קץ by itself in 8:17; 11:27 and 12:6, while 12:4 and 13 are the only instances where Th employs συντέλεια.

---

²⁵ 1:5, 14, 20; 9:2, 12, 23(2), 25; 10:1(3), 6, 9(2), 11, 12(2), 15; 12:4, 9. OG and Th both omit the second דבר in 10:9 which is probably an addition. The vocabulary we have examined has not been comprehensive enough to determine the nature of the link between the translator of chapters 1-2(3) and 7-12 in OG. However, OG has τρόπος for דבר in 1:14 and λόγος in 1:20, both of which are unique equivalents for OG (1:5 is an idiom).

²⁶ 4QDanᶜ has a singular (דברו) in 10:6 (lacuna for 10:9), but OG's equivalent implies the plural of MT.

²⁷ See also 6:18(17); 9:24(2). OG has σπανίζω and συντελέω in 9:24.

Chapter 12:1-13   201

Besides 12:4, OG renders קץ with συντέλεια 9/15.[28] Since OG and Th only have the shared reading of קץ in 12:4, and Th demonstrates a significantly different pattern of translation throughout Daniel; the agreement is more likely due to textual corruption than to Th borrowing from OG.

l. 49-The readings of OG (ἀπομαίνομαι "to rage violently" HL in LXX) and Th (διδάσκω "to teach") for the HL שוט "to rove about" (BDB, 1002) reveal that both had difficulties with the text.[29] OG has read a homonym שוט "treat with contempt." Charles, 332, suggests that Th's reading is a corruption from διαχθῶσιν, but διδαχθῶσιν is more likely a contextual guess based on the following clause "until many have been taught and knowledge is multiplied." Th's guess is clearly independent from OG, but both versions alter the intention of MT significantly.

l. 51-OG and Th employ different but appropriate equivalents. רבה only appears elsewhere in the Hebrew portion of Daniel in 11:39 where both OG and Th have πληθύνω.

l. 52-Th provides an equivalent for MT. OG is reading הרעת and has added ἡ γῆ to produce, "the earth be filled with iniquity" (see *Text-Critical*).

l. 56-ἵστημι is the expected equivalent for עמר, as in l. 3, 5, 144 of Th (see OG in l. 3, 140), but the common reading of the 3 plural

---

[28] See 9:26; 11:6, 13, 27, 35, 40, 45; 12:6, 13. קץ is also found in 8:17, 19; 9:26; 12:9, 13. OG=0 in 9:26; 12:9 (error), 13. Th=0 in 12:13; τέλος in 9:26; 11:13; ἐκκοπάω? in 9:26; μέρος in 11:45; and μετά in 11:6 (reading קצה, see 1:5, 15, 18; 4:26[29], 31[34]). OG also has an addition in 12:13 (l. 141) which includes συντέλεια, but the text that corresponds to MT is in all likelihood a later correction.

[29] Charles, 332, emends to ישׁוטו (based on Aramaic יסטון from √סטה) "till the many become apostates."

pluperfect active indicative is probably a distinctive agreement. However, there is no way to determine the direction of dependence, though it may be noted that Th employs ἵστημι and its compounds consistently for עמד; whereas OG uses variety (eg. l. 3; 1:4, 19).

l. 64, 75, 76-OG uses a variety of equivalents for לבש (στολίζω 5:7, 16; ενδύω 5:29; 10:5; περιβάλλω 12:6, 7), while Th employs ἐνδύω as a SE (6/6).

l. 65, 77-The same equivalents are found in the other occurrence of בד "linen" in 10:5. Th transliterates.

l. 71-OG and Th employ different and adequate renderings for פלא. פלא also appears twice elsewhere, in each case as a niphal participle, in 8:24 (OG-θαυμαστῶς, 1-4; Th-θαυμαστός) and 11:36 (OG=0; Th-ὑπέρογκος, 1-7, see OG 5:12) to refer to the boastings of Antiochus. The "end" being referred to in 12:6 is not solely the resurrection and judgment, but includes the conclusion of the events in chapter 11.[30]
Th's renderings are distinct.

l. 82-The verb רום appears 8x in Daniel and ὑψόω is the expected equivalent. OG has ὑψόω 3/4 and Th 6/8.[31]
l-87-שבע is a HL in Daniel. OG and Th both employ ὄμνυμι, which is the SE for שבע in the LXX.
l. 102-OG employs λύσις (1-3) as a dynamic equivalent for אחרית while Th has the expected SE ἔσχατος.[32]
l. 103-OG adds λόγος "matter," which is implicit in MT.

---

[30] Also Charles, 334; Collins, *Daniel*, 399.

[31] See also 4:34(37); 5:19, 20, 23; 8:11; 11:12, 36. OG=0 in 5:19, 20, 23 and in 4:34(37) the texts are vastly different, though ὕψιστος does occur. In 8:11 OG and Th have the common reading ἐρράχθη. Th also has ὑπερυψῶ in 4:34(37).

[32] See also 8:19, 23; 10:14; 11:4. OG has ἀλκή in 11:4, which may be an adjustment according to the sense of the context or based on an alternative *Vorlage* (BHS, ככחו, Collins, *Daniel*, 363, לחזקתו).

l. 107, 137-OG employs ἀποτρέχω (HL in Daniel) in l. 107 and a common SE (βαδίζω) for הלך in l. 137. Th's renderings with δεῦρο are unique in the prophetic corpus of the LXX and must be considered distinctive.³³

l. 113-McCrystall argues that the omission of יתבררו in 12:10(9) is probably due to the translator's desire to reserve ברר in 11:35 for an elite group within the *maskilim*.³⁴ Though McCrystall admits that the omission in 12:10(9) could be due to the fact that the verb is translated by πειράζω (in which case ויתלבנו was omitted) or that the three Hebrew verbs were rendered by two in the Greek, he clearly favours his hypothesis. It is the use of the passive infinitive of ἐκλέγω for ולברר in 11:35 that constitutes his proof that ברר was reserved for the elite group within the *maskilim*. He believes that there is a contrast in that verse between the voluntary decision of some of the wise to purify themselves and be elect according to OG, against the statement in MT that their affliction has the purpose of purifying.³⁵

To be fair, McCrystall does note with Montgomery, 460, that OG apparently reads ישכלו for יכשלו in 11:35, but he does not consider the ramifications of this reading on the translator's approach to the rest of the verse. Once the translator mistook the initial verb ישכלו "to consider/have in mind" for יכשלו "to stumble" he still had to make sense of the verse. It would have been a fairly easy step to translate the following infinitives as passives, and the remainder of the OG follows the Hebrew. This passage reflects what Tov refers to as a "pseudo-

---

³³ On the use of δεῦρο, see Eynikel and Lust, 59-62. Other occurrences of הלך are 3:25(92); 4:26(29), 34(37)-OG=0; 9:10. OG and Th share the reading περιπατέω in the first two instances and OG has κατακολουθέω in 9:10. Th employs πορεύομαι in 4:34(37) and 9:10, where the reference is to God's goings.

³⁴ McCrystall, 85-86; 228-231.

³⁵ Ibid., 229.

variant."³⁶ It does not reflect a variant *Vorlage*; neither does it reflect *Tendenz*. Furthermore, we have already seen that OG and Th betray no special significance in the vocabulary employed for translating משכלים (see *Lexicology*, 1. 32, 99, 119, 121, 122). The variant in 11:35 resulted from a simple *metathesis* in the verb יכשלו.

McCrystall's argument for an elite group within the *maskilim* is based on the intended restriction of the term ברר to 11:35 and an intentional change in the meaning of the verse in OG, but there is no basis to McCrystall's premise. As for the omission of ברר from 12:10(9) McCrystall fails to consider still another possibility: one of the first two verbs may have been omitted by the translator due to homoioarchton (יתבררו ויתלבנו), and the omission is part of a larger one beginning in 1. 111.

1. 114-OG's choice renders the sense of MT, while Th's is a closer formal equivalent. However, ἐκλευκαίνω is also a HL in the LXX! Th's distinctiveness is also demonstrated by the translation of לבן in its other occurrence in 11:35. OG has καθαρίζω, while Th might have ἀπολευκαίνω (HL in LXX).³⁷

1. 115-The only other occurrence of צרף in Daniel is in 11:35 where OG has καθαρίζω and Th again has πυρόω.
1. 120-Th's omission of כל appears to be an example of one of his occasional omissions, because it is rendered by OG.
1. 124-OG employs ἀφίστημι as a SE 4/4 for סור. Th demonstrates complete independence from OG. Th employs ἐκκλίνω (not in OG) in

---

³⁶ Tov, *Text-Critical Use*, 236-240.

³⁷ Ziegler reads ἀποκαλυφθῆναι in 11:35, but Montgomery, 460 suggests that Th's text is a corruption from ἀπολευκασθηναι. ἀποκαλύπτω cannot easily be explained as a variant reading of the *Vorlage*, yet it does make sense in the context. Therefore, a later scribe might have written the graphically similar ἀποκαλυφθῆναι for the rare ἀπολευκασθηναι. Th's reading is still distinct from OG.

9:5, 11; μεθίστημι in 11:31; παράλλαξις (1-2, see *Morphology*) in 12:11.

l. 125-MT has תמיד collocated with סר in 11:31. OG and Th employ the same equivalents there.[38] Th's use of ἐνδελεχισμός "daily sacrifice" (2-11) in l. 125 indicates his independence. Ziegler, 17, regards διὰ παντός in OG as a doublet and elsewhere OG does employ θυσία alone. However, as Jeansonne, 92, points out, the meaning of OG is the same with the addition "the eternal sacrifice" and Lev. 6:13(20) does employ θυσίαν διὰ παντός for תמיד.

l. 132-OG and Th employ appropriate equivalents for חכה (HL in Daniel), though Th's ὑπομενω is more common.

l. 133-The SE for נגע in the LXX is ἅπτω so both OG and Th employ unique renderings.[39]

l. 143-ἀναπαύω is a common equivalent for נוח (HL in Daniel) in the LXX.

l. 145-OG has the dynamic rendering δόξα for גרל, though it could be based on reading גדל (see *Syntax*, l. 138-142). Th has κλῆρος (HL), a SE in the LXX.

VI.2.iv. *Summary*

As in the other sections that we have examined, OG offers a faithful rendering of MT where it is present. For the most part, OG follows the word order of MT. Other than textual differences, OG only interrupts the word order of MT with the postpositive conjunction δὲ in

---

[38] Otherwise תמיד appears in 8:11, 12, 13, and both OG and Th employ θυσία. As previously mentioned, 8:11-13 has similar textual difficulties to 9:24-27.

[39] See the discussion of v. 7 in 8:1-10 above. Th's use of φθάνω is distinctive not only because of the equivalence he makes, but also because OG does not use the verb at all.

l. 28 (in l. 30 δὲ is an addition) and οὖν in l. 69. On two occasions OG altered the syntax (l. 10-11, 122-124), which did not affect the meaning of the text significantly; whereas in one case it did (l. 30, three groups at the resurrection). As elsewhere OG omits the pronominal suffix in some cases (l. 18, 83, 84), but has added a personal pronoun 2x (l. 37, 106). As usual, OG offers several dynamic translations (l. 17 against Ziegler's conjecture; l. 102, 107, 122, 138-142?, 145), though several others were occasioned by OG's difficulty in understanding MT or a textual problem (l. 30, 36, 49, 94, 105?, 145?). Several translations were also influenced to varying degrees by phonological considerations (l. 33-34, 117-118, 119).

There were a number of textual differences between OG and MT that are significant for our understanding of OG. The minuses were mainly due to the omission of redundant elements (l. 58, 61-62, 67-68) or textual problems (l. 111-113, 137). These omissions are characteristic of what we have found throughout this investigation and are not greatly important. Some of the additions are not that important either. For example, l. 39, 81 are probably due to harmonization and l. 89 was probably a scribal addition. However, the pluses in l. 70, 100, 126, though similar in nature to other places where OG makes an addition in order to make MT explicit, are significant. The significance of these pluses lies in their length and that there are three of them in close proximity. In particular, l. 70 and 100 read as explanatory additions. Of course, these additions would not be all that remarkable without the pluses in l. 72-73, 104-105, 138-142 (though there is good reason to question whether we should regard l. 138-142 as an addition). The presence of additions/translations like these should make us pause to consider how likely it is that other such additions/translations have not survived the transmission of OG, because of correction toward the MT and Th.

In 12:1-13 Th provides a formally equivalent translation to MT. Th is generally consistent in his choice of equivalents, but, at the same

Chapter 12:1-13

time, Th is sensitive to context and does not violate Greek grammar. There are two omissions against MT and OG (l. 19, 120), which is not unusual for Th, and one omission due to a textual problem (l. 95-96). Phonological considerations played a role in some of Th's translations (l. 33-34, 117-118, 120, 121), and Th has some good dynamic renderings as well (l. 107, 124, 137).

VI.3. *The Relationship Between OG and Th*

OG and Th share one distinctive agreement in 12:1-13, which is the addition in l. 70. We can also be fairly certain that Th has the OG reading in l. 47-48 and they share the reading in l. 129, but both of these are probably due to textual corruption. There are four other possible distinctive agreements where it might be argued that Th has borrowed from OG. The best candidate is l. 10-11, which some would cite as a classic example of Th's revision of OG toward MT. The difficulty is that Th does in fact correspond to MT, and the argument that Th is revising OG only has weight if accompanied by significant supporting evidence. The reading of the pluperfect in l. 56 could be due to borrowing, but such an agreement could easily have occurred through corruption/harmonization to a familiar form. The agreement in l. 23 may be coincidental and the addition in l. 92 is probably based on an alternative *Vorlage*.

There are, then, 7 instances in chapter 12 where Th may show evidence of direct borrowing from OG and a number of other expected verbal agreements in common vocabulary. On the other hand, there is substantial evidence to indicate Th's independence from OG as well as some evidence that Th readings have infiltrated OG. For example, the verbal agreement in l. 32 (also 11:35), and the addition of αἰσχύνην in l. 31 are almost certainly due to OG corruption by Th. It is less certain whether OG has been corrupted in l. 78, but the reading is definitely Th. Finally, it has also been suggested that l. 143-147 is a later correction of OG in the light of Th. Besides the 4 agreements that indicate Th readings in OG, there are 9 instances where Th employs distinct vocabulary from OG, some of which is rare in the LXX (l. 24, 33-34, 107, 114, 121, 124, 125, 133, 137). Furthermore, in two cases Th had trouble understanding MT and clearly employed his own renderings of MT (l. 49, 95-96). In addition there are 5x that Th transliterated MT, or exhibited minor textual differences against MT and OG (l. 19, 41, 65, 77, 120), which indicate Th was not following OG. Finally, there are 5 less impressive cases where Th's vocabulary is distinct from OG (l. 4, 57, 60, 71, 117-118).

The evidence of Th's independence from OG is overwhelming, and vindicates the original evaluation of the 7 readings that might have indicated Th borrowing from OG. The agreements in l. 47-48, 56, 129 are probably due to textual corruption. The same explanation or alternative *Vorlagen* accounts for l. 70 and 92. L. 10-11 and 23 are inconsequential.

VI.4. *Text-Critical Problems*

l. 12-OG omits, see *Morphology*, l. 12.
l. 39-See *Syntax*, l. 39.

l. 52-OG is reading הרעת and has added ἡ γῆ to produce, "the earth be filled with iniquity," (see 1 Macc 1:9 for a possible allusion). The difference is the interchange of ד/ר. As Charles, 333, writes, "the only certainty is the uncertainty of the text," but it seems more likely in the context of the book that wickedness rather than knowledge will multiply before the time of the end. MT should be emended.[40]

---

[40] So also Charles, 333; Collins, 369; Bevan, 203; Hartman and DiLella, 274.

l. 58, 61-62-Both OG and Peshitta omit these lines in l. 61-62, while OG also omits לשפה in l. 58. Although l. 61-62 could be a later harmonization in MT, such repetition is certainly characteristic of Daniel and Hebrew narrative in general.⁴¹ The fact that OG also omits l. 58 suggests that he has omitted for the purposes of Greek style, just as we have witnessed elsewhere.

l. 67-68-Collins, *Daniel*, 369, reconstructs OG without τῷ ἐπάνω in l. 66 from 88-Syh and regards l. 66-68 as a later addition in MT to harmonize with l. 78-80. Collins' reconstruction is possible, but would we not expect a complete description of the one to whom Daniel was speaking in the first instance? Once the figure is clearly identified, then the figure might be referred to in an abbreviated form. Furthermore, it could well be argued that the verbal agreement of OG with Th in l. 78-80 is due to corruption of the OG by Th (see *Syntax*, l. 66, 78), and we do not know what OG read! Perhaps OG omitted l. 78-80. It is also possible that the omission of l. 67-68 was simply a scribal error due to parablepsis (see *Syntax*, l. 67-68). For these reasons, the text of 88-Syh is accepted as OG in l. 66, and MT is not to be emended.

l. 70-The attestation by both OG and Th is strong evidence that they read אשר דבר in their *Vorlagen*, but the resulting Hebrew syntax would be awkward and the Greek looks like an addition by one of the translators (probably OG). In any case, the identification of the one clothed in linen with Michael is wrong when compared with 10:5, 13 (see *Syntax*). The common reading in OG and Th is probably due to textual corruption.

---

⁴¹ Cf. Taylor, 292-293. Collins, 369, wants to omit l. 61-62 and merely states that MT and Th "repeat 'on the bank of the river.'" Surprisingly, Charles does not even comment on the omission.

l. 72-73-The addition of καὶ ὁ καθαρισμὸς τούτων in OG is to clarify that the end will also bring the purification of the wise. The link is based on the two appearances of the verb καθαρίζω in 11:35 (see *Syntax*, l. 72-73 above); therefore, it is unlikely that it represents an alternative *Vorlage*.

l. 81-The addition in l. 81 would be retroverted into עד־עת קץ, but it probably resulted from harmonization.

l. 92-We would not expect OG, Th and P to have the addition of καιροῦ if it were not based on their *Vorlagen*, but the shorter reading of MT is to be preferred (cf. 7:25).

l. 100-This is a large addition in OG against MT, but it is similar to other additions in that it makes explicit what is implicit in MT. So OG can omit elements which are redundant or unnecessary (eg. l. 58, 61-62, 67-68), but also adds elements to make MT explicit.

l. 104-105-These lines originated as an additional comment by the translator or by a later hand (see *Syntax*). It is highly unlikely that such a plus existed in an alternative *Vorlage*, but even if it did, MT is to be preferred.

l. 126-The addition in OG is not based on a semitic *Vorlage* (see *Syntax*).

l. 137-Only OG and Th omit לקץ, but commentators are agreed in reading this as a doublet.[42]

---

[42] Montgomery, 478; Collins, 370; but see Plöger, 170 who regards the addition in OG as an expansion of לקץ.

Chapter VII
Summary

The investigation of OG and Th in the book of Daniel was concentrated on five sections: 1:1-10, 2:1-10, 3:11-20, 8:1-10, and 12:1-13, though significant portions of the remainder of Daniel were also examined. As a summary we will review the three main areas of our investigation: TT, textual criticism of MT, and the relationship between OG and Th.

For the most part, OG provided a faithful rendition of a *Vorlage*, which was very similar to, and, in most cases, basically identical with MT. We also found that OG's translation was not only faithful to the semantic content of his parent text, but also exhibited a relatively high degree of formal equivalence to MT. However, OG is usually regarded as a "free" translation, and there were particular features about his TT that were identified as characteristic of his dynamic approach. The most consistent characteristic of OG's dynamic approach was variety in the choice of lexical equivalents. OG also employed various methods to avoid excessive parataxis. The main way OG did so was to employ post-positive conjunctions, but the majority of these are confined to chapters 1-3, particularly chapter 2.[1] Occasionally OG employed hypotactic constructions with a subordinate participle, and in a few instances the genitive absolute. Another fairly consistent feature was

---

[1] There is not enough shared vocabulary in chapters 1-2 and 7-12 to determine whether chapters 1-2, like 4-6, originate from a separate translator. However, the dearth of the postpositive conjunctions δὲ and οὖν in the later chapters requires some explanation.

hand, OG often made small additions or introduced slight changes in the syntax in order to make something explicit that was implicit. Most of these changes should be regarded as attempts to remain faithful to the content and intention of the *Vorlage*. However, there were occasions, sometimes due to misunderstanding the parent text, that OG's theology was more evident in the translation (eg. 3:17).

The evidence from our research also supports two conclusions regarding the TT in the OG. First, it strengthens Albertz' conclusion that chapters 4-6 originate from a separate and distinct translator. Therefore, it cannot be assumed that a semitic equivalent of OG with an alternative structure in chapters 4-6 ever existed as a complete book.[2] Second, the TT in 3:20-30(97) is different in character from both the preceding and following chapters, which suggests that a later editor inserted the deutero-canonical material into chapter 3 of OG.

Generally speaking, Th prefers to follow a consistent pattern of formal equivalence, but he deviates from that pattern when required. Th's formal equivalence is subordinated to his concern for clarity and the demands of the target language. For example, Th usually does not represent the ל of the infinitive construct with an article and Th often omits a preposition that would be redundant in Greek (eg. partitive מן). Th tends to employ SE, but not when the semantic range of the SE does not overlap with the use of a word in a particular context. Th's sensitivity to the meaning of the parent text is also exemplified by occasional renderings of lexemes with dynamic equivalents.[3] A rather curious feature of Th's translation, to which A. Schmitt has already drawn attention, is the occasional omissions of words. Some of these

---

[2] Contrast Ulrich's conclusion that the Greek of chapters 1-12 "is of one piece." See E. Ulrich, "The Canonical Process, Textual Criticism, and Latter Stages in the Composition of the Bible," *Sha'arei Talmon* (ed. M. Fishbane, E. Tov, and W. W. Fields; Winona Lake: Eisenbrauns, 1992) 285.

[3] For additional examples, see Schmitt, "Stammt," 29-33.

omissions are due to textual problems, but not all.[4] For these reasons, it would be completely inaccurate to assume that Th intended to provide a translation by which we could retranslate back to the semitic *Vorlage*. Th's reverence for the text is evident in his basic technique of formal equivalence, but it was in an attempt to translate faithfully the meaning of the parent text.

In each passage of text that we analyzed for TT we examined specific text-critical differences with MT, but the results of the analysis provide us with additional guidelines for the use of the OG and Th for textual criticism of MT. The fact that both OG and Th exhibit a tendency to omit means that we have to be very careful in the evaluation of shorter readings in the Greek texts. This is particularly true of omissions of repeated elements in MT and those which are redundant when transmitted into Greek. However, an omission by both OG and Th is a weighty combination. At the same time, OG exhibits a definite tendency to introduce slight syntactical changes or small additions in order to clarify the meaning of MT. Therefore, many additions are not based on a semitic *Vorlage*. OG also had more difficulty reading and understanding the *Vorlage* than Th. Therefore, we ought to be slow to accept retroverted readings from OG as preferable to MT when OG's retroverted reading can be explained as an error. OG may be an older witness to Daniel than MT, but it certainly contains a number of mistakes. Finally, OG also employs dynamic equivalents more frequently than Th as well as more variety in lexical choices. However, there are other occasions when OG levels out distinctions in the *Vorlage* due to the literary context. For example, φοβούμεθα in 3:17 is a dynamic equivalent motivated by a previous use of the verb in 3:12.

---

[4] See Ziegler, 60-61 where he discusses the important minuses of the B group in Th against MT. In 8:2, 3, 5; 9:19; 11:36 of 88-Syh there are asterisked additions to bring OG in line with MT, but in these cases the B group also has the minus. This is a clear indication that Th had also undergone revision toward MT. There are possible hints of later revision of Th in the translation of עבד=παῖς/δοῦλος, מלה=ῥῆμα/λόγος, and פלח=λατρεύω/δουλεύω.

Yet, in 3:15 OG employs ἵστημι for עבד because throughout chapter 3 קום is usually collocated with צלם; and in 3:15 OG ignores that distinction (or perhaps OG did not notice). Like OG's inclination both to omit and to add, these tendencies are working at cross-purposes and complicate the use of OG for the evaluation of lexical variants against MT.

The examination of the relationship between the texts of OG and Th has proved to be one of the most interesting aspects of the investigation. It also has provided the most fruitful results. Two questions have dominated the discussion: 1) How faithfully has the OG text been preserved? 2) How great was Th influence on the OG witnesses that have survived? Unfortunately, we cannot give an accurate answer to either of these two questions. However, it is no doubt due to the fact that previous scholars have not examined the texts of OG and Th in detail with these questions in mind that many have surmised that Th is a revision of OG. There is certainly a relatively large percentage of verbal agreement shared by OG and Th, at times as high as 50% through most of chapters 1-3 and 7-12. Common readings do not necessarily prove anything though, unless one is already predisposed to view Th as a revision, because the majority of the common readings in Daniel exhibit the typical formal equivalence to MT that is found throughout the LXX. The common readings would only indicate Theodotionic revision of OG if they were accompanied by a significant number of distinctive agreements that also demonstrated dependence of Th upon OG.

The fact is, however, that the evidence from the texts of Daniel that we examined demonstrates the corruption of OG by Th readings. Although we cannot answer accurately how great the influence of Th readings has been upon OG, we do know that Th influence has been significant. This was evident in Ziegler's critical text prior to the publication of the remainder of the extant portions of 967 by Geissen, Hamm, and Roca-Puig, and is even more apparent now. It is also obvious that corruption of OG mss. towards Th and MT is not limited to 88-Syh, but includes 967, our best representative of OG.[5]

During the analysis of TT we discovered further certain examples of Th influence in the OG textual witnesses along with other instances where it seems only probable or merely possible.[6] These findings are entirely predictable. Given the fact that these two versions co-existed in the same time and geographical area we should expect corruptions and "cross-pollinization" of manuscripts, which produce mixed texts. However, if the Th version supplanted OG because OG was perceived to be inadequate as a translation, then we should be especially vigilant to discover corrections in OG from Th. After all, our knowledge of OG is limited from the outset because we only have **three** major witnesses to OG! How much of the OG has been irretrievably lost through successive revisions toward MT and Th? It is impossible to know, but the loss is no doubt substantial.

When it comes to the evaluation of verbal agreements, then, besides the presence of common agreements because of equivalence to MT we should expect some distinctive agreements between OG and Th. These distinctive agreements are present because either the OG or the Th reading has been erased from the textual evidence, or because we have failed to recognize original readings. In this research there were 24 distinctive agreements between OG and Th in which it is impossible to determine the direction of borrowing, and the majority of these are HL.[7] At the same time, there were only 5 distinctive agreements where there is a possibility that Th has the OG reading. Such agreements are entirely consistent with the view that the two texts are independent

---

[5] See the full evaluation of 967 in my thesis, pp. 48-100.

[6] The number of common readings is generally greater in chapters 7-12, but that may be due to greater corruption of OG.

[7] All of the distinctive agreements between OG and Th that were noted in the course of this volume, along with the evaluation of their significance, can be viewed in an appendix.

translations. On the one hand, we have expected common verbal agreement and little evidence of distinctive agreements in which Th has borrowed from OG. On the other hand, there were 29! distinctive agreements where the reading of Th had infiltrated the OG mss.

Besides the certain evidence that OG is corrupted with Th readings, there is ample evidence that Th was translating independently from OG. For the most part, Th employs the common SE for MT that are found throughout the LXX. However, we have seen how Th has his own pattern of translation equivalents for vocabulary sharing the same domain (eg. knowing, wisdom) and his own way of resolving conflicts when two words are collocated that he normally renders by the same lexeme. That Th's translation pattern is substantially his own is also verified by the numerous HL and translation equivalents employed by Th that are not shared with OG. Furthermore, we have seen how Th consistently makes his own contextual guess, rather than follow OG, when he does not understand MT. Finally, we have seen numerous omissions against MT and OG that would not be there if Th were revising OG toward MT. For these reasons, we can affirm that in the book of Daniel, the available evidence supports that Th is an independent translation of MT and not merely a revision of OG.[8]

To claim that Th is an independent translation does not necessarily deny that Th had any knowledge of OG or that he may have occasionally borrowed from OG. However, the evidence of such borrowing is scarce, and does not support a position that Th systematically revised OG toward MT. There simply is not enough data at this time for us to draw a firm conclusion. That Th is basically an independent translation also means that we have a different view of agreements where the direction of borrowing cannot be demonstrated, and of possible doublets

---

[8] For those interested in statistics, according to a search with LBASE there are 8859 words in Daniel MT. This figure includes all proper nouns, conjunctions, and prepositions. For example, the total includes 1150x where ו appears as the simple conjunction or with verbs in "converted" forms. In the course of this work we have examined the translation equivalents of almost 2000 of these words in OG and Th.

where a reading in OG corresponds closely to MT and Th (eg. 12:13). Nor can we assume that Th is a witness to OG in an attempt to reconstruct a critical text of OG.[9] On the contrary, where OG exhibits a marked agreement with Th and formal equivalence to MT (eg. 3:11-20), we have every reason to suspect that Th readings have corrupted the OG. Based on the extant manuscript evidence we can never know how much of OG has been obliterated by Th.

Finally, the assertion that Th is a translation in Daniel means that it is an independent witness to MT for textual criticism. There are also implications when Th is compared with other texts that are associated with the allusive figure of Theodotion and the so-called *kaige* recension.[10] It is to an evaluation of Th's relationship with *kaige* that we now must turn.

---

[9] Contrast Jeansonne, 8-10, who speaks more confidently of reconstructing OG readings from Th.

[10] Gentry, 381-382, also concludes that the Theodotion text in Job is an independent translation.

Chapter VIII

Th and Kaige

In the years since the publication of *Les Devanciers D'Aquila* a number of doctoral dissertations and studies have been published that have sought to delineate further characteristics of *kaige*. The list of possible characteristics has now grown to 97,[1] but this number gives a false impression of the homogeneity of *kaige*. This judgment will be vindicated as we examine Th's relationship to *kaige*.

Armin Schmitt had already argued in 1966 that Th did not belong to the *kaige* tradition,[2] but there are three reasons to look at this question again. First, it is clear that Schmitt's results have not been accepted as conclusive.[3] Second, the enumeration of more characteristics since *Les Devanciers* provides a larger base for comparison. The third reason to examine Th's relationship to *kaige* is that we are approaching the question from a different perspective.

---

[1] A list is provided by Greenspoon, *Joshua*, 270-273; Gentry, 400-405. See also the comments on p. 12 above.

[2] He has restated his position in "Danieltexte," 1-15. However, in the article (pp. 8-9) Schmitt only examines one of the *kaige* characteristics, גם/וגם=καίγε.

[3] Barthélemy, "Notes critiques sur quelqeus points d'histoire du texte," *Études d'histoire du texte de l'Ancien Testament* (OBO 21; Göttingen: Vandenhoeck & Ruprecht, 1978) 289-303 disputes Schmitt's findings and Jellicoe, "Some Reflections on the ΚΑΙΓΕ Recension," *VT* 23 (1973): 22 questions the reliability of Schmitt's data. Jeansonne, 22, also remains agnostic concerning this question. Contrast E. Tov, "Transliterations of Hebrew Words in the Greek Versions of the Old Testament," *Textus* 8 (1973): 79, who accepts Schmitt's arguments as "convincing."

The perspective of this evaluation is different, because it has been argued that Th is basically an independent translation; and not a revision of OG. At the same time, it has also been affirmed, though not argued in detail, that a *kaige* recension did not exist. The grounds for this conclusion are both negative and positive. Negatively, it has been pointed out that the *kaige* research since Barthélemy has not always been methodologically sound. For example, O'Connell attributes a number of characteristics to *kaige* that are technical terms rendering lexemes related to the cult and tabernacle. Or Bodine delineates characteristics of *kaige* that are probably OG.[4] Bodine's research was hindered because there is still no critical edition of the Greek text of Judges; however, there are other occasions when so-called *kaige* characteristics are nothing more than OG.[5] The failure to distinguish *kaige* readings from OG has also been replicated in the failure to contrast the *kaige* texts with one another. For example, numbers 83-93 in Greenspoon's list are named "Characteristics Peculiar to the Vaticanus Family of Judges" by Bodine, but Greenspoon includes them in the list of *kaige* characteristics. Greenspoon includes all the suggested traits of *kaige* in his list in order to be comprehensive, but this actually distorts some of the recognized distinctions between the texts.[6] *Kaige* research has concentrated on shared characteristics; consequently, the fact that none of the characteristics are found in all members of *kaige*, and that there are disagreements among the *kaige* texts, has largely been ignored. Even some of the agreements are not evidence of a relationship between the texts. For example, in many cases it is argued that *kaige* has simply employed a common or even the most frequent OG equivalent more consistently. However, unless that proposed characteristic is employed in significant numbers in any given text there are no statistical grounds

---

[4] See Pietersma, "Plea," 305-306.

[5] See, for example, the discussion of בין=ἀνὰ μέσον below.

[6] Greenspoon, *Joshua*, 270-273.

to distinguish a *kaige* characteristic from OG. For example, בתוך=ἐν μέσῳ, שוב(qal)=ἐπιστρέφω, and עבד=δουλ- are common and expected equivalents in the LXX. There would have to be significant consistency (eg. 10/12) in several texts to indicate that any of these equivalents might be evidence of a single recension. Far too many of the *kaige* characteristics only indicate that a revisor (or translator) of a text employed a SE.

The positive basis to deny the existence of a uniform *kaige* recension is the recent comparison of vocabulary in the Greek Minor Prophets Scroll, Theodotion Job, Aquila, and the Greek Psalter by Peter Gentry.[7] Gentry compares all attested nouns and verbs in the aforementioned texts and finds agreements and disagreements among all of them. He concludes that Theodotion Job does exhibit some dependence on the Greek Psalter,[8] and shares some equivalences with the Greek Minor Prophets Scroll; but the disagreements with the Minor Prophets' Scroll are so weighty that the similarities only indicate that these translators (revisor for the Minor Prophets' Scroll) shared a similar attitude to translation. He states:

> In fact, we must cease all together speaking of a *Kaige* Recension as if there were a monolithic revision behind the members of this group. There is no *Kaige* Recension as such. Instead, there is a continuum from the Greek Pentateuch to Aquila in which approaches and

---

[7] See Gentry, 410-484. Gentry first examines (386-410) Theodotion Job to determine how many of the *kaige* characteristics are present. Of those that could be assessed he finds that a total of 19 agree with *kaige* and 14 do not, though many of the agreements are actually of little significance. Of the 14 agreements with the characteristics proposed since Barthélemy, Gentry concludes that only four (36, 58, 67, 94) are of any value as *kaige* characteristics.

[8] Munnich argues that *kaige* employed the Psalter as a glossary or lexicon for the work of translation in O. Munnich, "Contribution à l'étude de la première révision de la Septante," *ANRW* II.20.1 (1986): 190-220.

attitudes to translation are on the whole tending toward a closer alignment between the Greek and the Hebrew.[9]

Ideally, we would want to compare and contrast Th's vocabulary with the material provided by Gentry, but that is beyond the immediate objectives of this research. However, a comparison of Th's vocabulary with the "characteristics" proposed by previous researchers will serve an important purpose. If *kaige* represents an approach to translation that is characterized by formal equivalence to MT, then we might expect to find some agreement between Th and *kaige*. On the other hand, given the thesis that *kaige* is not a uniform recension, we should expect disagreements. These findings would coincide with those of previous researchers. However, the degree of agreements and disagreements between Th and the proposed *kaige* characteristics will provide an indication of how closely Th is related to the *kaige* tradition.

VIII.1. *List of Kaige Characteristics*

Following is the list of 97 *kaige* characteristics that have been produced by Thackeray (1907, 1921),[10] Barthélemy (1963), Smith (1967),[11] Shenkel (1968), Grindel (1969),[12] O'Connell (1972), Tov (1973), Bodine (1980),[13] and Greenspoon (1983). Asterisks (60x) indicate that the Hebrew equivalent does not appear in Daniel, which leaves

---

[9] Gentry, 488.

[10] Barthelemy's monumental work was actually preceded by research carried out by Thackeray in "The Greek Translators of the Four Books of Kings," *JTS* 8 (1907): 262-78; H. St. J. Thackeray, *The Septuagint and Jewish Worship* (Oxford: University Press, 1920) 114-115.

[11] M. Smith, "Another Criterion for the καίγε Recension," *Bib* 48 (1967): 443-45.

[12] J. A. Grindel, "Another Characteristic of the *Kaige* Recension: נצח/νικος," *CBQ* 31 (1969): 499-513.

[13] Bodine adds what is the 97th characteristic in the list in his article, "*Kaige* and Other Recensional Developments in the Greek Text of Judges," *BIOSCS* 13 (1980): 52.

37 equivalents for discussion in the following section. Each equivalent is also marked in the right hand column to indicate the scholars who have discussed that particular equivalent. The names of the scholars are abbreviated as follows:

Thackeray=T
Barthélemy=B
Smith=Sm
Shenkel=Sh
Grindel=G
O'Connell=O
Tov=To
Ulrich=U
Bodine=Bod
Greenspoon=Gr
Gentry=Gen

1. וגם/גם=καίγε   T B O Bod Gr Gen
*2. רק=πλήν   Gr[14]
3. איש=ἀνήρ   B O Bod Gr Gen
4. מעל=ἐπάνωθεν (ἀπάνωθεν) + genitive   T B O Bod Gr
*5. נצב/יצב=στηλόω   B O Bod[15] Gr Gen
*6. חצצרה=σάλπιγξ/שופר=κερατίνη   T B O Bod Gr
*7. Elimination of Historical Present   T B O Bod Gr Gen[16]

---

[14] Greenspoon, *Joshua*, 277, only suggests that "in some tradition, perhaps the καιγε recension, πλήν was the preferred translation," of רק. Given the vagueness of the evidence, it is surprising that he includes it in his list of *kaige* characteristics. רק does not appear in MT in Daniel, but Th has πλήν 4x independently: 2:6 for להן; 4:12(15) for ברם, 4:20(23) for ברם; 11:18 for לו בלתי. OG never has πλήν.

[15] The Aramaic יצב is employed in 7:19 (OG=ἐξακριβόω; Th=ἀκριβῶς) and the noun נצבה appears in 2:41 (OG and Th have a shared reading ῥίζα).

[16] Although the historical present is frequent in the OG of Samuel-Kings it has been noted by O'Connell (208), Bodine (14), and Greenspoon (*Joshua*, 285) that it is non-existent (Exodus and Joshua) or rare (Judges once) in the OG of their books.

8. אין=οὐκ ἔστιν (in a series of aorist verbs.)   B O Bod Gr Gen
*9. אנכי=ἐγώ εἰμι   T B O Bod[17] Gr Gen
*10. לקראת=εἰς συνάντησιν/εἰς ἀπαντην   B O Bod Gr
*11. נדוד=μονόζωνος   T B Gen
*12. יהוה צבאות=κύριος τῶν δυνάμεων   B O Gr
13. אל=ἰσχυρός   B Gr Gen
14. נגד= forms of ἔναντι   B Bod Gr Gen
15. לפני=ἐνώπιον   B Bod Gr Gen
*16. על זאת/על כן=διὰ τοῦτο   B Bod[18] Gr Gen
17. לעלם=εἰς τὸν αἰῶνα   B Bod Gr
*18. הוי=οὐαί   B
19. אסף=συνάγω   B Bod Gr Gen
*20. כמר=χωμαρείμ   B
*21. אפלה=σκοτία/ערפל=γνόφος   B Gr Gen
*22. חוץ=ἔξοδος   B Gr Gen
23. הדרה/הדר=εὐπρέπεια   B Gen
*24. מהר=ταχύνω   B Sh Bod Gr
*25. הורה=φωτίζω   Sm Bod Gen
*26. בעיני=ἐν ὀφθαλμοῖς   Sh O Bod[19] Gr

Theodotion Job has two aorist indicatives where OG has the historical present (Gentry, 389). The historical present is not found in either OG or Th. In the one case in Judges, it is the B text that has the historical present.

[17] Th has ἐγώ ἤμην in 8:5 (אני) and 10:4 (ואני הייתי =OG). In 8:5 Th employs a periphrastic participle where OG has an imperfect.

[18] In 11:20, 21, 38 MT has עַל־כֵּנּוּ, which OG and Th recognize and translate correctly.

[19] There are no occurrences of this semi-preposition in MT. OG (8/9) and Th both employ ὀφθαλμός for עין. See 4:31(34) OG=0; 7:8(2), 20; 8:3 (OG omits), 5, 21; 9:18; 10:5, 6. See the discussion of the semi-preposition by Sollamo, *Renderings*, 123-146.

Th and Kaige 225

*27. פה=στόμα		Gr[20] Gen
*28. זבח=θυσιάζω		Sh O Bod[21] Gr
*29. רדף=διώκω		Sh Bod Gr
30. שׂר (ה)צבא=ἄρχων (τῆς) δυνάμεως		Sh Bod Gr
31. חכם=σοφ-		Sh Bod Gen
*32. חרשׁ=κωφεύω/חשׁה=σιωπάω		Sh Bod Gr Gen
33. עון=ἀνομία		Sh Gr
*34. הרה=ἐν γαστρὶ ἔχω or λαμβάνω		Sh Bod
*35. לא אבא=(ἐ)θέλω		Sh Bod Gr
*36. נצח=νῖκος		Grin Gen
*37. דכא(pual participle)=πεπυρ(ρ)ωμένος		O
38. אהל=σκέπη/משׁכן=σκηνή		O Gr Gen
*39. אורים=φωτισμοί		O
*40. אליה=κέρκιον		O
41. אלם=μογιλαλόν		O
*42. אשׁ=πυρ(ρ)όν		O Gr
43. בין=ἀνὰ μέσον		O Bod Gr Gen
*44. בקרב=ἐν μέσῳ		O Bod Gr
*45. בתוך=ἐν μέσῳ		Gr Gen
*46. בשׂמים=ἀρώματα		O
*47. בתים=θήκαι		O
*48. ווים=κόσμοι		O
49. חזק(piel)=ἐνισχύω		O Bod Gr
50. חרב=ῥομφαία		O Bod Gr
*51. חשׁב(noun)=μηχανώματος, μηχανήματος		O

---

[20] Greenspoon, *Joshua*, 293-294 suggests that στόμα might have been chosen as a more literal translation of פה in expressions like פי יהוה. It should be noted that Greenspoon does not produce any supporting evidence from Joshua that this is a characteristic of *kaige*, though he does cite Margolis as an authority that the substitution happens in Theodotion elsewhere. However, this is not sufficient evidence to prove a characteristic.

פה occurs twice in MT (10:3, 16) but both times it is in the literal sense of "mouth." Both OG and Th employ στόμα.

[21] Both OG and Th employ the expected θυσία for the noun זבח in 9:27.

*52. חשן=λόγιον O
*53. חָתָן=γαμβρός/חָתָן=νυμφίος O Bod
54. ילדים=παιδάρια, παιδία O Gr
*55. ירה=τοξεύομαι O Gr
*56. יתרת=περιττόν O
*57. כפרים=ἐξιλασμός O
*58. מעיל=ἐπενδύτης, ἐπιδύτης O Gen
*59. משבצ(ו)ת=συνεσφιγμένοι, συνεσφραγισμένοι O
60. ניחוח=εὐαρέστησις O
61. עבד=δουλ- O Bod Gr Gen
*62. עבת and עבתת=ἁλυσιδωτά and/or ἁλύσεις O
*63. ערף(verb)=νωτοκοπέω O Gr
*64. פרע=διασκεδάζω, διασώζω O
*65. קרסים=περόναι O
*66. קרש=σανίς O
*67. שהם=ὄνυξ O Gen
*68. שולים=πρὸς ποδῶν O
*69. שלם(piel)=ἀποτιννύω O Gen
*70. שרץ=ἐξέρπω O
*71. שרש/שרשת/שרשה=χαλαστά O
*72. תמים=τελειότητες O Gen
*73. תרומה=ἀπαρχή O
*74. יען אשר=ἀνθ' ὧν ὅσα T Bod Gr
75. Various=ἡνίκα T Bod Gr
*76. אחז=κρατέω Bod Gr Gen
*77. גלה=ἀποικίζω Bod[22]
78. טוב=ἀγαθος (cognates) Bod Gr Gen
79. ישר=εὐθύς Bod Gr
*80. לין=αὐλίζω Bod Gr Ul Gen

---

[22] גלה appears 8x in the Aramaic section, but never in the sense of exile. See 2:19, 22, 28, 29, 30, 47(2); 10:1. Th employs ἀποκαλύπτω 8/8, whereas OG employs various equivalents, but never ἀποκαλύπτω.

Th and Kaige 227

81. נצל=ῥύομαι   Bod Gr Ul
82. שׁוב(q.)=ἐπιστρέφω   Bod Gr Gen
83. אור=διαφαύσκω   Bod
84. הביא=φέρω, εἰσφέρω   Bod Gr Gen
85. זעק/צעק=βοάω   Bod Gr Gen
*86. חרה אף=ὀργίζομαι θυμῷ Bod Gr Gen
87. נלחם=παρατάσσομαι   Bod Gr
88. מלחמה=παράταξις   Bod Gr
*89. נתץ=καθαιρέω   Bod
*90. סרן=ἄρχων   Bod Gr
*91. פגע=συναντάω/ἀπαντάω Bod Gr Gen
92. קצין=ἀρχηγός   Bod Gr
93. רעה=πονηρία   Bod Gr Gen
94. Transliteration of Unknown Words   To Gr Gen
95. גדול (איש)=ἁδρός   T Gr
96. אבל=καὶ μάλα   T Gr
97. גבור=δυνατός   Bod

VIII.2. Evaluation of Readings in Daniel

The 37 characteristics of the *kaige* group which are found in Daniel will now be examined to determine Th's relationship to *kaige*. Disagreements are assumed to show independence from *kaige*, while agreements will be investigated as to whether they can be considered as bona fide *kaige* characteristics.

1. וגם/גם=καίγε

There are only two cases of וגם: 11:8, 22. Th has καίγε in 11:8, but only καί in 11:22. The evidence is mixed.

3. איש=ἀνήρ

Th employs ἀνήρ as a SE 8/8 while OG prefers ἄνθρωπος 5/8.[23] However, Barthélemy argues that the main trait of *kaige* for this characteristic is that it even employs ἀνήρ for the distributive sense of איש, but there are no cases of איש as a distributive in Daniel. The use of ἀνήρ may indicate a *kaige* characteristic, or it may just be the SE chosen by Th.[24]

4. מעל = ἐπάνωθεν (ἀπάνωθεν) + genitive
   Th employs ἐπάνω in 12:6, 7.

8. אין = οὐκ ἔστιν (in a series of aorist verbs)
   MT has אין 9x and in each case Th employs an equivalent which is contextually appropriate.[25] Th has οὐκ ἔστιν in 1:4; 9:26; 10:21; 11:16; 45; οὐκ ἦν in 8:4, 5, 27; οὐκ ἔσται in 11:15. In three instances Th renders אין where he employs a series of aorist verbs in the context (1:4; 8:4, 5),[26] but οὐκ ἔστιν is appropriate in 1:4 to describe the type of youths the king desired for training, "youths in whom there is no blemish."

13. אל = ἰσχυρός
   אל appears 4x in MT: 9:4; 11:36(3). OG and Th both employ θεός as SE, though Th omits 2x in 11:36 by parablepsis.

14. נגד = forms of ἔναντι

---

[23] See 9:7, 21; 10:5, 7, 11, 19; 12:6, 7. OG has ἀνήρ in 9:21, ἐνὶ in 12:6; omits in 12:7.

[24] Barthélemy, 54, argues that *kaige* also replaced ἄνθρωπός with ἀνήρ as a SE, but that is difficult to prove in Daniel when there is no other supporting evidence.

[25] OG and Th have common readings in 8:4; 11:15, 16, 45. OG has a dynamic equivalent in 1:4.

[26] Bodine, 15 offers 10:21 as evidence that Th exhibits the characteristic. However, though aorist verbs occur in the previous verses and OG employs an aorist for אין, 10:21 begins with the future and the present tense is applicable in the context.

Barthélemy suggests that this equivalence was developed in order to avoid confusion with the established equivalence לפני=ἐνώπιον (see below).²⁷ However, the LXX translators employed a variety of equivalents for נגד and that is what we find in OG and Th. Both have κατέναντι in 6:11(10) (Hebraism), and ἐνώπιον in 8:15; but they employ different equivalents in 10:13 OG=ἐναντίον, Th=ἐναντίας and 10:16 OG=ἀπέναντι, Th=ἐναντίον. At best this characteristic exhibits mixed findings, but there is no real distinction from the common Old Greek renderings employed throughout the LXX.

15. לפני=ἐνώπιον

Th does prefer to restrict ἐνώπιον to לפני (9/15), while OG only has it 3x and employs a greater variety of equivalents.²⁸ However, as Sollamo notes, ἐνώπιον is the most common equivalent for לפני in the LXX.²⁹ Therefore, Th's tendency to employ ἐνώπιον may be evidence of a *kaige* trait, but it is not definite. When we consider 14 and 15 together, it is perhaps best to consider them as offering mixed evidence for *kaige*.

17. לעלם=εἰς τὸν αἰῶνα

לעלם does appear in 12:3, but it is OG who has the *kaige* equivalent while Th has εἰς τοὺς αἰῶνας.³⁰ MT also has עלם 18x in the Aramaic section, but Th almost always follows the number of MT and is not dependent upon OG (see p. 78).

19. אסף=συνάγω

---

²⁷ Barthélemy, 84, discusses these under the one precursor pattern: נגד= forms of ἔναντι.

²⁸ See p. 52 for a breakdown of the equivalents.

²⁹ Sollamo, *Renderings*, 18.

³⁰ עולם is rendered by αἰώνιον in 9:24; 12:2(2); αἰῶνα in 12:7.

Barthélemy, 86, argues that אסף=συνάγω is a precursor to Aquila who employs συλλέγω. אסף does occur in 11:10 and both OG and Th employ συνάγω. OG also read אסף in error and employs συνάγω at 8:25.³¹ However, συνάγω is the most common equivalent for the verb אסף in the LXX (121/200; 24x in the Pentateuch), so it is questionable whether one could justify that this is a *kaige* characteristic.

23. הדרה/הדר=εὐπρέπεια

The nominal form appears 4x and Th has δόξα in 4:27(30)=OG; 5:18 OG=0; 11:20=OG. In 4:33(36) Th has ἦλθον?³² The verbal form appears 3x in the Aramaic and each time Th employs δοξάζω 4:31(34), 34(37); 5:23.³³

30. שר (ה)צבא=ἄρχων (τῆς) δυνάμεως

This title only appears in 8:11 where both OG and Th have ἀρχιστράτηγος.³⁴

---

[31] In Dan 8:25 the MT has the difficult reading, ובאפס יד "without hand," which OG renders with καὶ ποιήσει συναγωγὴν χειρὸς "and [then] he will make/cause a gathering by [his] hand." However we construe the Greek, the reading seems to be derived from the translator having read באסם as a hiphil perfect of אסם (והאסיף). Th had similar difficulties with the text, and produced a very different interpretation. See R. Hanhart, "The Translation of the Septuagint in Light of Earlier Tradition and Subsequent Influences," *Septuagint, Scrolls and Cognate Writings* (SCS 33; ed. G. J. Brooke and B. Lindars; Atlanta: Scholars Press, 1992) 364.

The argument that OG has reread the consonantal text is based on the fact that the addition of the auxiliary verb ποιέω was one of the means of the translator's to render causatives and συνάγω frequently renders אסף. See E. Tov, "The Representation of the Causative Aspects of the *Hiph'il* in the LXX. A Study in Translation Technique," *Bib* 63 (1982): 422-23. In effect, the translator read a ה for ב, transposed the letters פס, and read the changed letters as a hifil perfect with ו consecutive. The motivation for this change was that the translator did not know the meaning of the HL באסם.

[32] Collins, *Daniel*, 212, inexplicably states that Th omits.

[33] OG=0 in 4:31(34), 34(37); εὐλογέω? in 5:23.

[34] Th does employ δύναμις as a SE for צבא and ἄρχων for שר when they appear separately. See the discussion of 8:1-10.

31. חכם=σοφ-

Th employs σοφία as a SE for חכמה 8/9, while OG has it 5/7.[35] As Gentry notes, the equivalence is already found 139/171 in the LXX.[36] חכים appears 14x in the Aramaic section.[37] Th's SE is σοφός (14/14), while OG's SE is σοφιστής (7/10). OG has πάντας in 2:13; σοφός in 2:21; and spells out who the wisemen are in 5:8. It is obvious that forms of חכם=σοφ- is stereotyped throughout the LXX; therefore, it should be discarded as a *kaige* characteristic.

33. עון=ἀνομία

In all 3x Th has ἀδικία (9:13, 16, 24).[38]

38. אהל=σκέπη/משכן=σκηνή

אהל appears in 11:45 and OG and Th employ σκηνή.

41. אלם=μογιλαλόν(dumb)

אלם is only in 10:15 and Th has κατανύσσω where OG renders with σιωπάω. The characteristic is without foundation in the first place.[39]

43. בין=ἀνὰ μέσον

---

[35] See 1:4, 17, 20; 2:20, 21, 23, 30; 5:11(2), 14. OG=0 in 5:11(2), 14. Th has σύνεσις in 5:11 while OG has it in 1:20. OG has a free rendering in 1:17. Th shares the second OG minus in 5:11 which looks like a late addition to MT.

[36] Gentry, 406.

[37] 2:12, 13, 14, 18, 21, 24(2), 27, 48; 4:3(6), 15(18); 5:7, 8, 15. OG=0 in 4:3(6), 15(18); 5:7, 15.

[38] OG has ἁμαρτία in 9:13, 16; ἀδικία in 9:24.

[39] O'Connell, 287, proposes this characteristic on the basis of one reference in Exod 4:11.(?)

Both OG and Th employ ἀνὰ μέσον in all 4 cases (8:5, 16, 21; 11:45). This is also the most common equivalent in the LXX and should not be used as a criterion for *kaige*.[40]

49. חזק(piel) = ἐνισχύω

Forms of the verb חזק occur 13x in Daniel and compounds of ἰσχύω are the most common equivalents in OG and Th.[41] The piel is only in 10:18 and once in 10:19. In both places Th employs ἐνισχύω. OG has ἐνισχύω in 10:19, but κατισχύω in 10:18. However, OG does have ἐνισχύω in 11:1 where Th employs κρατός and in 11:5 Th employs ἐνισχύω twice for the qal.

The piel of חזק appears a total of 64x in MT, and 10x outside of Daniel it is translated by ἐνισχύω. O'Connell proposed this characteristic on the basis of one example and Bodine offers possible support from another example in the B family of Judges (9:24).[42] However, in two other cases of Judges all witnesses agree in reading ἐνισχύω (3:12; 16:28). O'Connell suggested that ἐνισχύω = חזק "may be part of a concerted effort at reinterpretation" since Reider-Turner lists 12 instances in which Aquila has ἐνισχύω for some form of חזק. Though Aquila might have made the equation between ἐνισχύω and forms of חזק, it is anachronistic to read it back into *kaige* on the basis of the scanty textual evidence. Th does not make the equation in any case.

50. חרב = ῥομφαία

Both OG and Th employ ῥομφαία in 11:33, and it is the most common equivalent in the LXX. Therefore, the agreement between Th and *kaige* should not be considered as evidence that Th belongs to *kaige*.

---

[40] Similarly Gentry, 407.

[41] 10:18; 19(4), 21; 11:1, 5(2), 6, 7, 21, 32.

[42] O'Connell, 28; Bodine, 26, 42.

54. ילדים=παιδάρια, παιδία

Th employs παιδάρια 4/6 against OG which prefers νεανίσκος 5/5.[43] The plural of ילד only occurs 47x in MT and O'Connell suggests this characteristic on the basis of one passage in Exod 1:18. The equivalence also occurs in Lam 4:10. ילדים does not occur or the plural is not rendered in Theodotion Joshua, Judges, or Job.[44] Furthermore, the equivalence ילדים=παιδάρια is made 3x in the γγ section of reigns (1 Kgdms 12:8, 10, 14 + 15x in the singular) and Zech 8:5, while γδ employs παῖς (2 Kgdms 2:24) and υἱός (2 Kgdms 4:1; also Ruth 1:5). In Genesis ילדים=παιδίον 8/10 and all forms of ילד=παιδίον 13x (see HR). Clearly, there is no basis here to establish any *kaige* characteristic.

60. ניחוח=εὐαρέστησις

The only reading is 2:46 where OG has σπονδή and Th employs εὐωδία.[45]

61. עבד=δουλ-

Th employs παῖς 6x and δοῦλος 6x for the noun עבד, while OG prefers παῖς (11/12).[46] In 7:14, 27 Th employs δουλεύω for פלח.[47] The criterion is a weak one in any case since עבד=δουλ- is common throughout the LXX.[48]

---

[43] See p. 40 for references.

[44] ילדים occurs 4x in Job, but it is not rendered by Theodotion.

[45] This is another reading proposed by O'Connell, 289 based on scanty evidence, Exod 29:18 and Lev 1:9.

[46] See p. 98. The Aramaic verb עבד occurs 12x, but is not counted because it is most naturally rendered by ποιέω.

[47] Th normally employs λατρεύω for פלח (7/9). See p. .

[48] Though עבד=δουλ- is consistent in Exodus, O'Connell notes that the equivalence is "a common pattern in the OG." While there is evidence of an increased use of this pattern among various witnesses in both Judges (Bodine, 27-28) and Joshua (Greenspoon, *Joshua*, 309-312), it is not consistent.

75. Various = ἡνίκα

ἡνίκα appears in 6:11(10) for כדי, but Bodine (p. 19) has already rejected it's use as a *kaige* characteristic.

78. טוב = ἀγαθός/cognates

Bodine argues that it is the consistency with which this equivalence appears in *kaige* that makes it a characteristic, and there may be some validity to this argument.[49] However, Th employs ἀγαθός only in 1:15 but κάλος in 1:4. Therefore, Th cannot be judged to exhibit this *kaige* characteristic.

79. ישר = εὐθύς

Once again, Bodine argues that it is the consistency of the usage that marks this equivalence, but the evidence is hardly compelling.[50] In any case, Th only has one reading in 11:17 (εὐθύς), which is not enough to prove a relationship to *kaige*.

81. נצל = ῥύομαι

Th has ἐξαιρέω 3/5 and ῥύομαι 2/5, so he does not support the equivalence.[51]

82. שוב(q.) = ἐπιστρέφω

Forms of שוב appear 16x in Daniel of which 12/13 are qal.[52] Th shares the common LXX equivalent with OG in 10:20; 11:13, 19, 28(2), 30(2). 3x Th reads it independently (9:25-OG=0; 11:18, 29).

---

[49] Bodine, 48-51; contrast Gentry, 410.

[50] Bodine, 52.

[51] See p. 141 for a discussion.

[52] 9:13, 16, 25(hi.), 25; 10:20; 11:9, 10, 13, 18, 18(hi.), 19(hi.), 28(2), 29, 30(2). In the first case in 11:18 OG reads with the *Qere* while Th reads the *Kethib*. Bodine, 55-56, admits that Th does not support the characteristic, and for some reason he does not include the occurrence in 11:10.

However, OG has ἐπιστρέφω independently 2x as well (11:9, 10), plus once for the hiphil in 11:18. The equivalence ἐπιστρέφω=שוב is common in the LXX, particularly in the qal form. For example, Bodine notes that the equivalence is made 11/19 in the βγ section of Reigns and 29/44 in γδ. However, he does not note that it occurs 22/33 in γγ. Therefore, the value of this criterion is highly suspect.

Numbers 83-93 in Greenspoon's list come from Bodine's chapter entitled "Characteristics Peculiar to the Vaticanus Family of Judges" so we would not expect there to be a marked equivalence in Th. Most of these examples involve common OG equivalences that are employed more consistently in Judges.

83. אור=διαφαύσκω
In 9:17 OG=ἐπιβλέπω; Th=ἐπιφαίνω.

84. הביא=φέρω, εἰσφέρω
הביא is found 10x in Daniel.[53] OG and Th share a common reading only in 9:12, 14 (ἐπάγω). Th has good renditions with forms of φέρω or εἰσφέρω only in 1:2(2); 11:6, 8, so it does not support Bodine's proposed characteristic.

85. זעק/צעק=βοάω
זעק only appears in 6:21(20) and Th does employ βοάω (OG=κλαυθμός). However, the equivalence is common throughout the LXX,[54] and βοάω is employed by Th also in 3:4 and 5:7 for קרא.

87. נלחם=παρατάσσομαι

---

[53] See p. 46 for a discussion.

[54] Bodine, 71, notes this as well.

נלחם appears in 10:20; 11:11 and in both cases Th employs πολεμέω. OG=Th in 11:11 and has διαμάχομαι in 10:20.

88. מלחמה=παράταξις
Both OG and Th employ πόλεμος as a SE (3/3) in 9:26; 11:20, 25.

92. קצין=ἀρχηγός
Th has ἄρχων in 11:18 (OG=ὀργή).

93. רעה=πονηρία
OG has the common LXX equivalent κακά 3/3 (9:12, 13, 14), while Th has κακά 2/3 and a more dynamic rendering with the pronoun αὐτά in 9:14.

94. Transliteration of Unknown Words

Tov offers an important contribution to the study of transliterations in the LXX. He groups transliterations into four categories: 1. proper nouns; 2. technical terms; 3. words unknown to the translator; 4. transliterations of common nouns erroneously transliterated as proper nouns because of the context.[55] Group 3 form the largest number of transliterations and it is to these that he devotes his attention. He concludes:

> The practice of leaving unknown words untranslated has been shown to be characteristic of *kaige* in Reigns γδ and of Th. (i.e. the notes referring to the contents of Origen's sixth column). . . Or, to phrase our conclusion, with due caution, in a different way: we were able to point out a new characteristic common to two members of the *kaige*-Th.

---

[55] Tov, "Transliterations," 82.

group. When used critically, this criterion may also be applied to other members of the same group.⁵⁶

"Critically" is the key word in the last sentence, because Tov is quick to point out that the practice was in use prior to *kaige*-Th; therefore, the presence or absence of transliterations is not determinative for inclusion within *kaige*. Nor does the presence of transliterations guarantee that a text is a revision.

As for the unknown words transliterated by Th, Tov provides a separate listing, because he accepts Schmitt's conclusion that Th is unrelated to *kaige*. They are פרתמים=φορθομμιν 1:3; עיר(ין)=ιρ 4:10 (13), 14(17), 20(23); אובל=Ουβαλ 8:2, 3, 6; פלמוני=φελ-μουνι 8:13; ברים=βαδδιν 10:5; 12:6, 7; מעזים=μαωζιν 11:38; אפדנו=εφαδανω 11:45.⁵⁷ However, Tov omits the transliteration of (ה)צבי-σαβιρ(αιν) 11:16, 41, 45 (δύναμιν, reading צבא in 8:9) from his list.

In his list of words from the LXX in group 3, Tov puts in a separate subsection transliterations of unknown words that were probably understood as proper nouns.⁵⁸ If we apply the same distinction to the transliterations in Th, all but אפדנו=εφαδανω could be classed in this category. For example, in 1:3 the king commands the chief eunuch to bring some of the captives of Israel "from the royal line and from the פרתמים." Th could easily have understood the Hebrew as some type of royal title or technical term (Tov's category 2). ברים may not have been understood exactly as a proper noun, but, given the context, Th might have understood that there was something intrinsically special about ברים, since it adorned heavenly beings. Similarly, מעזים was probably understood as a title, though Schmitt notes that מעוז is also transliterated

---

⁵⁶ Ibid., 85.

⁵⁷ Ibid., 92.

⁵⁸ See also the discussion by Greenspoon, *Joshua*, 334-336.

in Judg 6:26 (A μαωζ B Μαουεκ). The remaining transliteration (אפרנו) is a Persian loan word.[59]

The reason why the possible motivation for the majority of these transliterations is noted is in order to contrast them with other occasions where Th did not employ transliterations of unknown words. For example, in 2:5 and 3:29 Th does not transliterate הדמין and in 2:22 Th employs a contextual guess for שרא.[60] It seems that an important factor in Th deciding to transliterate was the fact that a word could be understood as a proper noun.

In Schmitt's investigation of the transliterations he argues that only ιρ and βαδδιν could have derived from previous transliterations in *kaige* elsewhere.[61] Schmitt states that the presence of these two transliterations is due to later revision of Th by "Theodotion."[62] However, ιρ does not actually appear anywhere else in *kaige*, so there is only one proven agreement between Th and *kaige*.

In conclusion, Tov's criterion is certainly viable as a *kaige* trait, but as he states, "The subject deserves to be treated in a detailed monograph."[63] Th does employ transliterations, particularly for terms which he understood as proper nouns, but it was also a common practice among the Greek translators.

95. גדול (איש)=ἁδρός

---

[59] Schmitt, "Stammt," 58-59.

[60] Th seems to have known שרא in the sense "to loose" (3:25[92]; 5:6, 12), but did not know the figurative sense "to dwell" (see BDB, 1117).

[61] Schmitt, "Stammt," 57-59. Schmitt does not note that the use of δύναμον for צבי in 8:9 could be equated with translations attributed to Theodotion in Isa 28:1; Ezek 20:6, 15 (δύναμις). However, the connection is unlikely given the use of transliteration in chapter 11 and the fact that צבא appears in 8:10.

[62] Ibid., 59.

[63] Tov, "Transliterations," 80.

Th employs μέγας as a SE (13/15) and πολύς in 11:28, 44.⁶⁴

96. אבל = καὶ μάλα

In both instances of this reading Th employs ἀλλά, whereas OG has καὶ in 10:7 and καὶ μάλα in 10:21.

97. גבור = δυνατός

Both OG and Th employ δυνατός in 11:3. Although the equivalence is fairly common in the LXX there is a marked increase in Judges, Kingdoms, and Psalms, so it may mark a *kaige* characteristic. The noun גבורה appears twice in the Aramaic section (2:20, 23) and Th employs δύναμις for both.

VIII.3. *Does Th belong to kaige?*

In Th there are 12 agreements with the proposed *kaige* characteristics (3, 19, 31, 43, 49, 50, 54, 75, 79, 85, 94, 97), 22 disagreements (4, 8, 13, 17, 23, 30, 33, 38, 41, 60, 61, 78, 81, 82, 83, 84, 87, 88, 92, 93, 95, 96), and 3 with mixed findings (1, 14, 15). There are only 2 (3, 19) agreements and 3 with mixed findings (1, 14, 15) that agree with Barthélemy's 9 core patterns and 12 precursor patterns, while there are five clear disagreements (4, 8, 13, 17, 23). Among the 12 agreements 6 are based on one reading (19, 50, 75, 79, 85, 97). The first 5 of these are common OG equivalents and at least 3 (75, 79, 85) should be discarded as *kaige* characteristics. The evidence for 5 of the 7 remaining agreements is tenuous, and it is extremely doubtful that 4 of these (31, 43, 49, 54) should even be considered *kaige* characteristics.

This examination of the *kaige* characteristics in Th vindicates the conclusion of A. Schmitt. The most that we can say that Th has in

---

⁶⁴ See p. 167 for references.

common with *kaige*-Theodotion is that they share a similar approach to translation, i.e. formal equivalence. If we were to depict their relationship in kinship terms, they might be described as distant cousins. In Gentry's terms, Th belongs within the continuum between the translation of the Pentateuch (c. 281 BCE)[65] and Aquila in which translations were tending to employ greater formal equivalence to the semitic *Vorlage*.[66] However, it is impossible to identify the translator or to date his work with any certainty. On the basis of Th's TT (frequent omissions, occasional dynamic renderings), and the inclusion of the deutero-canonical additions, it is probable that Th originated some time prior to the Greek Minor Prophets Scroll; therefore, before the common era.

---

[65] N. Collins, "281 BCE: the Year of the Translation of the Pentateuch into Greek under Ptolemy II," *Septuagint, Scrolls and Cognate Writings* (*SCS* 33; ed. G. J. Brooke and B. Lindars; Atlanta: Scholars Press, 1992) 403-503.

[66] For a discussion of the developing trend toward literalism, see any one of the articles by Sebastian Brock listed in the bibliography.

Conclusion

The primary concern of this research was to analyze the TT of the OG and Th versions of Daniel in order to determine how these two versions relate to one another and how they can be employed for textual criticism of the HA version. This aim was accomplished by examining five selected passages: 1:1-10; 2:1-10; 3:11-20; 8:1-10; 12:1-13.

Due to the fact that Ziegler only had access to part of Papyrus 967 when writing his critical edition, it was first necessary to reconstruct a critical text for OG before the analysis of each passage. The results of our textual criticism confirmed that the pre-hexaplaric 967 is the most reliable extant witness to the OG and also underscored the need for a revised critical edition of OG. The original readings of 967 reveal that 88-Syh has suffered corruption from Th and correction toward MT; yet, it was obvious that 967 had also suffered similarly.

Once we reconstructed a critical text for the OG we were able to analyze the TT for our five passages. For each section we compared the morphological, syntactical, and lexical elements of the source texts (OG and Th) with the target text (MT). Each of these passages was examined in detail, along with numerous related passages throughout the remainder of the book. By this means we were able to define more clearly the features of OG that make it more of a dynamic translation in contrast to the formal equivalence exhibited in Th. Besides some of the more outstanding results of the investigation, which are detailed below, there were many insights into the TT of both translators and how they understood the *Vorlage* they were translating. Though there were differences between the two translations, they were both concerned to provide a faithful rendering of the parent text.

The results of the analysis for each passage were then employed for textual criticism of MT. In several instances it was suggested that MT should be emended, but, generally speaking, it was found that OG and Th were translating a text virtually identical to MT.

There were four additional conclusions that emerged from the analysis of TT.

1. The analysis of OG supported the thesis of Albertz that chapters 4-6 originate from a translator different from the person(s) who translated 1-3; 7-12.

2. Based on the unique equivalents in 3:20-30(97) it is probable that a later translator/redactor inserted the deutero-canonical material into the text of OG. The Prayer of Azariah and The Song of the Three Young Men are additions to the OG text.

3. The analysis uncovered evidence that Th readings have displaced and replaced the OG text. On the basis of our present manuscript evidence it is impossible to know the extent of the corruption of OG, but in many cases the original reading is beyond recovery.

4. On the basis of the analysis of TT in Th, and in conjunction with the previous conclusion, it was demonstrated that the available evidence indicates that Th is an independent translation of Daniel. This conclusion has significant implications for the recovery of the text of OG as well as the understanding of the transmission history of the LXX.

The results of the analysis are based on detailed study of the OG and Th texts and, if they stand the test of future research, are by no means insignificant for LXX research. Both the linguistic principles upon which the model for TT was based, and the results that have been achieved through its application should encourage more extensive use of the model in future research on the LXX. It should be admitted that it would require a complete textual commentary to apply our methodology to the entirety of the OG and Th texts; so our results could be challenged

Conclusion 243

because they are not based on an exhaustive treatment of both texts. However, our analysis considered far more than the five select passages, because it treated the linguistic elements that were found in those passages exhaustively. The pattern of our results was also consistent throughout the course of the investigation; therefore, we can have a great measure of confidence that the results of further analysis will likewise conform to this pattern.

In the final chapter Th's text was compared with the characteristics that have been ascribed to *kaige*. Th exhibits significant disagreements and only superficial agreement with *kaige*. On this basis it can be concluded that Th and *kaige* have little, if anything at all, to do with one another. It is impossible at this stage to be more specific, because the relationship between the *kaige* texts as well as their relationship to OG has not been adequately defined. *Kaige* research has focused primarily on comparing agreements, and, in the process, has failed to contrast the significant disagreements that exist between the same texts. Consequently, the means do not yet exist to determine which texts are most closely related and many of the proposed characteristics of *kaige* are useless for this purpose. With respect to the *kaige* recension, as it has been defined in the majority of recent literature, we would do well to doubt that it ever existed except as a scholarly construct.

As one line of research draws to a close, several more avenues of research have been opened. The analysis of TT in the LXX has barely scratched the surface of the research that remains to be done. Continued analysis in this area will be of enormous benefit to the editors of critical texts for both the LXX and MT.

In the book of Daniel, Th has often been neglected in the research like a younger sibling following in the footsteps of the successful older brother. If we take the independence of Th seriously, then fresh approaches to the text are possible. Particularly significant in this regard are chapters 4-6. Perhaps our eyes (and minds) will be open to the possibility that other texts as well are translations rather than revisions of OG.

Finally, an exhaustive comparison of lexical and syntactical translation equivalents of each of the *kaige* texts would be an excellent foundation for the task of clarifying the relationship of the *kaige* texts to one another and their relationship to OG.

Appendix

The following three lists include all the distinctive agreements and cases of possible borrowing between OG and Th that were noted during the course of this volume. The first notes all of the instances where OG has probably been influenced by Th. We have included in this list all those instances where we determined 88-Syh have been corrupted by Th readings, because it helps to indicate the overall degree of corruption of OG mss. by Th readings. The second list has all instances where Th may be dependent upon OG. The third lists those instances of distinctive agreement where we cannot determine the direction of borrowing. Each reference is followed by a page number in brackets where the agreement is discussed. Occasionally, there are brief comments.

Though the number of Th readings in OG is somewhat inflated by the corruptions contained in 88-Syh, the fact that there are 29 does serve to underscore the point that we are severely limited in our ability to reconstruct a critical text of OG.

A. *OG influenced by Th*

1. 1:5 (see p. 57) τραπέζης Th, OG
This may be a Th reading since OG normally employs δεῖπνον.
2. 1:8 (see p. 39) ἀλισγηθῇ Th, 88-Syh
    ἀλ{ε}ισθῇ 967
3. 2:1 (see p. 72) ἐν τῷ ἔτει τῷ δευτέρῳ Th, 88-Syh
    ἐν τῷ δωδεκάτῳ ἔτει 967
    Ἔτους δευτέρου OG?

4. 2:1 (see p. 72) καὶ ὁ ὕπνος αὐτοῦ ἐγένετο ἀπ' αὐτοῦ Th, 88-Syh
   >καὶ ὁ ὕπνος αὐτοῦ ἐγένετο ἀπ' αὐτοῦ 967
5. 2:4, 28; 3:9 (see p. 73) ζῆθι Th, 88-Syh
   ζήσῃ 967
6. 2:4 (see p. 73) τὴν σύγκρισιν (+αὐτοῦ 88-Syh) Th
   αὐτό 967
7. 2:5, 6, 26 (see p. 73) σύγκρισιν Th, 88
   κρίσιν 967
8. 2:8 (see p. 74) οἶδα ὅτι Th, 88-Syh
   >οἶδα ὅτι 967
9. 2:8 (see p. 74) ὅτι ἀπέστη ἀπ' ἐμοῦ Th, 88-Syh (also 2:5)
   >ὅτι ἀπέστη ἀπ' ἐμοῦ 967
10. 2:9 (see pp. 88-91) ἀναγγείλητέ μοι Th
    ἀπαγγείλητέ μοι 88-Syh
    ἀπόδωτέ μοι 967
11. 2:10 (see p. 77) τοιοῦτο Th, 88-Syh
    τοῦτο τό 967
12. 2:10 (see p. 78) ἐπερωτᾷ Th, 88
    ἐρωτᾷ 967
13. 2:28? (see Chapter I, n. 23) ἃ δεῖ γενέσθαι Th, 88-Syh, 967 We question this reading on the basis of the differences in 2:29 (see below) and 2:45.
14. 2:29 (see p. 8) τί δεῖ γενέσθαι Th
    πάντα ἃ δεῖ γενέσθαι Syh (Ziegler's retroversion)
    ὅσα δεῖ γενέσθαι 967
15. 2:29 (see p. 8) ἃ δεῖ γενέσθαι Th, 88-Syh
    ἃ μέλλει γίνεσθαι 967
16. 3:22 (see p. 143) ἐξεκαύθη
17. 5:5 (see p. 141) ἐν αὐτῇ τῇ ὥρᾳ
18. 8:16 (see Chapter III, n. 39) κ. ἐκάλεσε καὶ . . . τ. ὅρασιν
19. 9:16 (see p. 137) ὁ θυμός σου καὶ ἡ ὀργή σου
The agreement is most likely due to textual corruption.

20. 10:13 (see p. 197) εἷς τῶν ἀρχόντων τῶν πρώτων
21. 11:14 (see Chapter VI, n. 17) καὶ ἐν τοῖς καιροῖς ἐκείνοις
22. 11:33 (see p. 199) συνήσουσιν
23. 11:35 (see p. 199) συνιέντων
24. 12:1 (see p. 186) σωθήσεται Th
   ὑψωθήσεται 88-Syh, 967
Ziegler wants to accept Th's reading as OG, but the conjecture should be rejected.
25. 12:2 (see p. 186) αἰσχύνη
26. 12:3 (see p. 199) συνιέντες
27. 12:7 (see p. 189) ὃς ἦν ἐπάνω
28. 12:13 (see p. 186, and below) ἀναπαύου Th, 88-Syh
   ἀπώθου 967
29. 12:13 (see p. 194) καὶ ἀναπαύου καὶ ἀναστήσῃ εἰς τὸν κλῆρόν σου εἰς συντέλειαν ἡμερῶν Th
   καὶ ἀναπαύου καὶ ἀναστήσῃ ἐπὶ τὴν δόξαν σου εἰς συντέλειαν ἡμερῶν OG
The reading in OG is a doublet added as a correction from Th.

B. *Th dependent on OG*

1. 2:8 (see p. 103) 'Επ' ἀληθείας
2. 3:19 (see p. 142) ἐπλήσθη
3. 8:6 (see p. 168) τὰ κέρατα ἔχοντα
   It is unlikely that Th is dependent upon OG for this reading.
4. 9:21 (see Chapter VI, n. 17) ὥραν θυσίας ἑσπερινῆς
5. 12:4 (see p. 200) συντελείας

C. *Direction of Dependence Unclear*

1. 1:3, 7, 8, 9, 10, 11, 18 (see p. 57) ἀρχιευνοῦχος
2. 1:7; 2:26; 5:1, 29, 30; 7:1; 8:1; 10:1 (see p. 58) βαλτασαρ

3. 1:10 (see pp. 51 and 59) τὸν ἐκτάξαντα τὴν βρῶσιν ὑμῶν καὶ τὴν πόσιν ὑμῶν
We believe it is more likely that OG has been influenced by Th in these readings, but there is insufficient evidence to make a decisive case.
4. 2:8 (see pp. 104 and 108) ἐξαγοράζω
5. 2:30 (see p. 133) οὖσαν
6. 3:15 (see p. 139) ἔχετε ἑτοίμως
7. 3:16 (see p. 141) χρείαν ἔχομεν
8. 3:17 (see p. 142) δύνατος
9. 7:3, 7, 19 (see p. 106) διαφέρω (διαφόρως appears in OG 7:7) The choice of the common translation equivalent in chapter seven of an otherwise rare term makes it difficult to assess what is happening. However, the number of such instances in chapter seven that are otherwise rare in the LXX suggests the work of later editors.
10. 7:10 (see p. 136) παρειστήκεισαν
11. 7:16 (see p. 103) ἀκρίβεια
12. 7:18 (see p. 78) καὶ ἕως τοῦ αἰῶνος τῶν αἰώνων Syh
    > καὶ ἕως τοῦ αἰῶνος Th, 88
    > τῶν αἰώνων 967
13. 7:25 (see p. 85) νομός Th, OG
14. 8:2 (see p. 162) ἐστιν ἐν χώρᾳ
15. 8:3 (see p. 163) ὑψηλά καὶ τὸ ἓν ὑψηλότερον . . . καὶ τὸ ὑψηλὸν ἀνέβαινε
16. 8:9 (see p. 171) ἰσχυρὸν
17. 8:14 (see Chapter VI, n. 7) καθαρισθήσεται
18. 9:27 (see p. 44) δοθήσεται Th, OG?
19. 9:27 (see p. 194) ἐρημώσεων 12:11 ἐρημώσεως
20. 10:1 (see p. 87) ἐπεκλήθη
21. 11:22 (see Chapter II, n. 41) ἀπὸ προσώπου αὐτοῦ
22. 12:2 (see p. 197) καθευδόντων
23. 12:5 (see p. 201) εἱστήκεισαν
24. 12:6 (see p. 190) ὧν εἴρηκας

Bibliography

I. *Primary Sources*

Baillet, M., J. T. Milik, and R. de Vaux, eds. *Les 'Petites Grottes'de Qumrân.* DJD 3. Oxford: Clarendon, 1962.

Barthélemy, D. and J. T. Milik. *Qumran Cave 1.* DJD 1. Oxford: Clarendon, 1955.

Benjamin, C. D. "Collation of Holmes-Parsons 23 (Venetus)-62-147 in Daniel from Photographic Copies." *JBL* 44 (1925): 303-27.

Burkitt, F. C. *The Old Latin and the Itala.* Text and Studies, IV.3. Cambridge: University Press, 1896.

Charlesworth, J. H., ed. *The Old Testament Pseudopigrapha.* 2 vols. Garden City: Doubleday, 1983.

Elliger, K. and W. Rudolph. *Biblia Hebraica Stuttgartensia.* Stuttgart: Deutsche Bibelstiftung, 1977.

Field, F. *Origenis Hexaplorum Quae Supersunt.* 2 vols. Oxford: University Press, 1867.

Geissen, A. *Der Septuaginta-Text des Buches Daniel Kap. 5-12, zusammmen mit Susanna, Bel et Draco, sowie Esther Kap. 1,1a-2,15 nach dem kölner Teil des Papyrus 967.* PTA 5. Bonn: Habelt, 1968.

Hamm, W. *Der Septuaginta-Text des Buches Daniel nach dem kölner Teil des Papyrus 967: Kap I-II.* PTA 10. Bonn: Habelt, 1969.

___. *Der Septuaginta-Text des Buches Daniel nach dem kölner Teil des Papyrus 967: Kap III-IV.* PTA 21. Bonn: Habelt, 1977.

Hanhart, R., ed. *Maccabaeorum liber III. Septuaginta* 9.3. Göttingen: Vandenhoeck & Ruprecht, 1960.

___, ed. *Judith. Septuaginta* 8.4. Göttingen: Vandenhoeck & Ruprecht, 1979.

___, ed. *Esther. Septuaginta* 8.3. 2nd ed. Göttingen: Vandenhoeck & Ruprecht, 1983a.

___, ed. *Tobit. Septuaginta* 8.5. Göttingen: Vandenhoeck & Ruprecht, 1983b.

___, ed. *Esdrae liber I. Septuaginta* 8.1. 2nd ed. Göttingen: Vandenhoeck & Ruprecht, 1991.

Holmes, R., and J. Parsons. *Vetus Testamentum Graecum*. 4 vols. Oxford: University Press, 1827.

Kappler, W. *Maccabaeorum liber I. Septuaginta* 9.1. 3rd ed. Göttingen: Vandenhoeck & Ruprecht, 1990.

Kappler, W., and R. Hanhart, eds. *Maccabaeorum liber II. Septuaginta* 9.2. 2nd ed. Göttingen: Vandenhoeck & Ruprecht, 1976.

Kenyon, Sir F. G. *The Chester Beatty Biblical Papyri. Fasc. VIII Ezekiel, Daniel, Esther (Plates)*. London: Emery Walker, 1937-38.

Koch, K. *Deuterokanonische Zusätze zum Danielbuch. AOAT* 38. 2 vols. Neukirchen-Vluyn: Neukirchener Verlag, 1987.

McLay, T. "A Collation of Variants from 967 to Ziegler's Critical Edition of *Susanna, Daniel, Bel et Draco*," *Textus* 18 (1995): 121-34.

Rahlfs, A. *Septuaginta, id est Vetus Testamentum Graece iuxta LXX Interpretes*. 2 vols. Stuttgart: Privilegierte   württembergische Bibelanstalt, 1935.

___, ed. *Psalmi cum Odis. Septuaginta* 10. 2nd ed. Göttingen: Vandenhoeck & Ruprecht, 1967.

Roca-Puig, R. "Daniel: Dos Semifolgi del Codex 967." *Aegyptus* 56 (1976): 3-18.

Sprey, T. and The Peshitta Institute eds. *The Old Testament According to the Peshitta Version: Daniel and Bel and the Dragon*. Leiden: Brill, 1980.

Swete, H. B. *The Old Testament in Greek According to the Septuagint*. 3 vols. Oxford: Clarendon, 1897.

Thackeray, H. St. J., R. Marcus, and L. H. Feldman, eds. *Flavius Josephus*. 9 vols. London: Clarendon, 1926-1965.

Tov, E., R. A. Kraft, and P. J. Parsons. *The Greek Minor Prophets Scroll from Nahal Hever (8HevXIIgr)*. DJD VIII. Oxford: Clarendon, 1990.

Ulrich, E. "Daniel Manuscripts from Qumran. Part 1: A Preliminary Edition of 4QDan^a." *BASOR* 268 (1987): 17-37.

___. "Daniel Manuscripts from Qumran. Part 2: A Preliminary Edition of 4QDan^b and 4QDan^c." *BASOR* 274 (1989): 3-31.

R. Weber et al., eds. *Biblia Sacra Iuxta Vulgatam Versionem*. 2 vols. Stuttgart: Deutsche Bibelgesellschaft, 1983.

Wevers, J., ed. *Genesis. Septuaginta*, 1. Göttingen: Vandenhoeck & Ruprecht, 1974.

__, ed. *Deuteronomium. Septuaginta* 3.2. Göttingen: Vandenhoeck & Ruprecht, 1977.

__, ed. *Numeri. Septuaginta* 3.2. Göttingen: Vandenhoeck & Ruprecht, 1982.

__, ed. *Leviticus. Septuaginta* 3.1. Göttingen: Vandenhoeck & Ruprecht, 1986.

__. ed. *Exodus. Septuaginta* 2.1. Göttingen: Vandenhoeck & Ruprecht, 1991.

Ziegler, J. ed. *Susanna, Daniel, Bel et Draco. Septuaginta* 16:2. Göttingen: Vandenhoeck & Ruprecht, 1954.

__, ed. *Sapientia Salomonis. Septuaginta* 12.1. Göttingen: Vandenhoeck & Ruprecht, 1962.

__, ed. *Sapientia Iesu Filii Sirach. Septuaginta* 12.2. Göttingen: Vandenhoeck & Ruprecht, 1965.

__, ed. *Duodecim Prophetae. Septuaginta* 13. 2nd ed. Göttingen: Vandenhoeck & Ruprecht, 1967a.

__, ed. *Ezechiel. Septuaginta* 16.1. 2nd ed. Göttingen: Vandenhoeck & Ruprecht, 1967b.

__, ed. *Isaias. Septuaginta* 14. 2nd ed. Göttingen: Vandenhoeck & Ruprecht, 1967c.

__, ed. *Ieremias, Baruch, Threni, Epistula Ieremiae. Septuaginta* 15. 2nd ed. Göttingen: Vandenhoeck & Ruprecht, 1976.

__, ed. *Iob. Septuaginta* 11.4. Göttingen: Vandenhoeck & Ruprecht, 1982.

II. *Grammars, Lexica, Concordances*

Barr, J. *Comparative Philology and the Text of the Old Testament*. Oxford: Univ. Press, 1968.

Bauer, H., and P. Leander. *Grammatik des Biblisch-Aramäischen*. Halle: Max Niemeyer, 1927.

Bauer, W. *A Greek-English Lexicon of the New Testament*. 2nd ed. Translated and adapted from W. Bauer's 4th edition by W.F. Arndt and F.W. Gingrich. Revised and augmented from the 5th edition by F.W. Gingrich and F.W. Danker. Chicago: Univ. of Chicago, 1979.

Blass, F., and A. Debrunner. *A Greek Grammar of the New Testament and other Early Christian Literature*. Translated and revised by R.W. Funk. Chicago: University Press, 1961.

Brooks, J. A., and A. L. Winbery. *Syntax of New Testament Greek*. Lanham: University Press of America, 1979.

Brown, F., S. R. Driver, and C. A. Briggs. *A Hebrew and English Lexicon of the Old Testament*. Oxford: Clarendon, 1906.

Clines, D. J. A., ed. *The Dictionary of Classical Hebrew*. Vol. 1. Sheffield: Sheffield Academic Press, 1993.

Dalman, G. *Grammatik des Jüdisch-Palästinischen Aramäisch*. Leipzig: J.C. Hinrichs, 1905.

Dos Santos, E. C., ed. *An Expanded Hebrew Index for the Hatch-Redpath Concordance to the Septuagint*. Baptist House, Jerusalem: Dugith, n.d.

Even-Shoshan, A., ed. *A New Concordance to the Old Testament*. Jerusalem: Kiryat Sepher, 1985.

Fanning, B. M. *Verbal Aspect in New Testament Greek*. Oxford: Clarendon, 1990.

Freedman, D. N., ed. *Anchor Bible Dictionary*. 6 vols. New York: Doubleday, 1992.

Hatch, E., and H. A. Redpath, eds. *A Concordance to the Septuagint and the Other Greek Versions of the Old Testament*. 2 vols. with a supplement. Oxford: University Press, 1897-1906.

Helbing, R. *Die Kasussyntax der Verba bei den Septuaginta*. Göttingen: Vandenhoeck & Ruprecht, 1928.

Jacques, X. *List of Septuagint Words Sharing Common Elements*. Rome: Biblical Institute, 1972.

Jastrow, M. *A Dictionary of the Targumim, the Talmud Babli, and Yerushalmi, and the Midrashic Literature*. New York: Judaica, 1971.

Johannessohn, M. *Der Gebrauch der Kasus in der Septuaginta*. Berlin: Weidmannsche, 1910.

Joüon, P. *Grammaire de l'Hébreu Biblique*. Rome: Institut Biblique Pontifical, 1947.

___. *A Grammar of Biblical Hebrew*. Translated and Revised by T. Muraoka. Roma: Editrice Pontificio Istituto Biblico, 1991.

Kautzch, E., ed. *Gesenius' Hebrew Grammar*. 2d ed. Translated by A.E. Cowley. Oxford: Clarendon, 1910.

Koehler, L., and W. Baumgartner. *Lexicon in Veteris Testamenti Libros*. 2nd ed. with a supplement. Leiden: Brill, 1958.

Lampe, G. W. H. *A Patristic Greek Lexicon*. Oxford: University Press, 1961.

Lee, J. A. L. *A Lexical Study of the Septuagint Version of the Pentateuch*. SCS 14. Chico: Scholars Press, 1983.

Liddell, H. G., and R. Scott. *A Greek-English Lexicon*. 10th ed. revised and enlarged by H.S. Jones and R. McKenzie. Oxford: University Press, 1968.

Louw, J. P., and E. A. Nida, eds. *Greek-English Lexicon of the New Testament*. New York: UBS, 1988.

Lust, J., E. Eynikel, and K. Hauspie. *A Greek-English Lexicon of the Septuagint*. Stuttgart: Deutsche Bibelgesellschaft, 1992.

Mayser, E. *Grammatik der griechischen Papyri aus der Ptolemäerzeit*. Berlin: De Gruyter, I.1 (2nd ed. by H. Schmoll, 1970), I.2 (1938), I.3 (1936), II.1 (1926), II.2 (1934), II.3 (1934).

Moulton, J. H., and G. Milligan. *The Vocabulary of the New Testament*. Reprint ed. Grand Rapids: Eerdmans, 1982.

Muraoka, T. *A Greek-Hebrew/Aramaic Index to I Esdras*. SCS 16. Chico: Scholars Press, 1984.

__. *Emphatic Words and Structures in Biblical Hebrew*. Jerusalem: Magnes, 1985.

__. *A Greek-English Lexicon of the Septuagint. Twelve Prophets*. Louvain: Peeters, 1993.

Porter, S. E. *Verbal Aspect in the Greek of the NT, with Reference to Tense and Mood*. New York: Peter Lang, 1989.

__. *Idioms of the Greek New Testament*. Sheffield: JSOT, 1992.

Qimron, E. *The Hebrew of the Dead Sea Scrolls*. Atlanta: Scholars Press, 1986.

Rehkopf, F. *Septuaginta-Vokabular*. Göttingen: Vandenhoeck & Ruprecht, 1989.

Reider, J., and N. Turner. *An Index to Aquila*. VTSup, 12. Leiden: Brill, 1966.

Rengstorf, K. H. *A Complete Concordance to Flavius Josephus*. 3 vols. Leiden: Brill, 1973-83.

Rosenthal, F. *A Grammar of Biblical Aramaic*. Porta Linguarum Orientalum, N.S, 5. Wiesbaden: Otto Harrassowitz, 1983.

Smyth, H. W. *Greek Grammar*. Rev. by G.M. Messing. Cambridge: Harvard Univ. Press, 1956.

Sokoloff, M. *A Dictionary of Jewish Palestinian Aramaic of the Byzantine Period*. Ramat-Gan: Bar Ilan University Press, 1990.

Thackeray, H. St. J. *A Grammar of the Old Testament in Greek*. Vol. 1. Cambridge: University Press, 1909.

Walters (Katz), P. *The Text of the Septuagint, Its Corruptions and Their Emendations.* Cambridge: University Press, 1973.

Waltke, B., and M. O'Conner. *An Introduction to Biblical Hebrew Syntax.* Winona Lake: Eisenbrauns, 1990.

Williams, R. J. *Hebrew Syntax: an Outline.* 2nd ed. Toronto: University of Toronto, 1976.

III. Translation Technique

Abercrombie, J. R. et al. *Computer Assisted Tools for Septuagint Studies: Volume 1, Ruth. SCS* 20. Atlanta: Scholar's Press, 1984.

Aejmelaeus, A. *Parataxis in the Septuagint. AASF,* DHL, 31. Helsinki: Suomalainen Tiedeakatemia, 1982a.

___. "*Participium Coniunctum* as a Criterion of Translation Technique." *VT* 32 (1982b): 385-93.

___. "OTI Causale in Septuagintal Greek." In *La Septuaginta en la Investigacion Contemporanea (V Congreso de la IOSCS),* edited by N. F. Marcos, 115-32. Madrid: Instituto Arias Montano, 1985.

___. "The Significance of Clause Connectors in the Syntactical and Translation-Technical Study of the Septuagint." In *VI Congress of the IOSCS. SCS* 23, edited by C. Cox, 361-79. Atlanta: Scholars Press, 1988.

___. "*OTI recitativum* in Septuagintal Greek." In *Studien zur Septuaginta - Robert Hanhart zu Ehren. MSU* 20, edited by D. Fraenkel, U. Quast, and J. Wevers, 74-82. Göttingen: Vandenhoeck & Ruprecht, 1990.

___. "Translation Technique and the Intention of the Translator." In *VII Congress of the IOSCS. SCS* 31, edited by C. Cox, 23-36. Atlanta: Scholars Press, 1991.

___. "Septuagintal Translation Techniques - A Solution to the Problem of the Tabernacle Account." In *Septuagint, Scrolls and Cognate Writings. SCS* 33, edited by G. J. Brooke and B. Lindars, 381-402. Atlanta: Scholars Press, 1992.

Barr, J. "The Typology of Literalism in Ancient Biblical Translations." *Mitteilungen des Septuaginta-Unternehmens der Akademie der Wissenschaften in Göttingen* 15 (1979): 275-325.

___. "Doubts about Homoeophony in the Septuagint." *Textus* 12 (1985): 1-77.

___. "Translators' Handling of Verbs in Semantically Ambiguous Contexts." In *VI Congress of the IOSCS,* edited by C. Cox, 381-403. Atlanta: Scholars Press, 1986.

___. "'Guessing' in the Septuagint." In *Studien zur Septuaginta - Robert Hanhart zu Ehren. MSU* 20, edited by D. Fraenkel, U. Quast, and J. Wevers, 19-34. Göttingen: Vandenhoeck & Ruprecht, 1990.

Bertram, G. "Der Sprachschatz der Septuaginta und der des hebräischen Alten Testaments." *ZAW* NF 16 (1939): 85-101.

Bludau, A. *Die Alexandrinische übersetzung des Buches Daniel und ihr Verhältnis zum Massorethischen Text*. Freiburg: Herder'sche Verlagshandlung, 1897.

Brock, S. P. "The Phenomenon of Biblical Translation in Antiquity." *Alta: The University of Birmingham Review* 2 (1969): 96-102.

___. "Aspects of Translation Technique in Antiquity." *Greek, Roman, and Byzantine Studies* 20 (1979): 69-87.

___. "To Revise or Not to Revise: Attitudes to Jewish Biblical Translation." In *Septuagint, Scrolls and Cognate Writings. SCS* 33, edited by G. J. Brooke and B. Lindars, 301-38. Atlanta: Scholars Press, 1992.

Caird, G. B. "Homoeophony in the Septuagint." In *Essays in Honour of W.D. Davies*, edited by R. Hammerton-Kelly and R. Scroggs, 74-88. Leiden: Brill, 1976.

De Waard, J. "'Homophony' in the Septuagint." *Bib* 62 (1981): 551-61.

Eynikel, E., and J. Lust. "The Use of ΔΕΥΡΟ and ΔΕΥΤΕ in the LXX." *ETL* 67 (1991): 57-68.

Flaschar, M. "Exegetische Studien zum Septugintapsalter." *ZAW* 32 (1912): 81-116, 161-89.

Frankel, Z. *Vorstudien zu der Septuaginta*. Leipzig: Vogel, 1841.

Fritsch, C. "Homophony in the Septuagint." In *Sixth World Congress of Jewish Studies*, edited by A. Shinan, 115-20. Jerusalem: Jerusalem Academic Press, 1977.

Gentry, P. J. "An Analysis of the Revisor's Text of the Greek Job." Ph.D. Dissertation, University of Toronto, 1994.

Grabbe, L. "The Translation Technique of the Greek Minor Versions: Translations or Revisions?" In *Septuagint, Scrolls and Cognate Writings. SCS* 33, edited by G. J. Brooke and B. Lindars, 505-56. Atlanta: Scholars Press, 1992.

Greenspoon, L. "Biblical Translators in Antiquity and in the Modern World." *HA* 60 (1989): 91-113.

Grindel, J. A. "Another Characteristic of the *Kaige* Recension: נצח/νῖκος." *CBQ* 31 (1969): 499-513.

Hanson, A. T. "The Treatment in the LXX of the Theme of Seeing God." In *Septuagint, Scrolls and Cognate Writings. SCS* 33, edited by G. J. Brooke and B. Lindars, 557-68. Atlanta: Scholars Press, 1992.

Heller, J. "Grenzen sprachlicher Entsprechung der LXX." *MIO* 5 (1969): 234-48.

Johannessohn, M. *Der Gebrauch der Präpositionen in der Septuaginta.* Berlin: Weidmannsche, 1925.

Kaupel, H. "Beobachtungen zur Übersetzung des Infinitivus absolutus in der Septuaginta." *ZAW* 61 (1948): 191-92.

Lee, J. A. L. "Equivocal and Stereotyped Renderings in the LXX." *RB* 87 (1980): 104-17.

Leiter, N. "Assimilation and Dissimilation Techniques in the LXX of the Book of Balaam." *Textus* 12 (1985): 79-95.

Lübbe, A. "Describing the Translation Process of 11QtgJob: A Question of Method." *RQ* 52 (1988): 583-93.

Marquis, G. "Consistency of Lexical Equivalents as a Criterion for the Evaluation Translation Technique." In *VI Congress of the IOSCS*, edited by C. Cox, 405-24. Atlanta: Scholars Press, 1986a.

___. "Word Order as a Criterion for the Evaluation of Translation Technique in the LXX and the Evaluation of Word-Order Variants as Exemplified in LXX-Ezekiel." *Textus* 13 (1986b): 59-84.

Martin, R. A. "Some Syntactical Criteria of Translation Greek." *VT* 10 (1960): 295-310.

___. *Syntactical Evidences of Semitic Sources in Greek Documents. SCS* 3. Missoula: Scholars Press, 1974.

___. "Syntax Criticism of Baruch." In *VII Congress of the IOSCS*, edited by C. Cox, 361-71. Atlanta: Scholars Press, 1991.

McGregor, L. J. *The Greek Text of Ezekiel: An Examination of Its Homogeneity. SCS* 18. Atlanta: Scholars Press, 1985.

McLay, T. "Translation Technique and Textual Studies in the Old Greek and Theodotion Versions of Daniel." Ph.D. Dissertation, University of Durham, 1994.

Muraoka, T. "Literary Device in the Septuagint." *Textus* 8 (1973): 20-30.

Nida, E. *Toward a Science of Translating.* Leiden: E.J. Brill, 1964.

Nida, E., and C. R. Taber. *The Theory and Practice of Translation.* Leiden: Brill, 1974.

Olofsson, S. *The LXX Version: A Guide to the Translation Technique of the Septuagint*. ConBib.OT 30. Stockholm: Almqvist & Wiksell, 1990a.

___. *God is My Rock*. ConBib.OT 31. Stockholm: Almqvist & Wiksell, 1990b.

___. "Consistency as a Translation Technique." *SJOT* 6 (1992): 14-30.

Pietersma, A. "The Greek Psalter. A question of methodology and syntax." *VT* 26 (1976): 60-69.

Rabin, C. "The Ancient Versions and the Indefinite Subject." *Textus* 2 (1962): 60-76.

___. "The Translation Process and the Character of the Septuagint." *Textus* 6 (1968): 1-26.

Rife, J. M. "The Mechanics of Translation Greek." *JBL* 52 (1933): 244-52.

Sailhamer, J. H. "The Translational Technique of the Greek Septuagint for the Hebrew Verbs and Participles in Psalms 3-41." Ph.D. dissertation, University of California, 1981.

Schehr, T. P. "The Perfect Indicative in Septuagint Genesis." *BIOSCS* 24 (1991): 14-24.

Smith, M. "Another Criterion for the καιγε Recension." *Bib* 48 (1967): 443-45.

Soisalon-Soininen, I. *Die Infinitive in der Septuaginta*. Helsinki: Suomalainen Tiedeakatemia, 1965.

___. "Verschiedene Wiedergaben der hebräischen status-constructus-Verbindung im griechischen Pentateuch." *SEA* 40 (1975): 214-23.

___. "The Rendering of the Hebrew Relative Clause in the Greek Pentateuch." In *Sixth World Congress of Jewish Studies*, edited by A. Shinan, 401-6. Jerusalem: Jerusalem Academic Press, 1977a.

___. "Die Wiedergabe einiger Hebräischer, mit der Präposition B^e ausgedrückter Zeitanggaben in der Septuaginta." *Annual of the Swedish Theological Institute* 11 (1977/78b): 138-46.

___. "Der Gebrauch des Verbes 'ÉXEIN in der Septuaginta." *VT* 28 (1978): 92-99.

___. "Die Konstruction des Verbs bei einem Neutrum Plural im griechischen Pentateuch." *VT* 29 (1979a): 189-99.

___. "Renderings of Hebrew Comparative Expressions with *MIN* in the Pentateuch." *BIOSCS* 12 (1979b): 27-42.

___. "ἐν für εἰς in der Septuaginta." *VT* 32 (1982): 190-200.

___. "Beobactungen zur Arbeitsweise der Septuaginta-Übersetzer." In *Isac Leo Seeligmann Volume*, edited by A. Rofé and Y. Zakovitch, 319-29. Jerusalem: Magnes, 1983.

___. "Die Wiedergabe des hebräischen, als Subjekt stehenden Personalpronomens im griechischen Pentateuch." In *De Septuaginta*, edited by A. Pietersma and C. Cox, 115-28. Mississauga: Benben, 1984.

___. "Die Wiedergabe des Partitiven מן im Griechischen Pentateuch." In *La Septuaginta en la Investigacion Contemporanea (V Congreso de la IOSCS)*, edited by N. F. Marcos, 83-100. Madrid: Instituto Arias Montano, 1985.

___. "Methodologische Fragen der Erforschung der Septuaginta-Syntax." In *VI Congress of the IOSCS*, edited by C. Cox, 425-44. Atlanta: Scholars Press, 1986.

___. *Studien zur Septuaginta-Syntax*. AASF, B, 237. Helsinki: Suomalainen Tiedeakatemia, 1987.

___. "Zurück zur Hebraismenfrage." In *Studien zur Septuaginta - Robert Hanhart zu Ehren*. MSU 20, edited by D. Fraenkel, U. Quast, and J. Wevers, 35-51. Göttingen: Vandenhoeck & Ruprecht, 1990.

Sollamo, R. "Some "improper" prepositions, such as ΕΝΩΠΙΟΝ, ΕΝΑΝΤΙΟΝ, ΕΝΑΝΤΙ, etc., in the Septuagint and early koine Greek." *VT* 28 (1975): 773-82.

___. *Renderings of Hebrew Semiprepositions in the Septuagint*. AASF DHL, 19. Tiedeakatemia: Suomalainen, 1979.

___. "The LXX Renderings of the Infinitive Absolute Used with a Paronymous Finite Verb in the Pentateuch." In *La Septuaginta en la Investigacion Contemporanea (V Congreso de la IOSCS)*, edited by N. F. Marcos, 101-13. Madrid: Instituto Arias Montano, 1985.

___. "The Koine Background for the Repetition and Non-Repetition of the Possessive Pronoun in Co-ordinate Items." In *Studien zur Septuaginta - Robert Hanhart zu Ehren*. MSU 20, edited by D. Fraenkel, U. Quast, and J. Wevers, 52-63. Göttingen: Vandenhoeck & Ruprecht, 1990.

___. "The Pleonastic use of the Pronoun in Connection with the Relative Pronoun in the Greek Pentateuch." In *VII Congress of the IOSCS*, edited by C. Cox, 75-85. Atlanta: Scholars Press, 1991.

Szpek, H. M. *Translation Technique in the Peshitta to Job*. SBLDS 137. Atlanta: Scholars Press, 1992.

Talshir, Z. "Double Translations in the Septuagint." In *VI Congress of the IOSCS*, edited by C. Cox, 21-63. Atlanta: Scholars Press, 1986a.

___. "Linguistic Development and the Evaluation of Translation Technique in the Septuagint." *Scripta Hierosolymitana* 31 (1986b): 301-20.

Taylor, R. *The Peshitta of Daniel*. (Leiden: Brill, 1994).

Thackeray, H. St. J. "The Bisection of Books in Primitive Septuagint MSS." *JTS* 9 (1907): 88-98.

___. "The Greek Translators of the Four Four Books of Kings." *JTS* 8 (1907): 262-78.

___. "Renderings of the Infinitive Absolute in the LXX." *JTS* 9 (1908): 597-601.

___. *The Septuagint and Jewish Worship*. Oxford: University Press, 1920.

Tov, E. "Transliterations of Hebrew Words in the Greek Versions of the Old Testament." *Textus* 8 (1973): 78-92.

___. "Three Dimensions of LXX Words." *RB* 83 (1976): 529-44.

___. "Compound Words in the LXX Representing Two or More Hebrew Words." *Bib* 58 (1977): 189-212.

___. "Loan-words, Homophony, and Transliterations in the Septuagint." *Bib* 60 (1979): 216-36.

___. "The Impact of the LXX Translation of the Pentateuch on the Translation of the Other Books." In *Mélanges Dominique Barthélemy*. OBO, 38, edited by P. Casetti, O. Keel, and A. Schenker, 577-92. Göttingen: Vandenhoeck & Ruprecht, 1981.

___. "The Representation of the Causative Aspects of the *Hiph'il* in the LXX. A Study in Translation Technique." *Bib* 63 (1982): 417-24.

___. "Did the Septuagint Translators Always Understand Their Hebrew Text?" In *De Septuaginta*, edited by A. Pietersma and C. Cox, 53-70. Mississauga: Benben, 1984.

___. "The Nature and Study of the Translation Technique of the LXX in the Past and Present." In *VI Congress of the IOSCS*, edited by C. Cox, 337-59. Atlanta: Scholars Press, 1986.

___. "Renderings of Combinations of the Infinitive Absolute and Finite Verbs in the LXX - Their Nature and Distribution." In *Studien zur Septuaginta - Robert Hanhart zu Ehren*. MSU, 20, edited by D. Fraenkel, U. Quast, and J. Wevers, 64-73. Göttingen: Vandenhoeck & Ruprecht, 1990.

Tov, E., and B. G. Wright. "Computer Assisted Study of the Criteria for Assessing the Literalness of Translation Units in the LXX." *Textus* 12 (1985): 149-87.

Troxel, R. L. "'ΕΣΧΑΤΟΣ and Eschatology in LXX-Isaiah." *BIOSCS* 25 (1992): 18-27.

De Waard, J. "Translation Techniques Used by the Greek Translators of Ruth." *Bib* 54 (1973): 499-515.

___. "Translation Techniques Used by the Greek Translators of Amos." *Bib* 59 (1978): 339-50.

___. "La Septante: une Traduction." In *Études sur le Judaïsme Hellénistique*, edited by R. Kuntzmann and J. Schlosser, 133-45. Paris: Les Éditions du CERF, 1984.

Weissert, D. "Alexandrian Word-Analysis and Septuagint Translation Techniques." *Textus* 8 (1973): 31-44.

Wevers, J. W. "Evidence of the Text of the John H. Scheide Papyri for the Translation of the Status Constructus in Ezekiel." *JBL* 70 (1951): 211-16.

___. "A Study in the Narrative Portions of the Greek Exodus." In *Scripta Signa Vocis.*, edited by H. L. J. Vanstiphout, K. Jongeling, F. Leemhuis, and G. J. Reinink, 295-303. Groningen: Egbert Forsten, 1986.

___. "The Göttingen Pentateuch: Some Post-Partem Reflections." In *VII Congress of the IOSCS*, edited by C. Cox, 51-62. Atlanta: Scholars Press, 1991.

Wifstrand, A. "Die Stellung der enklitischen Personalpronomina bei den Septuaginta." *Bulletin de la Société Royale des Lettres de Lund* 1 (1949-50): 44-70.

Wright, B. G. "The Quantitative Representation of Elements: Evaluating 'Literalism' in the LXX." In *VI Congress of the IOSCS*, edited by C. Cox, 311-35. Atlanta: Scholars Press, 1988.

___. *No Small Difference, Sirach's Relationship to Its Hebrew Parent Text*. SCS 26. Atlanta: Scholars Press, 1989.

Ziegler, J. "Der Gebrauch des Artikels in der Septuaginta des Ecclesiastes." In *Studien zur Septuaginta - Robert Hanhart zu Ehren*. MSU 20, edited by D. Fraenkel, U. Quast, and J. Wevers, 83-120. Göttingen: Vandenhoeck & Ruprecht, 1990.

IV. *Literature Consulted*

Aejmelaeus, A. "What Can We Know about the Hebrew *Vorlage* of the Septuagint?" *ZAW* 99 (1981): 58-89.

Albertz, R. *Der Gott des Daniel*. SBS 131. Stuttgart: Katholisches Bibelwerk, 1988.

Anderson, F. I. *The Hebrew Verbless Clause in the Pentateuch*. JBLMS 14. Nashville: Abingdon, 1970.

Ashley, T. R. "A Philological, Literary, Theological Study of Some Problems in Daniel Chapters I-VI; with Special Reference to the Massoretic Text, the Septuagint and Medieval Rabbinic Exegesis of Selected Passages." Ph.D. Dissertation, University of St. Andrews, 1975.

Baker, D. W. "Further Examples of the Waw Explicativum." *VT* 30 (1980): 12-36.

Barr, J. *The Semantics of Biblical Language*. Oxford: Clarendon, 1961.

___. "Vocalization and the Analysis of Hebrew among the Ancient Translators." *VTSup* 16 (1967): 1-11.

___. "Aramaic-Greek Notes on the Book of Enoch (I)." *JSS* 23 (1978): 184-98.

___. "Aramaic-Greek Notes on the Book of Enoch (II)." *JSS* 24 (1979): 179-92.

___. "Determination and the Definite Article in Biblical Hebrew." *JSS* 34 (1989): 307-35.

Barrera, J. T., and L. V. Montaner, eds. *The Madrid Qumran Congress*. 2 vols. Leiden: Brill, 1992.

Barthélemy, D. *Les Devanciers D'Aquila: Première Publication Intégrale du Texte des Fragments du Dodécaprophéton*. *VTSup* 10. Leiden: Brill, 1963.

___. "Notes critiques sur quelqeus points d'histoire du texte." In *Études d'histoire du texte de l'Ancien Testament*. *OBO*, 21, 289-303. Göttingen: Vandenhoeck & Ruprecht, 1978.

___. "L'enchevêtrement de l'histoire textuelle et de l'histoire littéraire dans les relations entre la Septante et la Texte Massorétique." In *De Septuaginta*, edited by A. Pietersma and C. Cox, 21-40. Mississauga: Benben, 1984.

Baumgartner, W. "Das Aramäische im Buche Daniel." *ZAW* 45 (1927): 81-133.

Beek, M. A. *Das Danielbuch*. Leiden: J. Ginsberg, 1935.

Bennett, J. *Linguistic Behaviour*. Cambridge: University Press, 1976.

Bentzen, A. *Daniel*. Erste Reihe 19, 2te Auf. Tübingen: J.C.B. Mohr, 1952.

Bevan, A. A. *A Short Commentary on the Book of Daniel*. Cambridge: University Press, 1892.

Bickerman, E. J. "The Septuagint as a Translation." *PAAJR* 28 (1959): 1-39.

Black, D. A. *Linguistics for Students of New Testament Greek*. Grand Rapids: Baker, 1988.

Bloomfield, L. *Language*. London: G. Allen & Unwin, 1935.

Bodine, W. *The Greek Text of Judges*. HSM 23. Chico: Scholars Press, 1980.

___. "*Kaige* and Other Recensional Developments in the Greek Text of Judges." *BIOSCS* 13 (1980): 45-57.

___. "How Linguists Study Syntax." In *Linguistics and Biblical Hebrew*, edited by W. Bodine, 89-107. Winona Lake: Eisenbrauns, 1992.

Bogaert, P. M. "Histoire et eschatologie dans le livre de Daniel." In *Apocalypses et Théologie de L'Espérance*. Lectio Divina 95, edited by Monloubou, 63-109. Paris: Éditions du CERF, 1975.

___. "Le témoignage de la Vetus Latina dans l'étude de la tradition des Septante. Ézéchiel et Daniel dans le Papyrus 967." *Bib* 59 (1978): 384-95.

___. "Relecture et refonte historicisantes du livre de Daniel attestées par la première version Grecque (Papyrus 967)." In *Études sur le Judaïsme Hellénistique*, edited by R. Kuntzmann and J. Schlosser, 197-224. Paris: Les Éditions du CERF, 1984.

Bréal, M. *Semantics: Studies in the Science of Meaning*. Translated by Mrs. H. Cust. New York: Dover, 1964.

Brock, S. P. "The Phenomenon of the Septuagint." *OTS* 17 (1972): 11-36.

Brock, S. P., C. T. Fritsch, and S. Jellicoe. *A Classified Bibliography of the Septuagint*. Leiden: Brill, 1973.

Brown, R. E., J. A. Fitzmeyer, and R. E. Murphy. *The Jerome Biblical Commentary*. Englewood Cliffs: Prentice-Hall, 1968.

Bruce, F. F. "The Earliest Old Testament Interpretation." *OTS* 17 (1972): 37-52.

___. "The Oldest Greek Version of Daniel." *OTS* 20 (1977): 22-40.

___. "Prophetic Interpretation in the Septuagint." *BASOR* 12 (1979): 17-26.

Busto Saiz, J. R. "Él Texto Teodocionico de Daniel y la Traduccion de Simaco." *Sef* 40 (1980): 41-55.

Cathcart, K. "Daniel, especially the Additions, and Chester Beatty-Cologne Papyrus 967." *Proceedings of the Irish Biblical Association* 15 (1992): 37-41.

Chafe, W. L. *Meaning and the Structure of Language*. Chicago: Univ. of Chicago, 1970.

Charles, R. H. *A Critical and Exegetical Commentary on the Book of Daniel*. Oxford: Clarendon, 1929.

Chiesa, B. "Textual History and the Textual Criticism of the Hebrew Old Testament." In *The Madrid Qumran Congress*, edited by J. T. Barrera and L. V. Montaner. Vol. 1, 257-72. Leiden: Brill, 1992.

Chomsky, N. *Reflections on Language*. New York: Pantheon, 1975.

___. *Rules and Representations*. Oxford: Basil Blackwell, 1980.

Colless, B. E. "Cyrus the Persian as Darius the Mede in the Book of Daniel." *JSOT* 56 (1992): 113-26.

Collins, J. J. "The Son of Man and the Saints of the Most High in the Book of Daniel." *JBL* 93 (1974): 50-66.

___. "Towards the Morphology of a Genre." *Semeia* 14 (1979): 1-20.

___. *Daniel*. FOTL 20. Grand Rapids: Eerdmans, 1984.

___. "The Meaning of "the End" in the Book of Daniel." In *Of Scribes and Scrolls*, edited by H. W. Attridge, J. J. Collins, and T. H. Tobin, 91-98. Lanham: University Press of America, 1990.

Collins, N. "281 BCE: the Year of the Translation of the Pentateuch into Greek under Ptolemy II." In *Septuagint, Scrolls and Cognate Writings*. SCS 33, edited by G. J. Brooke and B. Lindars, 403-503. Atlanta: Scholars Press, 1992.

Collinson, W. E. "Comparative Synomics: Some Principles and Illustrations." *Transactions of the Philosophical Society* (1939): 54-77.

Cook, E. M. "Word Order in the Aramaic of Daniel." *Afroasiatic Linguistics* 9 (1986): 1-16.

Cook, J. ""Ancient" Readings in the Translations of the Old Testament." *JNSL* 12 (1986): 41-51.

___. "Orthographical Peculiarities in the Dead Sea Biblical Scrolls." *RQ* 14 (1989): '293-305.

Coxon, P. W. "Greek Loan-Words and Alleged Greek Loan Translations in the Book of Daniel." *Transactions of the Glasgow University Oriental Society* 25 (1973-74): 24-40.

___. "Daniel III:17: A Linguistic and Theological Problem." *VT* 26 (1976): 400-409.

___. "The Syntax of the Aramaic of Daniel." *HUCA* 48 (1977): 107-22.

___. "The 'List' Genre and Narrative Style in the Court Tales of Daniel." *JSOT* 35 (1986): 95-121.

Crim, K., ed. *The Interpreter's Dictionary of the Bible, Supplementary Volume*. Nashville: Abingdon, 1976.

Cross, F. M. *The Ancient Library of Qumran and Modern Biblical Studies*. Westport: Greenwood, 1958.

___. "The Development of the Jewish Scripts." In *The Bible and the Ancient Near East*, edited by G.E. Wright, 133-202. London: Routledge, Kegan & Paul, 1961.

___. "The Contribution of the Qumran Discoveries to the Study of the Biblical Text." *IEJ* 16 (1966): 81-95.

___. "The Evolution of a Theory of Local Texts." In *Qumran and the History of the Biblical Text*, edited by F. M. Cross and S. Talmon, 306-20. Cambridge: Harvard University Press, 1975.

___. "Some Notes on a Generation of Qumran Studies." In *The Madrid Qumran Congress*, edited by J. T. Barrera and L. V. Montaner. Vol. 1, 1-14. Leiden: Brill, 1992.

David, P. S. "The Composition and Structure of the Book of Daniel: A Synchronic and Diachronic Reading." Ph.D. Dissertation, Katholicke Universiteit, Leuven, 1991.

Davies, P. R. "Daniel Chapter Two." *JTS* 27 (1976): 392-401.

___. "*Hasidim* in the Maccabean Period." *JJS* 28 (1977): 127-40.

___. *Daniel*. Old Testament Guides. Sheffield: JSOT, 1985.

Deissmann, A. *The Philology of the Greek Bible: Its Present and Future*. London: Hodder and Stoughton, 1908.

Delcor, M. "Les Sources du Chapitre VII de Daniel." *VT* 18 (1968): 290-312.

___. "Un cas de traduction 'Targumique' de la LXX à propos de la statue en or de Dan. III." *Textus* 7 (1969): 30-35.

Dorival, G., M. Harl, and O. Munnich. *La Bible Grecque des Septante*. Paris: Éditions du CERF, 1988.

Driver, G. R. "The Aramaic of the Book of Daniel." *JBL* 45 (1926): 110-19.

Driver, S. R. *The Book of Daniel*. Cambridge Bible for Schools and Colleges. Cambridge: University Press, 1900.

Eißfeldt, O. "Daniel und seiner drei Gefährten Laufbahn im babylonischen, medischen und persischen Dienst." *ZAW* 72 (1960): 134-48.

___. *The Old Testament: An Introduction*. Translated by Peter Ackroyd. Oxford: Basil Blackwell, 1965.

Eitan, I. "Some Philological Observations in Daniel." *HUCA* 14 (1939): 13-22.

Emerton, J. A. "The Participles in Daniel v. 12." *ZAW* 72 (1960): 262-63.

Ferch, A. J. "The Book of Daniel and the Maccabean Thesis." *AUSS* 21 (1983): 129-41.

Fernández Marcos, N. "The Use of the Septuagint in the Criticism of the Hebrew Bible." *Sef* 47 (1987): 60-72.

___. "Some Reflections on the Antiochian Text of the Septuagint." In *Studien zur Septuaginta - Robert Hanhart zu Ehren. MSU* 20, edited by D. Fraenkel, U. Quast, and J. Wevers, 219-29. Göttingen: Vandenhoeck & Ruprecht, 1990.

___. *Scribes and Translators: Septuagint and Old Latin in the Books of Kings.* VTSup 54. Leiden: E. J. Brill, 1994.

Fodor, J., and J. Katz. *The Structure of Language.* Prentice-Hall: Englewood Cliffs, 1964.

Fox, M. *The Redaction of the Books of Esther. SBLMS* 40. Atlanta: Scholars Press, 1991.

___. "The Redaction of the Greek Alpha-Text of Esther." In *Sha'arei Talmon*, edited by M. Fishbane, E. Tov, and W. W. Fields, 207-20. Winona Lake: Eisenbrauns, 1992.

Freedman, D. N. "The Prayer of Nabonidus." *JAOS* 145 (1957): 31-32.

Frölich, I. "Pesher, Apocalyptical Literature and Qumran." In *The Madrid Qumran Congress*, edited by J. T. Barrera and L. V. Montaner. Vol. 1, 295-305. Leiden: Brill, 1992.

Gammie, J. G. "The Classification, Stages of Growth, and Changing Intentions in the Book of Daniel." *JBL* 95 (1976): 191-204.

___. "On the Intention and Sources of Daniel I-VI." *VT* 31 (1981): 282-92.

Gaster, M. "The Unknown Aramaic Original of Theodotion's Additions to the Book of Daniel." *Proceedings of the Society of Biblical Archeology* 16 (1894): 280-90, 312-17; 17 (1895): 75-94.

Garr, W. R. "On the Alternation Between Construct and *DI* Phrase in Biblical Aramaic." *JSS* 35 (1990): 213-31.

___. "The Linguistic Study of Morphology." In *Linguistics and Biblical Hebrew*, edited by W. Bodine, 49-64. Winona Lake: Eisenbrauns, 1992.

Gehman, H. S. "Adventures in Septuagint Lexicography." *Textus* 6 (1966): 125-32.

Gibson, A. *Biblical Semantic Logic.* Oxford: Basil Blackwell, 1981.

Giese, R. L. "Qualifying Wealth in the Septuagint of Proverbs." *JBL* 111 (1992): 409-25.

Ginsberg, H. L. *Studies in Daniel.* New York: Jewish Theological Seminary of America, 1948.

___. "The Composition of the Book of Daniel." *VT* 4 (1954): 246-75.

Gleason, H. A. *An Introduction to Descriptive Linguistics.* Rev. ed. London: Holt, Rinehart and Winston, 1961.

Gnuse, R. "The Jewish Dream Interpreter in a Foreign Court: The Recurring Use of a Theme in Jewish Literature." *JSP* 7 (1990): 29-52.

Goldingay, J. *Daniel*. WBC 30. Dallas: Word, 1989.

Gooding, D. W. "A Recent Popularization of Professor F. M. Cross' Theories on the Text of the Old Testament." *Tyndale Bulletin* 26 (1975): 113-32.

___. "An Appeal for a Stricter Terminology in the Textual Criticism of the Old Testament." *JSS* 21 (1976): 15-25.

___. "The Literary Structure of the Book of Daniel and Its Implications." *Tyndale Bulletin* 32 (1981): 43-79.

Goshen-Gottstein, M. "Theory and Practice of Textual Criticism." *Textus* 3 (1963): 130-58.

___. "The Textual Criticism of the Old Testament: Rise, Decline, Rebirth." *JBL* 102 (1983): 365-99.

___. "Hebrew University Editions of the Bible—Past and Future." In *Sha'arei Talmon*, edited by M. Fishbane, E. Tov, and W. W. Fields, 221-42. Winona Lake: Eisenbrauns, 1992.

Grabbe, L. L. "Aquila's Translation and Rabbinic Exegesis." *JJS* 33 (1982): 527-36.

Greenspahn, F. *Hapax Legomena in Biblical Hebrew*. SBLDS 74. Chico: Scholars Press, 1984.

Greenspoon, L. *Textual Studies in the Book of Joshua*. HSM 28. Chico: Scholars Press, 1983.

___. "The Use and Abuse of the Term 'LXX' and Related Terminology in Recent Scholarship." *BIOSCS* 20 (1987): 21-29.

___. "Sharon Pace Jeansonne, The Old Greek Translation of Daniel 7-12." *JBL* 108 (1989): 700-702.

___. "It's all Greek to Me: The Septuagint in Modern English Translations of the Hebrew Bible." In *VII Congress of the IOSCS*, edited by C. Cox, 1-21. Atlanta: Scholars Press, 1991.

Grelot, P. "Les Versions grecques de Daniel." *Bib* 47 (1966): 381-402.

___. "Le Chapitre v de Daniel dans la Septante." *Sem* 24 (1974): 45-66.

___. "La Septante de Daniel iv et son substrat sémitique." *RB* 81 (1974): 1-23.

___. "L'Orchestre de Daniel III 5, 7 10, 15." *VT* 29 (1979): 23-38.

Gwynn, J. "Theodotion." In *Dictionary of Christian Biography*, edited by W. Smith and H. Wace. Vol. 4, 970-79. London: John Murrow, 1887.

Haag, E. *Die Errettung Daniels aus der Löwengrube.* SBS 110. Stuttgart: Katholisches Bibelwerk, 1983.

Hall, R. A. "Post-Exilic Theological Streams and the Book of Daniel." Ph.D. Dissertation, Yale, 1974.

Haller, M. "Das Alter von Daniel." *TSK* 93 (1921): 83-87.

Halliday, M. A. K. "Lexis as a linguistic level." In *In Memory of J.R. Firth*, edited by C. E. Bazell, J. C. Catford, M. A. K. Halliday, and R. H. Robins, 148-62. London: Longmans, 1966.

Hanhart, R. "Zum gegenwärtigen Stand der Septuaginta- forschung." In *De Septuaginta*, edited by A. Pietersma and C. Cox, 3-18. Mississauga: Benben, 1984.

___. "The Translation of the Septuagint in Light of Earlier Tradition and Subsequent Influences." In *Septuagint, Scrolls and Cognate Writings*. SCS 33, edited by G. J. Brooke and B. Lindars, 339-79. Atlanta: Scholars Press, 1992.

Harris, R. *Synonymy and Linguistic Analysis.* Oxford: Basil Blackwell, 1973.

Hartman, L. F., and A. A. Di Lella. *The Book of Daniel.* AB 23. Garden City: Doubleday, 1978.

Heaton, E. W. *The Book of Daniel.* Torch Bible Commentary. London: SCM, 1956.

Hengel, M. *Judaism and Hellenism.* 2 vols. Translated by John Bowman. Philadelphia: Fortress, 1974.

Hirst, G. *Semantic Interpretation and the Resolution of Ambiguity.* Cambridge: Cambridge University Press, 1987.

Hölscher, G. "Die Entstehung des Buches Daniel." *TSK* 92 (1919): 113-38.

Humphreys, W. L. "A Lifestyle for Diaspora: A Study of the Tales of Esther and Daniel." *JBL* 92 (1973): 211-23.

Jackendoff, R. *Semantics and Cognition.* London: MIT, 1990.

Jackson, H. *Words and Their Meanings.* New York: Longman, 1988.

Jahn, G. *Das Buch Daniel nach der Septuaginta hergestellt.* Leipzig: Pfeiffer, 1904.

Janzen, J. G. *Studies in the Text of Jeremiah.* HSM 6. Cambridge: Harvard, 1973.

___. "A Critique of Sven Soderlund's *The Greek Text of Jeremiah*." *BIOSCS* 22 (1989): 16-47.

Jaubert, A. "Le Calendrier des Jubilés et de la secte de Qumran: Ses origines bibliques." *VT* 3 (1953): 250-64.

___. "Le Calendrier des Jubilés et de les jours liturgiques de la semaine." *VT* 7 (1957): 35-61.

Jeansonne, S. Pace. *The Old Greek Translation of Daniel 7-12*. CBQMS 19. Washington: Catholic Biblical Association, 1988.

Jeffrey, A. "The Exegesis of the Book of Daniel." In *The Interpreter's Bible*, edited by G. Buttrick. Vol. VI, 341-59. Nashville: Abingdon, 1956.

Jellicoe, S. "The Hesychian Recension Reconsidered." *JBL* 82 (1963): 409-18.

___. *The Septuagint and Modern Study*. Oxford: Clarendon, 1968.

___. "Some Reflections on the ΚΑΙΓΕ Recension." *VT* 23 (1973): 15-24.

___, ed. *Studies in the Septuagint: Origins, Recensions, and Interpretations*. New York: KTAV, 1974.

Kallarakkal, A. G. "The Peshitto Version of Daniel — A Comparison with the Massoretic Text, the Septuagint and Theodotion." Ph.D. Dissertation, Hamburg, 1973.

Kasher, A. *The Chomskyan Turn*. Oxford: Basil Blackwell, 1991.

Keil, C. F. *The Book of the Prophet Daniel*. Translated by M. G. Easton. Edinburgh: T & T Clark, 1884.

Kirk, R. *Translation Determined*. Oxford: Clarendon, 1986.

Kitchen, K. A. "The Aramaic of Daniel," in *Notes on Some Problems in the Book of Daniel*, ed. D. J. Wiseman et al., 31-79. London: Tyndale, 1965.

Koch, K. "Die Herkunft der Proto-Theodotion-übersetzung des Danielbuches." *VT* 23 (1973): 362-65.

Kogut, S. "On the Meaning and Syntactical Status of חנה in Biblical Hebrew." *Scripta Hierosolymitana* 31 (1986): 133-54.

van der Kooj, A. "The Old Greek of Isaiah in Relation to the Qumran Texts of Isaiah: Some General Comments." In *Septuagint, Scrolls and Cognate Writings*. SCS 33, edited by G. J. Brooke and B. Lindars, 195-213. Atlanta: Scholars Press, 1992.

Kraeling, E. G. "The Handwriting on the Wall." *JBL* 63 (1944): 11-18.

Kraft, R. A., ed. *Septuagintal Lexicography*. Missoula: Scholars Press, 1972.

Kratz, R. G. *Translatio Imperii: Untersuchungen zu den aramäischen Danielerzählungen und ihrem theologiegeschichtlichen Umfeld*. WMANT 63. Neulirchen-Vluyn: Neukirchener Verlag, 1991.

Kuhl, C. *Die Drei Männer im Feuer*. BZAW 55. Giessen: Alfred Töpelmann, 1930.

Lacocque, A. *The Book of Daniel*. Atlanta: John Knox, 1979.

___. *Daniel in His Time*. Translated by D. Pellauer. Atlanta: John Knox, 1979.

Lehrer, A. *Semantic Fields and Lexical Structures*. London: North-Holland, 1974.

Leupold, H. C. *Exposition of Daniel*. Grand Rapids: Baker Book House, 1974.

Louw, J. P. *Semantics of New Testament Greek*. Atlanta: Scholars Press, 1982.

Lust, J. "Daniel VII and the Septuagint." *ETL* 54 (1978): 62-69.

___. "A Concise Lexicon of the Septuagint." *ETL* 68 (1992): 188-94.

___. "Translation Greek and the Lexicography of the Septuagint." *JSOT* 59 (1993): 109-20.

Lyons, J. *Structural Semantics*. Oxford: Basil Blackwell, 1963.

___. "Firth's Theory of Meaning." In *In Memory of J.R. Firth*, edited by C. E. Bazell, J. C. Catford, M. A. K. Halliday, and R. H. Robins, 288-302. London: Longmans, 1966.

___, ed. *New Horizons in Linguistics*. Middlesex: Penguin, 1970.

___. *Semantics*. 2 vols. Cambridge: University Press, 1977.

___. *Language and Linguistics*. Cambridge: University Press, 1981.

___. *Language, Meaning and Context*. Suffolk: Fontana, 1981.

MacDonald, P. "Discourse Analysis and Biblical Interpretation." In *Linguistics and Biblical Hebrew*, edited by W. Bodine, 153-75. Winona Lake: Eisenbrauns, 1992.

Marquis, G. "CATSS-Base: Computer Assisted Tools for Septuagint and Bible Study for All—Transcript of a Demonstration." In *VII Congress of the IOSCS*, edited by C. Cox, 165-203. Atlanta: Scholars Press, 1991.

McAlpine, T. H. *Sleep, Divine and Human in the Old Testament*. JSOTS 38. Sheffield: JSOT, 1987.

McCarter, P. K. *Textual Criticism: Recovering the Text of the Hebrew Bible*. Philadelphia: Fortress, 1986.

McCrystall, A. "Studies in the Old Greek Translation of Daniel." D.Phil. Dissertation, Oxford University, 1980.

Meadowcroft, T. J. "A Literary Critical Comparison of the Masoretic Text and Septuagint of Daniel 2-7." Ph.D. Dissertation, University of Edinburgh, 1993.

Milik, J. T. *The Books of Enoch.* Oxford: Oxford Press, 1976.

Miller, J. E. "The Redaction of Daniel." *JSOT* 52 (1991): 115-24.

Mitchell, T.C. and R. Joyce, "The Musical Instruments in Nebuchadrezzar's Orchestra," in *Notes on Some Problems in the Book of Daniel*, ed. D. J. Wiseman et al., 19-27. London: Tyndale, 1965.

Montaner, L. V. "Computer-Assisted Study of the Relation Between *1QpHab* and the Ancient (Mainly Greek) Biblical Versions." *RQ* 14 (1989): 307-23.

Montgomery, J. A. "The Hexaplaric Strata in the Greek Texts of Daniel." *JBL* 44 (1925): 289-302.

___. *A Critical and Exegetical Commentary on the Book of Daniel.* ICC. New York: Charles Scribner's Sons, 1927.

Moore, C. A. *Daniel, Esther and Jeremiah: The Additions.* AB 44. New York: Doubleday, 1977.

Müller, M. "The Septuagint as the Bible of the New Testament Church: Some Reflections," *SJOT* 7 (1993): 194-207.

Munnich, O. "Indices d'une Septante originelle dans le Psautier Grec." *Bib* 63 (1982): 406-16.

___. "La Septante des Psaumes et la Groupe *Kaige*." *VT* 33 (1983): 75-89.

___. "Contribution à l'étude de la première révision de la Septante." *ANRW* II.20.1 (1986): 190-220.

___. "Origène, éditeur de la *Septante* de *Daniel*." In *Studien zur Septuaginta - Robert Hanhart zu Ehren.* MSU 20, edited by D. Fraenkel, U. Quast, and J. Wevers, 187-218. Göttingen: Vandenhoeck & Ruprecht, 1990.

Muraoka, T. "Notes on the Syntax of Biblical Aramaic." *JSS* 11 (1966): 151-67.

___, ed. *Melbourne Symposium on Septuagint Lexicography.* SCS 28. Atlanta: Scholars Press, 1990.

___. "Hebrew Hapax Legomena and Septuagint Lexicography." In *VII Congress of the IOSCS*, edited by C. Cox, 205-22. Atlanta: Scholars Press, 1991.

Nida, E. *Morphology: The Descriptive Analysis of Meaning.* Ann Arbor: University of Michigan, 1949.

___. *Componential Analysis of Meaning.* Paris: Mouton, 1975.

___. *Exploring Semantic Structures.* Munich: Fink, 1975.

___. *Language Structure and Translation.* Stanford: University Press, 1975.

Nida, E., and J. P. Louw. *Lexical Semantics of the Greek New Testament.* Atlanta: Scholars Press, 1992.

Nida, E. A., J. P. Louw, A. H. Snyman, and J. Cronje. *Style and Discourse: With Special Reference to the Text of the Greek New Testament.* Cape Town: Bible Society, 1983.

Niditch, S. *The Symbolic Vision in Biblical Tradition.* HSM 30. Chico: Scholars Press, 1980.

___. "The Visionary." In *Ideal Figures in Ancient Judaism.* SCS 12, edited by J. J. Collins and G. W. E. Nickelsburg, 153-80. Chico: Scholars Press, 1980.

Nötscher, F. *Daniel.* Die Heilige Schrift in Deutscher übersetzung, Echter-Bibel. 3 Auf. Würzburg: Echter-Verlag, 1963.

O'Connell, K. G. *The Theodotionic Revision of the Book of Exodus.* HSM 3. Cambridge: Harvard University Press, 1972.

O'Connor, M. *Hebrew Verse Structure.* Winona Lake: Eisenbrauns, 1980.

Ogden, C. K., and I. A. Richards. *The Meaning of Meaning.* 3rd rev. ed. London: Kegan Paul, 1930.

Orlinsky, H. M. "The Origin of the Kethib-Qere System: A New Approach." *VTSup* 7 (1959): 184-92.

___. "The Textual Criticism of the Old Testament." In *The Bible and the Ancient Near East*, edited by G. E. Wright, 113-32. London: Routledge & Kegan, 1961.

___. "The Septuagint as Holy Writ and the Philosophy of the Translators." *HUCA* 46 (1975): 89-114.

Pace, S. (see Jeansonne) "The Statiography of the Text of Daniel and the Question of Theological *Tendenz* in the Old Greek." *BIOSCS* 17 (1984): 15-35.

Parker, F. *Linguistics for Non-Linguists.* London: Taylor & Francis, 1986.

Pickering, W. *A Framework for Discourse Analysis.* Dallas: Summer Institute of Linguistics, 1980.

Pietersma, A. "Septuagint Research: A Plea for a Return to Basic Issues." *VT* 35 (1985): 296-311.

___. "Ra 2110 (P. Bodmer XXIV) and the Text of the Greek Psalter." In *Studien zur Septuaginta - Robert Hanhart zu Ehren. MSU* 20, edited by D. Fraenkel, U. Quast, and J. Wevers, 264-86. Göttingen: Vandenhoeck & Ruprecht, 1990.

Plöger, O. *Das Buch Daniel.* KAT. Gütersloh: Mohn, 1965.

Polak, F. "Statistics and Textual Filiation: the Case of 4QSamª/LXX." In *Septuagint, Scrolls and Cognate Writings. SCS* 33, edited by G. J. Brooke and B. Lindars, 215-76. Atlanta: Scholars Press, 1992.

Porteous, N. *Daniel.* OTL. Philadelphia: Westminister, 1965.

Porter, P. A. *Metaphors and Monsters. ConBib.OT* 20. Uppsala: Uppsala University, 1983.

Porter, S. E. "Studying Ancient Languages from a Modern Linguistic Perspective: Essential Terms and Terminology." *FN* 2 (1989): 147-72.

Porzig, W. *Das Wunder der Sprache.* Bern: Francke, 1950.

Radford, A. *Transformational Syntax: A student's guide to extended standard theory.* Cambridge: University Press, 1981.

Revell, E. J. "LXX and MT: Aspects of Relationship." In *De Septuaginta*, edited by A. Pietersma and C. Cox, 41-51. Mississauga: Benben, 1984.

___. "The Conditioning of Word Order in Verbless Clauses in Biblical Hebrew." *JSS* 34 (1989): 1-24.

Riessler, P. *Das Buch Daniel.* Stuttgart: Roth'sche, 1899.

Rife, J. M. "Some Translation Phenomena in the Greek Versions of Daniel." Ph.D. Dissertation, University of Chicago, 1931.

Rosén, H. B. "On the Use of the Tenses in the Aramaic of Daniel." *JSS* 6 (1961): 183-203.

Salvesen, A. *Symmachus in the Pentateuch. JSSM* 15. Manchester: University Press, 1991.

Sanders, J. A. "The Dead Sea Scrolls and Biblical Studies." In *Sha'arei Talmon*, edited by M. Fishbane, E. Tov, and W. W. Fields, 323-36. Winona Lake: Eisenbrauns, 1992.

de Saussure, F. *Cours de linguistique générale (ed. Ch. Bally and A. Sechehaye).* 5th ed. Paris: Payot, 1955.

Scanlin, H. "The Study of Semantics in General Linguistics." In *Linguistics and Biblical Hebrew*, edited by W. Bodine, 125-36. Winona Lake: Eisenbrauns, 1992.

Schmitt, A. "Stammt der sogennante θ' Text bei Daniel wirklich von Theodotion?" *MSU* 9 (1966): 281-392.

___. "Die griechischen Danieltexte («θ» und ό) und das Theodotionproblem." *BZ* 36 (1992): 1-29.

Schüpphaus, J. "Das Verhältnis von LXX- und Theodotion-Text in den apokryphen Züsätzen zum Danielbuch." *ZAW* 83 (1971): 49-72.

Shenkel, J. D. *Chronology and Recensional Development in the Greek Text of Kings.* HSM 1. Cambridge: Harvard University, 1968.

Silva, M. "Semantic Change and Semitic Influence in the Greek Bible: With a Study of the Semantic Field of Mind." Ph.D. Dissertation, University of Manchester, 1972.

___. "Describing Meaning in the LXX Lexicon." *BIOSCS* 11 (1978): 19-26.

___. "Bilingualism and the Character of Palestinian Greek." *Bib* 61 (1980): 198-219.

___. *Biblical Words and Their Meaning.* Grand Rapids: Zondervan, 1983.

___. "Internal Evidence in the Text-Critical Use of the LXX." In *La Septuaginta en la Investigacion Contemporanea (V Congreso de la IOSCS)*, edited by N. F. Marcos, 151-67. Madrid: Instituto Arias Montano, 1985.

Soderlund, S. *The Greek Text of Jeremiah.* JSOT 47. Sheffield: JSOT, 1985.

Soisalon-Soininen, I. *Die Textformen der Septuaginta-übersetzung des Richterbuches.* AASF, B, 72. Helsinki: Suomalainen Tiedeakatemia, 1951.

___. "Der *infinitivus constructus* mit ל im Hebräischen." *VT* 22 (1972): 82-90.

Stefanovic, Z. *The Aramaic of Daniel in the Light of Old Aramaic.* JSOT 129. Sheffield: JSOT, 1992.

Stinespring, W. F. "The Active Infinitive with Passive Meaning in Biblical Aramaic." *JBL* 81 (1962): 391-94.

Swete, H. B. *An Introduction to the Old Testament in Greek.* Revised by R.R. Ottley. Cambridge: University Press, 1914.

Szörényi, A. "Das Buch Daniel, ein kanonisierter Pescher?" *VTSup* 15 (1966): 278-94.

Talmon, S. "Double Readings in the Massoretic Text." *Textus* 1 (1960): 144-84.

___. "The Textual Study of the Bible—A New Outlook." In *Qumran and the History of the Biblical Text*, edited by F. M. Cross and S. Talmon, 321-400. Cambridge: Harvard University Press, 1975.

Taylor, B. A. "The CATSS Variant Database: An Evaluation." *BIOSCS* 25 (1992): 28-37.

Thumb, A. *Die griechische Sprache im Zeitalter des Hellenismus.* Strassburg: Karl J. Trübner, 1901.

Tigay, J., ed. *Empirical Models for Biblical Criticism.* Philadelphia: University of Pennsylvania Press, 1985.

Torrey, C. C. "Notes on the Aramaic Part of Daniel." *Transactions of the Connecticut Academy of Arts and Sciences* 15 (1909): 241-82.

___. "Stray Notes on the Aramaic of Daniel and Ezra." *JAOS* 43 (1923): 229-38.

Tov, E. *The Septuagint Translation of Jeremiah and Baruch.* HSM 8. Missoula: Scholars Press, 1976.

___. "Some Thoughts on a Lexicon of the LXX." *BIOSCS* 9 (1976): 25-33.

___. "The Nature of the Hebrew Text Underlying the Septuagint. A Survey of the Problems." *JSOT* 7 (1978): 53-68.

___. *The Text-Critical Use of the Septuagint in Biblical Research.* JBS 3. Jerusalem: Simor, 1981.

___. "Criteria for Evaluating Textual Readings: the Limitations of Textual Rules." *HTR* 75 (1982): 429-48.

___. "A Modern Textual Outlook Based on the Qumran Scrolls." *HUCA* 53 (1983): 11-27.

___. "The Rabbinic Tradition Concerning the 'Alterations' Inserted into the Greek Pentateuch and Their Relation to the Original Text of the LXX." *JSJ* 15 (1984): 65-89.

___. "Computer Assisted Alignment of the Greek-Hebrew Equivalents of the Masoretic Text and the Septuagint." In *La Septuaginta en la Investigacion Contemporanea (V Congreso de la IOSCS),* edited by N. F. Marcos, 221-42. Madrid: Instituto Arias Montano, 1985a.

___. "The Literary History of the Book of Jeremiah in the Light of Its Textual History." In *Empirical Models for Biblical Criticism,* edited by J. H. Tigay, 211-37. Philadelphia: University of Pennsylvania Press, 1985.

___. "The Nature and Background of Harmonization in Biblical Manuscripts." *JSOT* 31 (1985): 3-29.

___. "Die griechischen Bibelübersetzungen." *ANRW* II.20.1 (1986): 121-89.

___. "The Growth of the Book of Joshua in the Light of the Evidence of the LXX Translation." *Scripta Hierosolymitana* 31 (1986): 321-39.

___. "Some Sequence Differences Between the MT and LXX and Their Ramifications for the Literary Criticism of the Bible." *JNSL* 13 (1987): 151-60.

___. "Hebrew Biblical Manuscripts from the Judean Desert: Their Contribution to Textual Criticism." *JJS* 39 (1988): 5-37.

___. "The CATSS Project: A Progress Report." In *VII Congress of the IOSCS*, edited by C. Cox, 157-63. Atlanta: Scholars Press, 1991a.

___. "The Original Shape of the Biblical Text." *VTSup* 43 (1991b): 345-59.

___. "The Contribution of the Qumran Scrolls to the Understanding of the LXX." In *Septuagint, Scrolls and Cognate Writings. SCS* 33, edited by G. J. Brooke and B. Lindars, 11-47. Atlanta: Scholars Press, 1992.

___. "Interchange of Consonants Between the Masoretic Text and the *Vorlage* of the Septuagint." In *Sha'arei Talmon*, edited by M. Fishbane, E. Tov, and W. W. Fields, 255-66. Winona Lake: Eisenbrauns, 1992.

___. "Some Notes on a Generation of Qumran Studies: A Reply." In *The Madrid Qumran Congress*, edited by J. T. Barrera and L. V. Montaner. Vol. 1, 15-21. Leiden: Brill, 1992.

___. *Textual Criticism of the Hebrew Bible*. Minneapolis: Fortress, 1992.

Ullmann, S. *The Principles of Semantics*. Glasgow: Jackson, Son & Co., 1951.

___. *Language and Style*. Oxford: Basil Blackwell, 1964.

Ulrich, E. *The Qumran Text of Samuel and Josephus*. HSM 19. Chico: Scholars Press, 1978.

___. "The Biblical Scrolls from Qumran Cave 4: An Overview and a Progress Report on their Publication." *RQ* 14 (1989): 207-28.

___. "Orthography and Text in 4QDan^a and 4QDan^b and in the Received Masoretic Text." In *Of Scribes and Scrolls*, edited by H. W. Attridge, J. J. Collins, and T. H. Tobin, 29-42. Lanham: University Press of America, 1990.

___. "The Canonical Process, Textual Criticism, and Latter Stages in the Composition of the Bible." In *Sha'arei Talmon*, edited by M. Fishbane, E. Tov, and W. W. Fields, 267-91. Winona Lake: Eisenbrauns, 1992.

___. "Pluriformity in the Biblical Text, Text Groups, and Questions of Canon." In *The Madrid Qumran Congress*, edited by J. T. Barrera and L. V. Montaner. Vol. 1, 23-41. Leiden: Brill, 1992.

___. "The Septuagint Manuscripts from Qumran: a Reappraisal of Their Value." In *Septuagint, Scrolls and Cognate Writings. SCS* 33, edited by G. J. Brooke and B. Lindars, 49-80. Atlanta: Scholars Press, 1992.

Vööbus, A. *The Hexapla and the Syro-Hexapla*. Wetteren: Cultura, 1971.

Weingreen, J. "Rabbinic-Type Commentary in the LXX Version of Proverbs." In *Sixth World Congress of Jewish Studies*, edited by A. Shinan, 407-15. Jerusalem: Jerusalem Academic Press, 1977.

Wenthe, D. O. "The Old Greek Translation of Daniel 1-6." Ph.D. Dissertation, University of Notre Dame, 1991.

Wesselius, J. W. "Language and Style in Biblical Aramaic: Observations on the Unity of Daniel II-VI." *VT* 38 (1988): 195-209.

Wevers, J. W. "Septuaginta Forschungen." *TR* 33 (1968): 18-76.

___. "Text history and text criticism of the Septuagint." *VTSup* 29 (1977): 392-402.

___. "An Apologia for Septuagint Studies." *BIOSCS* 18 (1985): 16-38.

___. "The Use of the Versions for Text Criticism: The Septuagint." In *La Septuaginta en la Investigacion Contemporanea (V Congreso de la IOSCS)*, edited by N. F. Marcos, 15-24. Madrid: Instituto Arias Montano, 1985.

___. "Barthélemy and Proto-Septuagint Studies." *BIOSCS* 21 (1988): 23-34.

Wikgren, A. P. "A Comparative Study of the Theodotionic and Septuagint Translations of Daniel." Ph.D. Dissertation, University of Chicago, 1932.

Williams, J. G. "A Critical Note on the Aramaic Indefinite Plural of the Verb." *JBL* 83 (1964): 180-82.

Wong, S. "What Case is This Case? An Application of Semantic Case in Biblical Exegesis." *Jian Dao* 1 (1994): 75-107.

Woude, A. S. van der. "Erwägungen zur Doppelsprachigkeit des Buches Daniel." In *Scripta Signa Vocis*, edited by H. L. J. Vanstiphout, K. Jongeling, F. Leemhuis, and G. J. Reinink, 305-16. Groningen: Egbert Forsten, 1986.

Würthwein, E. *The Text of the Old Testament*. Rev. ed. Translated by E. F. Rhodes. Grand Rapids: Eerdmans, 1979.

Yule, G. *The Study of Language*. Cambridge: University Press, 1985.

Ziegler, J. *Untersuchungen zur Septuaginta des Buches Isaias*. Münster: Aschendorffschen Verlagsbuchhandlung, 1933.

___. *Beiträge zur Ieremias-Septuaginta*. *NAWG* 2. Göttingen: Vandenhoeck & Ruprecht, 1958.

Author Index

Abercrombie 26
Aejmelaeus 4, 16, 20, 74, 80, 81, 82, 85, 193
Albertz 8, 10, 78, 90, 96, 98, 100, 109, 125, 133, 145, 212, 242
Arnold 50
Ashley 130
Barr 3, 5, 20, 105 227-229
Bevan 54, 140, 208
Bludau 1, 38, 39, 61, 93, 131
Bodine 12, 166, 220, 222, 223, 228, 232-234, 235
Bogaert 166
Brock 15, 240
Brooke and Lindars 15
Bruce 8
Busto Saiz 13
Chafe 21
Charles 41, 61, 110, 196, 201, 208, 209
Chiesa 10
Chomsky 19
Collins 10, 11, 51, 61, 110, 113, 151, 186, 194, 196, 202, 208, 209, 210, 230, 239
Cross 10
Coxon 130, 139, 140
De Waard 2, 4
Delcor 128
Eitan 103
Elliger and Rudolph 25
Eynikel and Lust 138, 203
Fernández Marcos 10
Fields 10
Geissen 7, 44, 101, 214
Gentry 12, 16, 20, 166, 217, 219, 221, 222, 223, 224, 231, 232, 234, 240
Goshen-Gottstein 2, 5
Grabbe 13
Greenspoon 5, 12, 15, 16, 166, 219, 220, 223, 224, 226, 233, 235, 237
Grelot 139
Grindel 222, 223
Halliday 48

Hamm 7, 38, 39, 40, 72, 73, 75, 77, 110, 125, 214
Hanhart 230
Hartman and Di Lella 196, 208
Jackson 48
Jahn 110
Janzen 10
Jeansonne 1, 8, 13, 25, 28, 153, 160, 161, 162, 164, 170, 171, 172, 173, 188, 194, 205 217, 219
Jellicoe 12, 219
Kenyon 7
Kitchen 139
Kraft 26
Lacoque 194, 196
Leiter 96
Lyons 17, 18, 19
Marquis 3, 27
Mayser 57
McAlpine 197
McCrystall 1, 11, 72, 93, 94, 95, 96, 100, 101, 128, 191, 192, 203, 204
McGregor 14
McLay 1, 7, 11, 16, 21, 215
Meadowcroft 1, 7, 105, 132, 151
Miller 97
Montgomery 41, 52, 61, 100, 105, 130, 134, 167, 168, 171, 186, 187, 189, 194, 196, 197, 204, 210
Munnich 8, 12, 39, 75, 99, 221
Muraoka 133, 138
Nida 17
O'Connell 12, 166, 220, 222, 223, 231, 232, 233
Olofsson 3
Orlinsky 18
Porzig 47
Pietersma 6, 220
Plöger 61, 210
Porter 16
Radford 17
Rahlfs 6, 26, 74, 167
Roca-Puig 7
Sailhamer 9
Schmitt 13, 108, 212, 219, 237, 238, 239, 240
Shenkel 222

Smith 222, 223
Smyth 129, 131
Soderlund 10
Soisalon-Soininen 3, 4, 16, 17, 18, 20, 43, 84, 92, 93
Sollamo 4, 20, 21, 224, 229
Szpek 4, 21
Sprey 26
Swete 4, 6
Talmon 10, 198
Talshir 9
Taylor, B. 27
Taylor, R. 26, 46, 113, 126, 209
Thackeray 4, 23, 101, 222
Tigay 10
Torrey 130, 139
Tov 3, 6, 9, 10, 12, 13, 14, 26, 110, 203, 219, 222, 223, 230, 236, 237, 238
Ulrich 10, 11, 212, 223
Vööbus 6
Weber 26
Wenthe 1, 11
Wevers 10, 12, 14, 18, 20
Wifstrand 80
Wooden 46
Wright 3, 27, 111
Ziegler 6, 7, 8, 11, 26, 27, 38, 47, 72, 74, 76, 78, 87, 91, 108, 125, 139, 153, 186, 188, 204, 205, 206, 213, 214, 241

Index of Biblical References

Genesis

7:17 164
15:1 95
32:28(29) 142
35:3 196
37-42 94
41:1 95
41:8 86
46:2 95

Exodus

1:18 233
4:11 231
21:28 165
21:31 165
21:32 165
29:18 233

Leviticus

1:9 233
6:13(20) 205

Numbers

12:6 95
13:31(30) 142
22:38 142

Deuteronomy

1:5 88
33:17 165

Judges

3:12 232
6:26 237
9:24 232
13:25 86
16:28 232

Ruth

1:5 233

1 Kgdms

2:3 163
12:8, 10, 14 233
16:7 163

2 Kgdms

2:24 233
4:1 233
19:3 196

3 Kgdms

7:17 169
7:20 169
14:9 169
9:33 169
22:11 165

Isaiah

5:15 163
21:2 95
28:1 238
29:8 95
37:3 196
66:24 198

Jeremiah 95

39(32):21 95

Ezekiel

1:15 167
1:19 167
3:14 168
6:11 102
20:6 238
20:15 238
34:21 166
40:2 164

Obadiah

1:12, 14 196

Micah

3:7 95

Nahum

1:7 196
3:14 169

Habakkuk

3:16 196

Zechariah

8:5 233

Malachi

1:7, 12 52

Psalms

44(43):5 165
68:31 45
77:5 86
101(100):5 163

Ecclesiastes

7:13(12) 167
8:20 173

Sirach 95

40:29 53

Lamentations

4:10 233

Daniel

Chapters 1-2 211
1:1 72
1:1; 2:1; 7:1; 8:1; 9:1; 10:1 72
1:1-10 22, 28, 29, 60, 107, 115, 134, 136, 144, 161, 166, 198, 211

1:2 8, 43, 44, 50, 126, 135, 235
1:3 7, 8, 9, 10, 11, 18, 73, 110, 237, 247
1:4 13, 15, 17, 19, 40, 46, 49, 50, 89, 110, 142, 165, 166, 199, 202, 228, 231, 234
1:5 44, 52, 200, 245
1:7 58, 159, 129, 245
1:8 57, 58, 245
1:9 43, 52, 53, 54
1:10 43, 46, 247
1:11 45, 46, 51, 57, 134, 136
1:12 43, 98
1:13 39, 40, 46, 47, 51, 52, 57, 98, 142
1:14 200
1:15 40, 43, 45-47, 51, 57, 142, 234
1:16 43, 44, 51, 57, 59, 164
1:17 38, 43, 46, 47, 49, 81, 86, 89, 94, 95, 166, 231
1:18 45, 46, 51, 52, 57, 81, 87
1:19 42, 52, 92
1:20 45, 48, 49, 53, 77, 200, 231

Chapters 2-3 76, 81, 82, 99
2:1 64, 95, 109, 245
2:1-10 22, 28, 58, 63, 73, 88, 98, 99, 107, 108, 115, 143, 144, 147, 211
2:1-3:21 137, 145
2:2 43, 51, 52, 64, 80, 87
2:3 65, 74, 81
2:4 65, 72, 73, 79, 91, 98, 110, 113, 246
2:4-11 89
2:5 50, 58, 66, 75, 81-83, 85, 90, 98, 99, 100-103, 110, 113, 140, 146, 147, 238, 246
2:5-6 113
2:6 53, 67, 74, 81, 89, 98, 168, 223, 246
2:7 68, 81, 82, 96, 98
2:8 68, 74, 76, 81, 82, 99, 109, 246-248
2:8-9 77, 113
2:9 39, 51, 69, 74, 75, 76, 81, 85, 89, 90, 96, 97, 98, 99, 105, 246
2:10 70, 76, 82, 89, 99, 110, 246
2:11 76, 89, 99, 133

Index of Biblical References

2:12 38, 51, 170, 231
2:13 49, 81, 85, 231
2:14 51, 134, 136, 142, 231
2:15 76, 82, 85, 90, 99, 107, 136, 137
2:16 43, 53, 81, 89, 98
2:17 45, 50, 76, 89, 90, 99, 136, 137
2:18 54, 231
2:19 45, 96, 136, 137, 224
2:20 49, 78, 82, 231, 239
2:21 43, 48, 49, 50, 105, 135, 136, 231
2:22 45, 226, 238
2:23 43, 49, 53, 76, 77, 90, 99, 139, 229, 239
2:24 51, 81, 89, 98, 129, 134, 136, 231
2:24-25 98
2:25 61, 82, 89, 93, 98, 133, 136
2:26 73, 77, 81, 82, 89, 96, 97, 98, 114, 133, 246, 247
2:27 81, 82, 89, 229
2:28 8, 45, 73, 77, 90, 95, 96, 109, 133, 226, 246
2:29 8, 45, 77, 90, 226, 246
2:30 43, 45, 49, 77, 81, 90, 98, 133, 226, 231, 248
2:31 135, 142, 167, 170
2:32 128, 142
2:33 81, 129
2:34 126, 142
2:35 136, 142, 164
2:36 74, 81, 96, 98
2:37 43, 53, 128
2:38 43, 44, 126, 136
2:39 135
2:40 104
2:41 81, 129, 223
2:42 45, 129
2:43 81
2:44 38, 78, 79, 81, 135
2:45 8, 74, 90, 96, 98, 103, 104, 113, 126, 246
2:46 51, 87, 132, 136, 233
2:47 45, 82, 226
2:48 43, 45, 84, 134, 136, 137, 162, 165, 170, 197, 231
2:49 51, 53, 134, 136, 162

Chapter 3 11
3:1 72, 134, 135, 140, 142, 162
3:1; 4:1; 7:1; 8:1; 9:1 41
3:1-18 135
3:1-20 82
3:2 134, 135, 138, 140, 142, 162
3:3 38, 52, 129, 134-137, 140, 142, 162
3:4 87, 91, 235
3:5 132, 135, 139, 140, 142, 163
3:6 127, 132, 133, 140, 143, 146, 148, 149
3:7 132, 135, 139, 140, 142, 163
3:8 133, 110
3:9 73, 78, 82, 111, 246
3:10 51, 58, 129, 132, 134, 139, 140, 142, 147, 163
3:10-11 127
3:11 116, 132, 143
3:11-20 22, 28, 42, 47, 102, 126, 144, 149, 167-169, 211, 217
3:12 51, 58, 81, 116, 132-135, 136, 140, 142, 162, 213
3:13 51, 117, 133, 136, 138
3:14 82, 118, 132, 133, 135, 140, 142
3:15 81, 119, 126, 129, 132, 133, 139, 140, 142, 143, 163, 167, 213, 248
3:16 72, 81, 82, 121, 167, 248
3:17 85, 121, 126, 132, 133, 141, 144, 145, 212, 213, 248
3:17-18 115, 130, 144
3:18 46, 122, 131, 132, 133, 135, 142
3:19 40, 47, 51, 72, 77, 82, 83, 87, 105, 106, 123, 127, 136, 142, 147, 247
3:20 51, 87, 124, 131, 132, 133, 143, 147
3:20-30(97) 102, 125, 146, 147, 212, 242
3:21 38, 127, 132, 133, 136, 143
3:21-26(93) 127
3:21-30(97) 146, 147
3:22 76, 99, 127, 133, 143, 148, 246
3:23 74, 81, 125, 127, 128, 129, 133, 143, 146, 147

3:24(91) 27, 51, 74, 81, 83, 87, 93, 103, 127, 132, 133, 135-137, 143, 146
3:24(91)-3:26(93) 83
3:24(91)-7:2 83
3:24(91)-7:19 137, 145
3:25(92) 81, 83, 127, 133, 146, 203, 238
3:26(93) 74, 81, 83, 98, 127, 128, 133, 136-138, 146
3:27(94) 105, 106, 127, 133, 134
3:28(95) 38, 43, 44, 57, 76, 81, 83, 85, 98, 99, 105, 132, 146, 147
3:29(96) 44, 50, 58, 74, 85, 100-104, 112, 133, 134, 140, 141, 146, 147, 238
3:30(97) 74, 81, 134, 136, 137, 146, 162, 197
3:32(99) 44, 89, 140
3:33(100) 78, 79
3:34 44
3:36 92
3:38 197
3:40 52
3:41 40
3:42 57
3:43 57
3:44 45
3:46 81, 129
3:49 81
3:51 81
3:57 134
3:79 87
3:88 141

Chapters 4-6 10, 11, 38, 81, 82, 91, 98, 99, 104, 109, 125, 127, 133, 137, 145, 147, 212, 242, 243
Chapters 4-7 99
4:1(4) 50, 105
4:2(5) 86, 96
4:3(6) 58, 90, 98, 134, 231
4:4(7) 90, 98, 110, 136
4:6(9) 96, 98
4:7(10) 96, 133, 163, 170
4:8(11) 167, 169
4:9(12) 52, 170
4:10(13) 96, 237

4:11(14) 51, 85, 87
4:12(15) 223
4:13(16) 43, 44, 105
4:14(17) 43, 44, 107, 135, 142, 237
4:14(17), 22(25), 29(32) 44, 107
4:15(18) 45, 89, 90, 98, 104, 197
4:16(19) 81, 83, 86, 87, 98, 105, 111, 136, 137, 140, 194
4:17(20) 92, 169
4:18(21) 170
4:19(22) 40, 81, 134, 169
4:20(23) 223, 237
4:21(24) 98, 169
4:22(25) 43, 44
4:23(26) 107
4:24(27) 85, 93, 103, 105
4:25(28) 169
4:26(29) 45, 50, 201, 203
4:27(30) 50, 53, 83, 230
4:28(31) 81, 99, 105
4:29(32) 43, 44, 92
4:30(33) 38, 40, 81, 140
4:30a 53, 105
4:31(34) 45, 49, 78, 79, 142, 201, 224, 230
4:32(35) 133, 140
4:33(36) 49, 53, 142, 230
4:34(37) 92, 105, 139, 202, 203, 230
4:34a 85, 105
4:34b 81
4:34c 45, 81, 89, 131, 145
4:34c(37) 125

5:preface 81
5:1 140, 247
5:2 50, 134, 138
5:3 50, 136, 137, 138
5:4 46
5:5 50, 140, 148, 244
5:6 74, 81, 86, 105, 106, 136, 137, 142, 143, 238
5:7 45, 83, 87, 89, 90, 91, 98, 110, 202, 231, 235
5:8 87, 90, 91, 98, 136, 137, 231
5:9 45, 86, 89, 91, 105, 136, 137, 142, 143, 170
5:10 50, 73, 78, 79, 83, 86, 105, 142
5:11 47, 49, 110, 133, 135, 136, 231

Index of Biblical References

5:12 45, 47, 49, 58, 87, 89, 90, 98, 104, 139, 193, 202, 238
5:13 83, 136-138
5:14 47, 49, 231
5:15 87, 89, 90, 98, 99, 139, 231
5:16 45, 87, 89, 90, 98, 139, 202
5:17 43, 44, 83, 84, 87, 90, 98, 136, 137
5:18 43, 44, 53, 230
5:19 43, 44, 202
5:20 53, 202
5:21 44, 100, 107, 135
5:22 104
5:23 46, 50, 138, 202, 230
5:24 51, 136, 137
5:25 51
5:26 51, 98, 99
5:28 43
5:29 87, 107, 136, 137, 202, 247
5:30 247

6:1(5:31) 38, 103
6:2(1) 135, 136
6:3(2) 43, 44, 134
6:4(3) 38, 104, 135-137
6:5(4) 53, 57, 81, 104, 136, 137
6:6(5) 81, 85, 133, 136, 137
6:7(6) 73, 78, 79, 136, 137
6:8(7) 53, 132, 135
6:9(8) 85, 105, 135, 139
6:10(9) 51
6:11(10) 38, 40, 50, 51, 52, 81, 104, 140, 229, 234
6:12(11) 53, 133, 136, 137
6:12a 135
6:13(12) 40, 51, 53, 81, 83, 85, 99, 103, 105, 132, 136, 137
6:14(13) 40, 51, 58, 83, 128, 134, 136, 137
6:15(14) 58, 99, 136, 137, 167, 170
6:16(15) 85, 105, 133, 135-137, 141
6:17(16) 81, 83, 132, 136-138
6:18(17) 58, 105, 132, 138, 200
6:19(18) 50, 136, 137
6:20(19) 93, 135, 136, 137
6:21(20) 82, 83, 98, 132, 141, 147, 235
6:22(21) 78, 92, 136, 137

6:23(22) 81, 101, 104, 105, 140
6:24(23) 136, 137, 170
6:25(24) 132, 133, 169
6:26(25) 136, 137
6:27(26) 58, 78, 85, 134
6:28(27) 38, 46, 85, 140, 141, 147
6:29(28) 38

Chapters 7-12 81, 211
7:1 77, 96, 97, 99, 136, 137, 247
7:1-2a 97
7:2 83, 96
7:3 106, 248
7:4 43, 135, 198
7:5 135, 170
7:6 43
7:7 81, 96, 106, 161, 169, 171, 248
7:8 47, 92, 163, 224
7:9 127
7:10 40, 127, 135, 136, 248
7:11 43, 92, 99, 136, 137, 163
7:12 43
7:13 96, 138, 169
7:14 43, 53, 105, 132
7:14 78, 132, 233
7:15 96, 133
7:16 74, 81, 90, 98, 99, 103, 135, 167, 248
7:17 135
7:18 78, 86, 103, 248
7:19 43, 106, 136, 137, 169, 171, 223, 248
7:20 92, 96, 161, 224
7:21 140, 163
7:22 43, 44, 138, 169
7:23 43, 106, 169
7:24 106, 135, 163
7:25 43, 85, 92, 106, 126, 191, 248
7:27 43, 51, 78, 132, 233
7:28 86, 99, 106, 142, 143, 170
7:28(27) 99

8:1 44, 152, 159, 247
8:1-10 13, 22, 28, 49, 149, 163, 172, 174, 198, 205, 211, 230
8:2 93, 94, 134, 154, 162, 213, 237, 248

8:3 43, 52, 155, 163, 164, 167, 213, 224, 237, 248
8:4 52, 81, 92, 126, 141, 155, 163, 165, 167, 170-172, 228
8:5 39, 156, 163, 166, 169, 213, 224, 228, 232
8:6 52, 138, 156, 163, 166, 167, 237, 247
8:7 52, 138, 141, 157, 163, 168
8:8 158, 163-165, 168-170
8:9 158, 163, 165, 170, 237, 238, 248
8:10 159, 165, 171, 238
8:11 78, 165, 202, 205, 230
8:11-14 165
8:12 43, 172, 205
8:13 43, 92, 169, 172, 190, 194, 205, 237
8:14 190, 248
8:15 48, 52, 53, 92, 133, 229
8:16 87, 166, 232, 246
8:17 39, 85, 92, 167, 193, 196, 200
8:18 39, 92, 169
8:19 77, 85, 89-91, 138, 193, 202
8:20 163, 167, 168
8:21 163, 166, 170, 224, 232
8:22 168
8:23 39, 202
8:24 104, 170, 202
8:25 45, 47, 89, 104, 126, 165, 168, 186, 197, 229
8:26 85, 193, 200
8:27 134, 135, 165, 194, 228

9:2 142, 166, 200
9:3 39, 43, 53
9:4 53, 170, 228
9:5 204
9:6 77, 98, 197
9:7 39, 105, 227
9:8 39, 197
9:9 54, 86, 193
9:10 43, 52, 85, 98, 203
9:11 85, 86, 98, 201, 204
9:12 46, 92, 135, 170, 188, 200, 235, 236
9:13 39, 47, 85, 89, 231, 234
9:14 46, 86, 193, 235, 236
9:15 163
9:16 86, 139, 140, 193, 198, 231, 234, 246
9:17 39, 98, 194, 235
9:18 52, 54, 85, 87, 88, 193, 194, 224
9:19 86, 87, 88, 193, 213
9:20 52, 92
9:21 92, 162, 169, 190, 196, 227, 247
9:22 45, 47, 48, 89, 92, 166, 167
9:23 45, 47, 86, 89, 162, 166, 193, 200
9:24 45, 46, 78, 200, 229, 231
9:24-27 44, 165, 191, 205
9:25 38, 47, 89, 196, 200, 234
9:26 104, 138, 165, 194, 201, 228, 236
9:27 44, 194, 198, 225, 248

10:1 45, 48, 87, 88, 166, 170, 200, 226, 247, 248
10:3 142, 225
10:4 167, 170, 224
10:5 164, 190, 202, 209, 224, 227, 237
10:6 39, 101, 200, 224
10:7 93, 170, 227, 238
10:8 170
10:9 39, 200
10:10 169
10:11 85, 92, 193, 200, 227
10:12 40, 43, 52, 86, 166, 193, 200
10:13 197, 209, 229, 246
10:14 45, 85, 89, 166, 193, 202
10:15 39, 43, 57, 92, 200, 231
10:16 92, 169, 169, 225, 229
10:17 92, 98
10:18 167, 232
10:19 86, 92, 193, 227, 232
10:20 197, 234, 236
10:21 45, 51, 85, 89, 165, 193, 197, 228, 232, 238

11:1 232
11:2 45, 89, 170
11:3 51, 142, 165, 239
11:4 51, 57, 86, 168, 193, 202

Index of Biblical References

11:5 51, 197, 232
11:6 8, 43, 44, 46, 196, 201, 232, 235
11:7 233
11:8 46, 227
11:9 234, 235
11:10 105, 186, 229, 234, 235
11:11 43, 44, 126, 138, 236
11:12 86, 164, 202
11:13 170, 196, 201, 234
11:14 164, 196, 246
11:15 165, 228
11:16 52, 57, 126, 165, 167, 171, 228, 237
11:17 39, 43, 45, 51, 58, 104, 134, 234
11:18 39, 45, 58, 138, 186, 198, 223, 234, 236
11:19 39, 45, 234
11:20 138, 166, 224, 230, 236
11:21 43, 224, 232
11:22 39, 52, 168, 227, 248
11:23 51, 164, 170
11:24 45, 134, 162, 196
11:25 86, 101, 169, 170, 193, 198, 236
11:26 51, 105, 168, 186
11:27 85, 92, 169, 193, 200
11:28 170, 234, 238
11:29 234
11:30 138, 166, 234
11:31 43, 194, 204
11:32 232
11:33 47, 48, 89, 166, 198, 199, 232, 247
11:34 93, 186
11:35 47, 85, 89, 190, 193, 196, 199, 200, 201, 203, 204, 207, 247
11:35-36 190
11:36 57, 85, 92, 138, 165, 190, 193, 202, 213, 228
11:37 51, 86, 132, 165, 166, 193
11:38 39, 53, 87, 224, 237
11:39 51, 201
11:40 105, 165, 196, 200, 201
11:41 141, 171, 186, 237
11:42 141
11:43 51

11:44 39, 86, 170, 186
11:45 165, 166, 171, 201, 228, 231, 232, 237
12:1 105, 141, 170, 176, 196, 247
12:1-13 22, 28, 175, 206, 211
12:2 78, 81, 129, 177, 198, 229, 247, 248
12:3 47, 78, 89, 178, 199, 229, 247
12:4 49, 142, 178, 190, 196, 200, 247
12:5 179, 187, 190, 248
12:5-13 196
12:6 74, 81, 180, 192, 200, 202, 227, 228, 237, 248
12:7 78, 85, 126, 180, 191-193, 227, 228, 229, 237, 247
12:8 166, 182
12:9 85, 182, 193, 196, 200, 201
12:10 47, 48, 89, 166, 183, 186, 198, 199, 203, 204
12:11 43, 183, 194, 196, 204, 248
12:12 168, 169, 184
12:13 85, 184, 200, 201, 217, 247

Ezra

8:5 166

Nehemiah

2:6 167
3:23 167

2 Chronicles

18:10 165
29:21 166

1 Esdras

6:31 103

Judith

1:1 74

1 Maccabees

1:9 208
1:54 194

2 Maccabees

1:16 101

4 Maccabees

13:21, 24 54

Mark

13:14 194

Matthew

15:14 194

www.ingramcontent.com/pod-product-compliance
Lightning Source LLC
Chambersburg PA
CBHW021137230426
43667CB00005B/145